"Rumors of a kingdom and reality beyond ourselves have fascinated philosophers for centuries, if not millennia. *Soul Whisperer* goes directly to the subject and brings significant new perspectives from the Christian tradition. It is a work of brilliance and highly relevant to the contemporary debate about living life fully with all of our heart, soul, mind and strength."

—**James Catford**, founding chair, Center for Christianity and Public Life.

"Building on the work of philosopher Dallas Willard, the thesis of *Soul Whisperer* is simple—the kingdom of God which Jesus proclaimed is the underlying Reality of life. To live a good life is to align our lives to this Reality. Daniel Napier provides key—and often profound—exegetical insights into the teachings of Jesus coupled with practical wisdom and guidance for those who desire to discover and experience the truth of the gospel."

—**Eric M. Riesen**, president, North American Lutheran Seminary

"What has Athens to do with Jerusalem? Daniel Napier knows. At the heart of ancient Greek philosophy was the question of how to live rightly, but no Greek thinker answered that question as well as did Jesus of Nazareth. In an era when philosophy was not just an intellectual exercise, but a way of life, the Way of Jesus presented itself as philosophy *par excellence*. Napier's account of Jesus' own philosophy stands as a modern *enchiridion* for the Christian life, in the tradition of Epictetus, Augustine, and Erasmus."

—**Aaron Preston**, professor of philosophy, Valparaiso University

"Many of us have inadvertently put Jesus in a box. He is the God-man who secured salvation for us when we die. We may affirm that Jesus cares about our life, but we don't know why or how this works. In this book, Daniel Napier gives us a very readable and nourishing framework for why the here-and-now matter and precisely how Jesus teaches us to live. I'm so grateful for this book."

—**Jon Guerra**, singer-songwriter

"Daniel Napier's *Soul Whisperer* is a book about spiritual and moral forma-tion that also spiritually and morally forms us. Jesus was, in the ancient sense, a philosopher: having brought us to God's love, he taught us how to live in it. In *Soul Whisperer*, Jesus appears as the philosopher of God's kingdom and we discover that this radical, dangerous, and truly joyful philosophy, is humanly livable, a way we may trust and follow, with hope."

—**Alan P. R. Gregory**, principal, St. Augustine's College of Theology

"In *Soul Whisperer*, Daniel Napier makes a more than significant contribu-tion to the philosophical understanding of Jesus and his message for today. Without any exaggeration I can say this book is the first new spiritual and devotional classic in the twenty-first century. Read and reread this book if you want to love and know God with all your heart, soul, mind, and strength. This book is a major achievement of intellectual honesty written from the point of view of an (extra)ordinary everyday follower of Christ."

—**Boris Gunjevic**, director of theological studies, Westfield House,
Cambridge Theological Federation

Soul Whisperer

SOUL WHISPERER

—— Jesus' Way among the Philosophers ——

Daniel Austin Napier

CASCADE *Books* • Eugene, Oregon

SOUL WHISPERER
Jesus' Way among the Philosophers

Cascade Books
An Imprint of Wipf and Stock Publishers
199 W. 8th Ave., Suite 3
Eugene, OR 97401

www.wipfandstock.com

PAPERBACK ISBN: 978-1-6667-6835-0
HARDCOVER ISBN: 978-1-6667-6836-7
EBOOK ISBN: 978-1-6667-6837-4

Cataloguing-in-Publication data:

Names: Napier, Daniel Austin [author].

Title: Soul whisperer : Jesus' way among the philosophers / by Daniel Austin Napier.

Description: Eugene, OR: Cascade Books, 2023 | Includes bibliographical references.

Identifiers: ISBN 978-1-6667-6835-0 (paperback) | ISBN 978-1-6667-6836-7 (hardcover) | ISBN 978-1-6667-6837-4 (ebook)

Subjects: LCSH: Jesus Christ—Philosophy. | Jesus Christ—Teachings. | Christian ethics. | Philosophical counseling. | Conduct of life. | Ethics. | Wisdom.

Classification: BT306 N37 2023 (print) | BT306 (ebook)

10/03/23

Contents

Section III—Kingdom Practices

Section IV—Kingdom Social Relations

Acknowledgments

As THIS MANUSCRIPT GOES to publication, I am particularly mindful of those who contributed to its completion and improvement over the course of writing and editing.

I would like to thank my students and colleagues at Austin Graduate School of Theology and, before that, at the Biblijski Institut in Zagreb, Croatia, for interacting with substantial portions of this material in seminar and lecture settings. I'm also grateful for the dialogue surrounding presentations of some chapters at Aristotle University of Thessaloniki's post-graduate "Exegeticum" seminar, at a conference for the Dallas Willard Center of Westmont College in Montecito, California, and at the Chrétiens en Mission program in Marseilles, France.

About six or seven years ago, Michael Thompson, then as an acquisition editor at Eerdmans, took the time to sit in my office at Austin Graduate of Theology. "What are you working on?" he asked. Then he lit up when I described my philosophy of Jesus project. Thank you, Michael, for reaching out, for your enthusiasm for this project, and for facilitating its publication at Cascade Books. I'm also grateful for Emily Callihan's work in formatting the manuscript and Robin Parry's work as copy editor.

Several scholarly friends have read prior drafts of the manuscript, in whole or part, and offered significant feedback. Bob Sweetman, Gary Moon, Nathan Moser, Boris Gunjevic, Dimitri Constant, Alan P. R. Gregory, Aaron Preston, Scott Lisea, Stephen Coney, Dimitrios Christidis, James Henderson, and Mike Robb—what can I say? No doubt this manuscript would have been better had I managed to incorporate all your suggestions. While still flawed due to the limitations of my hand, it is certainly better for having received your insightful comments along the way. Thank you.

From deep editorial experience, personal devotion, and cultural sensitivity, James Catford coached me through the process of transforming an initial draft into something more fitted for public consumption. And he did so with grace and skill. James, I'm touched and honored at the time you devoted to exploring Jesus' teachings with me and to helping me communicate more clearly.

A special word of gratitude goes to the apprentices in Ashrei's Spiritual Formation Institute in Mexico City and in Ashrei Europe's cohorts in Thessaloniki, Greece, and Skopje, Republic of N. Macedonia. Through your feedback both in our "intensive" retreat settings and in the practical experimentation of your everyday life you've helped me hone these insights and test their lived viability. This is your book. The warmth of your fellowship made this work joyful. Thank you for walking this portion of the journey together.

Finally, to Karly, my partner in life, family, and ministry, you truly are my God-designed "helper over against" me (Gen 2:18, 20). You so often see and hear what I miss, and you bring it to my attention with love. Thank you for carrying so much of the detail of our lives and thus freeing me for the ministry of teaching. But most of all, thank you for filling our lives with so much that has nothing to do with work or ministry or intellectual reflection. You make life richer and worth living. With all my love this book is dedicated to you.

PREFACE

The Backstory

Jesus, Dallas, and Me

THIS IS A BOOK about Jesus—not about me. But when I teach, I find that people often want to know the backstory. "Who is this guy that is talking to us?" And insofar as this is a different kind of book—crossing over disciplinary lines—perhaps there is good reason for readers to expect an answer to the question.

This Is Me

Fundamentally, I am a seeker. I'm a guy who long ago realized that he had much to learn from Jesus and embarked on a long life-experiment.

By temperament, and through the quirks of my journey, I also have acquired some intellectual tools, familiarity with Second Temple Jewish literature (i.e., what Jews in Jesus' era were writing), and facility in some ancient languages and philosophies. This has led me to formulate some new questions. My PhD ultimately came from the *Vrije Universiteit*, or Free University, in Amsterdam and my first book focused on Augustine of Hippo's concept of what a human being is and how persons change.[1] Ministerial service also has taken me into a couple dozen countries.

All this has allowed me to search within a somewhat different horizon than is common among writers of spiritual books today. But at bottom I'm just a guy trying to make sense of human life in this world, and who has been repeatedly surprised at how helpful Jesus' approach is for doing so.

The roots of this book go back to my early years of ministry and scholarship—and to an unusual book I was given. Here's the story.

The Backstory

In late 2000, the senior minister of a church at which I was serving in Austin, Texas, handed me a copy of Dallas Willard's *The Divine Conspiracy*. Maybe you are familiar with Dallas' teachings. I had never heard of Dallas or his books. But it must be important, I figured, because the senior minister gave it to me. So, I took it home and read the first few chapters.

I hate to admit it now, but I was repulsed. Dallas, whom I did not then know, struck me as naïve and utterly lacking in the marks of intellectual respectability into which I had been inducted through a pair of seminary degrees. I blush now to tell the story.

Later I discovered just how deep and broad Dallas' learning was and how sophisticated and thorough was his refutation of the late twentieth-century philosophic mythemes that I had simply imbibed. Dallas was not naïve but hyperaware of the issues. He had sorted through the intellectual thickets and come to a clear, consistent position that he presented as such—without affectation. So, I'm embarrassed to admit my first impressions. "A little learning is a dangerous thing. . . ." But that's how it happened.

For all his vast learning, Dallas hadn't bothered to connect the exegetical dots between his contemporary expositions and the broader intellectual features of the ancient world. He wasn't primarily writing for seminary-inoculated people like myself. I've since come to realize, through reading in Dallas' personal archives, that he could have written that sort of book. But he was aiming at a different audience. I do not fault him, but I do note that it was a stumbling block for me at the time.

The disconnect I felt is captured well by Michael Stewart Robb in his doctoral dissertation on Dallas' theology. "If one has received one of the standard theological educations of the late 20th century it is impossible to intelligently agree with Dallas' books and continue in that formation."[2]

Rediscovering Dallas

I did not, at the time, intelligently agree with Dallas. I set the book down and didn't come back to it for several years. In the intervening years, I moved up to Toronto for a graduate program in the history of philosophy, focusing on the ancient philosophers and the early church fathers. After a few years, I moved back to California to preach for a small church in Santa Barbara.

That's were something unexpected happened. As I taught through Matthew 5, and was groping for helpful resources, I recalled that the later chapters of *The Divine Conspiracy* were supposed to be an exposition of the Sermon on the Mount. It might be worth a quick glance, I thought. So, I picked up *The Divine Conspiracy* and began reading, this time, at chapter 6.

I was astounded at the depth of Dallas' insight as he unfolded Jesus' teachings about everyday human emotions and moral intuitions. By the time I finished the book, I knew that I must have missed something in the opening chapters years before. Dallas' philosophically sophisticated, phenomenologically trained mind, which I had discovered in the later chapters, could not be what I'd imagined when I read the opening chapters. On a second read, now with a bit more philosophical training of my own, the profundity of Dallas' work shone through to me.

I was hooked and began searching out all I could find of his writings and recorded teachings. As far as my appreciative learning from Dallas is concerned, the rest is, as they say, history. If you are familiar with Dallas' writings, you'll recognize my grateful debt to him as you read. If you are not familiar with Dallas' writings, don't worry. This book is written to stand on its own.

Just How Smart Is Jesus?

But one more element forms an essential part of the backstory. On my first reading, Dallas' book had seemed full of pious category mistakes. One of those stuck with me. Dallas delighted in telling people that Jesus was "the most intelligent person who ever lived." Also, Dallas everywhere insisted that such things were testable. Jesus' brilliance could be assessed experientially and learned to be factual. Could that be true?

I began to wonder. Just how smart is Jesus? How could one test it? We don't have a time machine from which to administer the Stanford-Binet or the Wechsler exams. And I was increasingly dubious as to whether those exams would provide an adequate answer anyway.

This Dallas-evoked question soon intersected with another one, which arose from a similar claim that was often thought to be a pious category mistake.

The early church, which I was studying, also insisted on highlighting Jesus' brilliance. They identified themselves as philosophers within the school of Christ's philosophy. So, a second question arose. Was that legitimate? Did Jesus really address the major questions of ancient philosophy in a coherent and original manner? I'll describe that question, and detail my discoveries regarding it, in the chapters to follow.

The convergence of those two questions—"Just how smart is Jesus?" and "Does Jesus, in historical context, really offer a coherent philosophy?"—has birthed a research and teaching project. For want of a better term I've been calling it my "philosophy of Jesus" project.

That was twenty years ago. It has been growing. I've been testing it personally in my life, academically in university seminars and conference presentations, and pastorally in dozens of congregations on several continents. I remain convinced of the project's cogency and needfulness.

This is the first book-length installment in the project.

This Book

What motivated this book? Well, many people have asked me to write the things I have been teaching in university courses, churches, and retreat centers. But I've also felt a growing personal urge to do so. My own life-experiments in Jesus' philosophy and my experiences in mentoring others seem worth sharing.

I decided to write in a voice as close as possible to my usual speaking voice. This is how I interact with people in retreats and seminars, churches and conferences, and in conversations of daily life.

I've provided my own translations of ancient texts. All translations, unless otherwise noted, are my own. I have tried to make those translations accessible to ordinary people.

Based on the assumption that my readers will also be seekers—whether from inside or outside organized religious groups—I've also provided annotations. Anyone so inclined may follow the notes to drill deeper into the topics and the scholarship behind my exposition. Nonetheless, I have not attempted to exhaustively survey and critique the numerous alternatives to every position I've taken. That would require a different, much longer type of book.

That's enough about me. In the coming pages I'll mostly fade into the background and simply speak as your tour guide—highlighting features of Jesus' teachings along this path that we're exploring together.

The book in your hands was written for thoughtful non-specialists—people who would like to know both what Jesus really taught and why he's worth considering today. Maybe that describes you? Although I make no effort to hide my admiration for and trust in Jesus, I don't assume anything but basic interest on the part of my readers. If you're curious about Jesus, this book is for you. I hope you find it helpful on your journey.[3]

Daniel Austin Napier

Thessaloniki, Greece
March 10, 2023

PROLOGUE

Why Philosophy?

On Jesus and Socrates

Two Seminal Figures

NEITHER HELD PUBLIC OFFICE. Neither, as adults, traveled very far from home. Neither wrote any literary work, though both occasionally made their points by writing on the ground.

Rather than writing books, both spoke to their contemporaries, aiming at transforming their individual and collective lives. They left the literary productions to their followers.

Both exercised an uncanny influence over not only their contemporaries, but also over the lives and imaginations of distant people for centuries to follow. This influence was not merely literary, but visceral. Those who spent time with these men were deeply changed and went on to change others. And both died by execution, condemned by their own people, because of the deep changes they were prompting in their societies.

Of course, I am speaking of Socrates and Jesus.[4]

This book is about Jesus and his ability—then and now—to change human lives. However, I cannot speak of Jesus' *philosophy* without a word about Socrates and Jesus' relation to him. So, perhaps I should point out that philosophy is not merely my choice of category for the life and thought Jesus introduced. It goes back to the beginning.

"The Way" and Ancient Philosophy

Three hundred years before Christianity became a religion, Jesus and his earliest followers taught "the Way."[5] They self-identified as philosophers and taught Jesus' way as a lived philosophy to be compared with other philosophic ways of life.[6] This self-identification remains implicit, though clear enough, in the movement's earliest writings, collectively known as the New Testament.[7] Beginning in the second century, however, we find copious, explicit, and near universal self-descriptions of Jesus' followers as philosophers.[8] Of course, a long, venerable tradition of Hellenistic Jews had self-presented as adherents of an ancestral philosophy.[9] When early Christians self-identified as adherents of a philosophy, the term philosophy referred to a coherent and comprehensive way of living. This they held in common with the broader range of philosophic schools in antiquity.[10]

Surprisingly, if asked the nature of their teachings, the earliest followers of Jesus would not use the term "theology."[11] Rather, their teachings were *philosophy*—expressions of a love for wisdom adapted to the specifics of human existence.

Frequently, the philosophical self-depiction of early Christians has been taken as nothing more or less than a rhetorical move aimed to leverage socially recognized categories for their own advantage—what today is sometimes called virtue signaling.[12] Given this community's commitment to truthfulness, however, this assumption seems highly questionable to me.[13] It is much more likely that they believed what they claimed. Of course, acknowledging their sincerity still leaves open the question of the suitability of their self-identification.

But what if their self-description were an accurate translation into the Greco-Roman categories of the import of Jesus' teachings? Could the life and teachings of Jesus of Nazareth, as preserved in the earliest accounts of his life, be fruitfully interpreted through the lens of ancient philosophy? Does his personal teaching fit with such a reading?

In short, I have found the answer is *yes*. This book is an attempt to make that fact more commonly known. So, back to Socrates and the relation of Jesus' philosophy to his.

Jesus and Socrates—What Are Their Philosophies?

Although many have attempted to characterize the core of these teachings, both Jesus and Socrates employed metaphors—*related* metaphors—to depict what they were doing when they taught. These provide us an inside perspective into what *they* thought they were doing. Moreover, these may guide us in discerning the relation between their distinctive approaches to human development.

Socrates—Midwife for the Soul

In a dialogue named for the bright youth, Theaetetus, with whom he is conversing, Socrates claims to be a midwife for the soul. Socrates' mother was a stout, no-nonsense midwife who was successful at helping women bring forth healthy physical children. Socrates, by analogy, was called by "the god" to be a midwife of men's souls. He notices the deep concern or preoccupation that some have for truth as being a "pregnancy of soul" (*Theat.* 148e). Then, Socrates employs his method of questioning to either abort the stillborn notions or to successfully birth those that are living and true.

Socrates himself, however, cannot place a seed inside the soul. Rather, he is like Artemis, whom the Greeks considered the patron of childbirth but who was herself childless (149b–c). Socrates characterizes his method this way:

> I am sterile in point of wisdom. The reproach which has often been brought against me, that I question others but make no reply myself about anything, because I have no wisdom in myself, is a true reproach. The reason of it is this: God compels me to act as midwife but has never allowed me to beget. I am, then, not at all a wise person myself, nor have I any wise invention, the offspring born of my own soul. But those who associate with me, although at first some of them seem very ignorant, yet, as our acquaintance advances, all of them to whom God is gracious make wonderful progress—not only in their own opinion, but in that of others as well. And it is clear that they do this, not because they have ever learned anything from me, but because they have found in themselves many beautiful things and have birthed them. But the delivery is due to God and to me. (*Theat.* 150c–d)[14]

Socrates thinks that innate, but indistinct and confused, ideas were already present within the soul of his dialogue partners. Questions, properly applied, enabled these deep, prior acquaintances with reality to emerge as truthful definitions. Or, alternatively, Socrates' questioning led his partners to realize that they had not yet managed a truthful definition and thus didn't yet possess real knowledge. In that case, the stillborn or false pregnancy was helpfully expelled.

Moreover, Socrates' philosophical project depended on revelation—at least negatively so.[15] His *daemon*—a messenger spirit whose voice he obeyed as that of the one God—intervened when he was going down the wrong path.[16] So, Socrates followed revelation in spotting untruth and stripping it away from himself and others. Falsehood, or at least the beginnings of an inner deceit, was indicated to Socrates from above. Obedience to that voice steered him away from lying and from bluster.

Such a pruning of false pretensions was a significant contribution to human life. Both in Socrates' own day and in subsequent centuries, this capacity to alert people to false claims and relieve them of any inclination to follow them enables them to "make wonderful progress" (150d). Merely removing falsehood (and deflating those who would sell it) must be recognized as a great gift to humanity.

By his own account, however, Socrates never received any positive revelation. God led him into a method of spotting falsehood, but the seed for new life would have to come from elsewhere. Socrates was sterile when it came to introducing the information needed for wisdom—for a life fully transformed.

Jesus—Teaching as the Seed of a New Existence

Jesus also tells us what he is doing when he speaks with people. In fact, he uses a metaphor that is related to Socrates' metaphor of midwifery. In his parables, Jesus identified his message of the kingdom[17] as "seed" or "sperm" of a new type of life.

The same words (*sperma*, *spora*, and cognate verbs) can be used either in a horticultural context or in a biological context. Ancients did not draw a sharp line between the tiny bits of matter that initiated a plant life and an animal life. We'll unpack how both senses appear in Jesus' teaching, but first let's consider the main point of the metaphor.

Jesus speaks the Father's word, which is the seed or sperm containing the vital information needed for a new type of human life. In modern parlance, we would say that Jesus' teaching provides the DNA for a new form of human existence. We might unpack (or should we say, "unfold"?) his claim this way: Jesus offers determinate information that supplies the coordinates for learning what is really there, how we can know it, and what makes for the best kind of human life. These are the three topics every ancient philosophy sought to understand. In other words, the core of Jesus' philosophy is positively revealed by the Father.

In the parables of the Synoptic Gospels[18] Jesus employs horticultural or plant imagery.[19] The "seed" falls on various types of soil, which determines its reception and effect. Likewise, Jesus' message will find varied reception and effect depending on what type of heart it encounters. Here the seed produces a new form of botanical life. Yet the botanical seed metaphor explicitly refers to the beginnings of a new kind of *human* life.[20]

The same words function in metaphorically biological contexts. Jesus, and some of his early followers, speak about God's word producing of a new type of life. In this context, they use the metaphor of "seed" as that which produces an embryo or the beginnings of a new human body.[21] By extending the metaphor, evangelizing could be described as a "begetting" or "generating" of a new life.[22] A person in whom this new form of life had been engendered has been "sired again" or "sired from above."[23] The same root word (*gennaō*) could mean either "to birth" or "to beget, sire"[24] depending on whether the subject is a male or female.[25] In the context of John's Gospel, the one who begets is God the Father and is thus metaphorically masculine. Attentive readers of John's Gospel will have been alerted at the beginning to this masculine sense of begetting. For the true light gives to believers the right to become children of God. Such are begotten, not from blood nor from the desire of the flesh nor from the choice of a man, but from God (John 1:12–13).

It's important to distinguish the notion of "begetting" or "generating" from "being born." Here is the reason. When we use the common language of "born again," our imaginations conjure a short, intense period of emergence. Birth typically lasts from a few hours to perhaps a full day. On the other hand, when one speaks of being generated from above, we naturally expect a longer, more involved process of growth and transformation, from initial conception to infancy. Conversion imagined as "being born again" conjures a quick change—perhaps like Saul of Tarsus' "road to Damascus" experience. Conversion understood as "being generated from above" prepares a person for what might be a year of awkward, searching, incremental morphing into a new life.[26] Jesus is preparing people for the second type of experience.

The Relation of Socrates' and Jesus' Philosophies

When we understand that Jesus' teaching begets a new life, it clarifies his relation to Socrates' philosophy. By his own account, Socrates' teaching is sterile. He cannot deliver the information ("seed") that shapes a new life.

Socrates is gifted, however, at identifying when someone is seized by an incoherent and lifeless idea (a stillbirth). Likewise, Socrates sees when someone is posturing and blustering—pretending to know something but lacking any coherent insight. By detailed and prolonged questioning, Socrates can help these types of people abort their false pregnancies. Likewise, Socrates' questions can help true ideas to reach term and be healthily born into the world.

Jesus' teachings impregnate with understandings of God's character and God's manner of working in the world. The life information he implants guides humans into a life of co-working with God and of deep moral transformation. Information, to be clear, is not just what fills one's head but what gives form to something (i.e., what in-forms it). Jesus gives us the best information about the most important things in human life.

Moreover, Jesus too seeks understanding rather than mere deference from his students. In a manner like Socrates, Jesus disrupts people's false understandings and tries to keep them searching for insight into his teachings. Jesus does not want anyone to emptily affirm the truth of something that they have not understood.

The proper relation of Jesus and Socrates, in a human life, is as that of the begetter and the midwife. Jesus' teaching provides the basic material of life. As that teaching begins to produce a new kind of person, Socrates' questions help that person dislodge any unhelpful, false preconceptions. They also help her or him to clearly express the truthful insights from Jesus that have been maturing within.

This handmaid relation does justice to both Socrates and Jesus, in the roles to which God called each and which each explicitly claimed for himself. Moreover, it fits with the way that Jesus' subsequent followers, for the next thousand years or so, made use of Socrates and his philosophical heirs. They used Socrates' method to articulate and develop Jesus' teachings—his life-giving information.

Among the second or third generation of Jesus' early followers, we find some impressive teachers at the church in Alexandria, Egypt. Clement of Alexandria, writing in the late second or early third century, expressed a similar view to the one I am suggesting. Clement was a Greek who converted to Jesus as the culmination of a philosophical journey. He noted the words of Paul, a Jewish follower of Jesus. "The Torah has become our tutor leading us to Christ so that we may be justified by faith" (Gal 3:24). Clement then observed that just as the Torah was the child-conductor that led the Jews to Christ, so philosophy was the child-conductor, or stepping stone, that led the Greeks to Christ.[27]

Whatever one thinks of that as a theological claim, historically it is quite accurate. In the second through the fifth centuries, throughout Greco-Roman society, the world witnessed a mass conversion of the philosophically trained intelligentsia to Christ. By their own accounts, they turned to Jesus because he effectively answered the questions which the philosophers had been fruitlessly wrestling with for several centuries.[28]

Both intellectually and morally, Jesus brought the new life—planted the seed—that the other philosophers simply could not produce. Socrates knew he could not produce it and, I'm pretty sure, he would have been grateful to Jesus for doing it.

So, on to Jesus and his life-giving information.

SECTION I

Jesus' Theory of Lasting Personal Change

CHAPTER ONE

The Parable of the Soils and the Formation of Human Attention

A Basic Life Issue

I WANT TO ASK you a really basic question. Who is your teacher? One thing is certain. You are somebody's student. I know that because it is characteristic of human beings to require a teacher or set of teachers.

The knowledge base needed for human life is just too extensive, and human life is too fragile and short, physically speaking, to be able to learn everything alone. In fact, humans require the longest period of instruction of any species out there. Lizards scratch their way out of an egg and immediately hunt for themselves. No teacher required. It's all hardwired. A baby wolf needs about seven or eight months before it can hunt with the pack. Giraffe calves stick around for one year and three months with their parents. Late bloomers might take a year and a half.

How long do your kids take to grow up and move out?

Throughout the ages reflective people have pondered this uniquely human condition. Aristotle noticed: "We owe more gratitude to our teachers than to our parents, because whereas our parents enable us to live, our teachers show us how to live well."[29] There is probably nothing more significant that one could know about a person, by which to predict the effect his or her life will have upon the world, than to know who taught that person how to live. Teachers are vital to life.

Ancient adherents of "the Way" embraced Jesus as their teacher. They were convinced that Jesus understood human life like nobody else. They were eager to compare his teachings and example with those of other significant thinkers and teachers. They learned from everyone. Indeed, nothing was off-limits to explore. But Jesus, they claimed, possessed a depth of insight (and today, one might add, a historical track-record of effectiveness) that set him apart from the philosophic crowd.

In this book—as well as the studies and life-experiments that gave rise to it—I want to know if a bridge could be built between their world and ours. Could one become Jesus' apprentice in living a flourishing human life in the twenty-first century?

Part of knowing how to live is knowing how to change. Jesus' teaching provides unparalleled insight into the dynamics of change for human beings. We can introduce this topic by posing the philosophic question to which it responds.

The Question of Moral Weakness and Transformation

How do people change over time and, more specifically, how might they change for the better? Few find satisfaction in answers to a question like "what is the best way to live?" if there is not an accompanying answer to "how could a person be sufficiently changed so as to live that way?"

Throughout the ages great philosophic minds have pondered the question of moral development and transformation, along with its corollary question of moral weakness. The questions are corollaries because in order to ask how people can morally grow or be changed for the better, one must also consider why people often find themselves incapacitated or stunted in their genuine efforts at moral improvement.

As we embark on this journey together, we're going to examine Jesus' answer to these questions and how Jesus remakes a person. My choice to attend to Jesus' teaching is not merely a matter of personal preference or religious prejudice. Philosophy, from Socrates on, has been committed to producing a superior human life.

Historically, nobody has succeeded at enabling broad swathes of people to grow morally and spiritually like Jesus has. People noticed that in the ancient world too, and it drove a mass conversion to Christ. For two thousand years, Jesus has enabled ordinary people to undergo substantial and lasting change for the better. The life that we read about in the New

Testament is not just religious fiction. It's a life for actual human beings—perhaps even for you and me.

This topic—personal change—matters because, if Jesus' account holds, then it would mean that it *is possible* for someone like you or me to become like Jesus. Personal transformation really can happen. It is available right where you are, . . . whatever your family, resources, education, life conditions. Nobody can keep you from having this sort of life. Nobody can take it away from you.

Those are lofty promises, but this is what Jesus taught, so we should consider his teaching carefully.

Jesus' Moral Theory—Where, in the Human Person, Does Transformation Begin?

Jesus' theory, like that of other philosophers, focuses on a key anthropological structure or element.[30] But Jesus' focal element, conceptually speaking, introduces something new when it enters the history of Western thought. (Of course, Jesus is not a Western thinker, but his teachings have exercised vast influence on the development of Western thought.) For Jesus, the central element is the human heart.[31]

According to Jesus, the most salient features of a human life spring from, or ultimately originate in, the heart or attention of a person. In placing the center of moral transformation in the heart, Jesus inherits and hones a concept native to Hebrew thought. In the Hebrew Bible, the heart (*leb, lebab*) is what sets human beings apart from the beasts and connects them with the divine.[32] The heart was the center of self-awareness as a whole.[33] We might call it *attention*. As such, it was broader than the more self-contained categories of reason, appetite, and emotion used by the Greek philosophers. One's attention, or heart, may at any moment be a mixture of all those and many other things, including speech, judgments, evaluations, fantasies, memories, anticipations, self-descriptions, aspirations, self-deceptions, etc.

In particular, the heart possesses a distinctive capacity of choice, which is not fully reducible to either reason, emotion, or appetite as the Greek philosophers had conceived them. When a person really "shows up" or consciously engages with something (which is not a continuous state for any human being), choice can be exercised through that attention. As such, the heart is the primary site of moral transformation.[34] Perhaps more to the point, attention and its various focal points are the raw materials out of which human lives are fashioned. More on this below.

Jesus' Theory of Moral Transformation

Through his parable of the sower and its interpretation, Jesus articulated a wide-angled theory of the necessary components of lasting personal change or moral transformation. The parable of the sower and the soils is all about how people change through interacting with the message of the kingdom of God.

This parable is recorded along with Jesus' interpretation in all three of the earliest accounts of his life (Matt 13:1–9, 18–23; Mark 4:1–9, 10–12; Luke 8:4–8, 11–15). For the sake of space, I will fully quote only the version found in Matthew, then comment on some variations in the other accounts in the discussion below.

> And Jesus spoke many things to them in parables saying, "Behold the Sower went out to sow. And while he was sowing some seeds fell upon the path and the birds came and devoured them. Other seeds, however, fell upon rocky places where there wasn't much soil and immediately it sprang up, because there was no depth of soil. But when the sun had risen, the plant was scorched and dried up because it did not possess a root. Other seeds fell upon the thorns, and when they came up the thorns choked them. Yet other seeds fell on the good soil and produced fruit, one a hundred, another sixty, and another thirty times as much. He who has ears, let him hear." (Matt 13:1–9)

> Therefore, hear the parable of the sower. Whenever someone hears the word of the kingdom without understanding, the evil one comes and seizes that which is sown in his heart. This one is the seed sown along the path. That which is sown upon the rocky places, he is the one who hears the word and immediately receives it with joy. However, he does not possess a root in himself, but is temporary. When difficulties or persecutions occur because of the word, immediately he is floored by them. And the one sown in the thorns, he is the one who hears the word and the worries of the social order (*lit.* age) and the illusory lure of wealth choke the word and it becomes fruitless. The one sown on the good soil, however, is the one who hears and understands, who also bears fruit and produces one hundred, sixty, or thirty times as much. (Matt 13:18–23)

The Parable of the Sower—It's All about
Moral Transformation

Let's begin with the most basic question. What is this parable *about*?[35] The title does not help with this question. In Matthew, Jesus titles it the "parable of the sower" (13:18). But titles, among the ancient Jews, identify the first words of a text, *not its theme*. The title only tells us that this is the parable that begins "The sower went out to sow. . . ."

What, then, is this parable *about*? Moral transformation. The parable is about how people change to become morally fruitful through attentive interaction with the "word of the kingdom." The key to its theme is in the contrasting images of fruit-bearing versus being unfruitful.

In the course of his story, Matthew has already employed these images of producing fruit and being barren of fruit. They always refer to moral life results. Our key terms enter the story with John the Baptist demanding of the Pharisees and Sadducees that they "produce fruit worthy of repentance"—literally, "do fruit . . . !" (3:8).

Later in Matthew, Jesus culminates his Sermon on the Mount by explaining that moral change is the outcome of "hearing and doing" his words. Conversely, moral failure and life disaster follow from hearing without doing (7:15–20). Jesus returns to the image of moral life results as fruit in Matthew 12:33.

Hence, moral transformation is the obvious meaning of "fruit bearing and doing" in our parable and its interpretation (13:8 and 23).[36] Incidentally, the earliest interpreters of the parable of the sower, often referred to as the church fathers, read it this way too.[37]

If moral transformation (and its failure) is the general theme, how does this parable depict the process of moral change? Two key elements are interacting in this process. They are symbolized in the story by the seed and the soil. Let's focus there.

Attention: Soil of the Heart

We'll concentrate one the basic element, in you and me, upon which God's word works. In the parable this is called *soil*. Jesus tells us that the soil refers to the heart.

What is a heart? This word requires a little clarification because in our world we tend to identify the heart primarily with emotion. But, in the scriptures, "heart" refers to something much broader and more basic than emotion. In scriptural terms, your heart is your *attention* or *present awareness*—the whole range of what you are personally engaged in at any given moment.

In the Bible, you *think* and *plan* and *hope* and *desire* with your heart. Of course, some emotion happens there too. But it's bigger than just emotion. It also includes whatever you are focused on or paying attention to at any moment.

Moral change for the better begins, Jesus explains, when one's attention (or "heart") acquires a new focal point—in this case, in his teaching concerning the kingdom. Some focal point (a teaching) is necessary for the attention to move a person towards moral improvement. On its own, human attention is unformed and easily altered—like soil. While humans have a capacity to focus their awareness and maintain, or return to, that focus over time, this capacity has distinct limits posed by its own lack of endurance, surrounding conditions that compete for focus, and the necessity of adequately significant content.

The raw material of human life, which is reshaped through spiritual formation, is simply attention. Carpenters reshape wood. Metal workers fashion new things out of iron, copper, lead, and such. Painters create out of canvas and paint. God remakes humans by working, at least initially, on our attention—our heart. Jesus' teachings work upon the unformed, and often malformed, stuff of human attention. As our attention is given to his teachings they fashion a life of moral fruitfulness.

Moral transformation begins when our attention, by God's grace, is given a new focal point by interacting with "the word of the kingdom," or in Luke's variation, the "word of God."

These are phrases that refer to a vast body of teaching. A few words about that body of teaching are therefore in order.

The core of Jesus' message was his announcement that God's kingdom—or present activity in this world—is immediately available for ordinary people to enter.[38] In other words, it is possible to take one's personal agency, centered in the heart or attention, and join it to God's personal project in this world. The result is a distinct form of collaboration with God in one's everyday life.

In other teaching settings, Jesus describes the experience of collaboration with God as a timed interaction with an unseen force, which is reliable but uncontrollable (see Mark 4:26–29). He also describes the experience of divine collaboration, in any given instance, as being marked by a distinct disproportion between visible causes (in one's own action) and the ultimate effects, which are much greater (Mark 4:30–32). These and many other teachings, mostly in parables, are designed to sensitize his students to the possibility and promise of living in an interactive, collaborative manner with God.

Jesus' teaching on the kingdom also contains significant portions of ethical exhortation. In order to collaborate with God, over an extended period of time, one must come to share something of God's moral character. So, Jesus teaches about love—or benevolence—and compassion as the guiding moral principles of God's own decisions. These core virtues can also be developed in human persons. Subsidiary teachings offer descriptions of and exhortations concerning such core vices as retained anger, disproportionate or twisted desires, and various misuses of speech. This entire body of moral teaching is encapsulated in Jesus' phrase "the word of the kingdom."

When these teachings become the enduring focus for one's attention, potentially lasting and positive change begins. Moral growth requires sustaining a broad enough range of awareness to effectively counteract the intense narrowing of focus that ordinary desires instigate as they arise from or pass through a person. Moral descriptions and exhortations, such as found in Jesus' teachings, *while actively attended to* produce a broadening of the perceptual horizon and allow a form of choice that is not a mere yielding to impulse. This is the seminal moment. Change starts here.

Seed of the Word

According to Jesus, his teaching of the kingdom contains the life-structure for a new type of human existence. It is seed.[39] It's worth reflecting on what a seed is. A seed is something with the capacity to reshape part of the world into a life-form. That's what seeds do. Right? If you drop a tomato seed into usable soil, it will eat the dirt, absorb the water, and utilize the light of the sun. From those raw materials, the seed produces a tomato plant—something completely different and something very much alive.

In the same way, Jesus' message about the kingdom of God has the capacity to take the raw materials of your attention—your personal experience—and remake them into a new kind of human existence. This metaphor of the word of God as the seed (in modern parlance we might call it the DNA) of a new human existence runs from Jesus' own teachings through early Christian thought and constitutes a distinctive claim of this philosophic movement.[40] Like all such claims, it should be tested against experience, but it must first be identified in order to become testable.

When received properly, Jesus' teaching initiates a process that changes human life. Metaphorically, we might say that it contains the DNA of a new kind of human existence.

How People Change

Through focusing our attention on a uniquely potent set of teachings, a fundamental change in us begins. But this seminal event, essential as it may be, is far from self-sufficient. The broadening of perceptual horizons, which occurs during attending to such teaching, is, by its nature, a temporary event. It produces a real, though transient, effect on the person that enables a choice. However, a life of moral fruitfulness cannot be a transient, temporary affair. Moral challenges do not wait for a person to possess an attentive readiness for choice. For the change enabled and structured by moral teaching to last, several other things must occur.

Jesus' story tells us that three things can go wrong with our attention, each of which would prevent the new life nestled in the word from growing to maturity within us. Thereby, Jesus implicitly informs us of three activities that need to work properly for the seed to sprout, develop, and bear fruit.

According to Jesus, the three necessary components are alterations in an individual's ideas, the introduction of regular bodily practices, and a re-negotiation of one's social relations. In Jesus' parable, these three components are presented first as what goes wrong with the receptions of particular "seeds." However, this failure implicitly indicates how things might go right. Three activities, rightly employed, allow the seed to grow to maturity. Let's consider the role of each.

Understanding: The Role of Ideas

Jesus says that the first type of soil is too hard, so the seed cannot penetrate. Consequently, the evil one comes and removes it. In his explanation of the parable, we learn that this simply refers to a lack of understanding in the hearer, which results in him or her forgetting the message.

> Behold the sower went out to sow. And while he was sowing some seeds fell upon the path and the birds came and devoured them. (Matt 13:3b–4)

> Whenever someone hears the word of the kingdom without understanding, the evil one comes and seizes that which is sown in his heart. This one is the seed sown along the path. (Matt 13:19)

Without finding basic sense in an utterance, the memory will not retain it and any potency within it will be negated. It's that simple. However, the consequences are great.

Ideas are important. In fact, they are indispensable for human life and for moral change. One might refashion the behavior of many animals through pure stimulus and response. A dog, for instance, can be trained without instilling a single idea within him. (Indeed, I must confess that it is unclear to me what it would mean for a dog to possess an idea at all.) Human beings, however, live under the guidance and control of their ideas—for better and for worse. That is the type of being that humans are.

According to Jesus, there are a few basic ideas that must *make sense* to a person for the whole process of change, in Jesus' Way, to begin. Jesus' central message, what he calls "the gospel of the kingdom," is *a set of ideas*. Specifically, it is a set of ideas about God and how close God's activity is to you—to ordinary human existence. The kingdom of God—God's own action—is close to you. He's personally engaged and working right where you are at. That's one cluster of ideas that we must make sense of and trust or we won't be able to grow.[41]

The gospel is good *news* or a good *message*. It's not a good *mood*. There is information in Jesus' teaching that's vitally important for your life. Humans live under the guidance and control of their ideas—for better and for worse.

As Dallas Willard used to point out, "When Satan came to Eve in the garden of Eden, he didn't hit her with a club. He hit her with an idea." In fact, the snake confronted her with an idea about God. "Maybe God's withholding something good from you, . . . making your life worse instead of better." Once human beings accepted that false idea of God, everything started going wrong.

When Jesus comes to remake human beings, he brings us true ideas about God and ourselves and the world. For instance, we learn from Jesus that God is love. His character is marked by humility and gentleness. That's a very important truth. If you really grasp it, it can change your life. It has changed the lives of many, many people over the last two thousand years.

So, gospel ideas are important. You can train a dog without that dog knowing anything. But human beings will never live much better than the ideas they believe in and comprehend. If you want the best life possible, it starts with acquiring *the best ideas*. Jesus has some for you try.

Disciplines: The Role of Bodily Practices

The second type of soil in Jesus' story lacks the depth needed for roots. A thin layer of dirt over rocks will allow a seed to penetrate, but just a little.

Once the seed has digested the nutrients from that thin layer, it's incapable of acquiring any more nutrients, so it is weak and easily destroyed by the heat.

> Other seeds, however, fell upon rocky places where there wasn't much soil and immediately it sprang up, because there was no depth of soil. But when the sun had risen, the plant was scorched and dried up because it did not possess a root. (Matt 13:5–6)

> That which is sown upon the rocky places, he is the one who hears the word and immediately receives it with joy. However, he does not possess a root in himself, but is temporary. When difficulties or persecutions occur because of the word, immediately he is floored by them. (Matt 13:20–21)

This shallow soil and lack of "roots" refers to a life in which initial understanding brings joy. The broadening of perception enables a genuine choice. However, any person's attention is quickly passing. Cognitive apprehension alone doesn't allow the message to move from an initial change into lasting bodily habits. That's what is meant by Jesus' phrase "he does not possess a root in himself" (Matt 13:21). Ideas, or rather the practices associated with them, must be transposed from the mind to the body through a process of habituation and tempering. Bodily practices produce "roots."[42]

Jesus had already advocated "hearing *and doing*" in Matthew 7:24–27. In that context, the doing would include the kinds of practices or disciplines Jesus had just taught in Matthew 6:1–18 (almsgiving, praying, and fasting, all in secret). In the parable of the sower, these practices deepen the attention (soil) and develop a root or stable connection between the attention and the teaching. In contemporary terms, consider that even the minimal habits of regularly reading one's Bible or engaging in morning or evening prayer are all *bodily* practices—something you do with your limbs and eyes and in a favorite seat.

Of course, this is the sort of activity that each individual must do for him- or herself.[43] Many may hear, but I alone can engage in the work needed to inscribe these actions in *my* bodily habits. Just as you might explain an idea to me, but you cannot understand it for me, likewise your practice cannot instill habits in my body. These things one must do for oneself.

Consider the metaphor. Roots absorb dirt and transfer its nutrients into the plant—the new life form. Remember that the dirt, metaphorically, is our attention or awareness. Corresponding bodily practices attach more of a person's attention to the content of the moral vision. By habituating the body, they prime it to act in keeping with the moral vision, even at times when the energy for genuine choice is lacking.

In Matthew 6:1–18, Jesus has given instructions to his students about how to engage in spiritual disciplines such as giving and fasting and praying in secret. These sorts of practices are designed to close the gap between our understandings and our bodies. They move the message of the gospel from the mind into our nerves and muscles, our chest and belly.

Here is Jesus' wisdom: As soon as you learn something, act bodily in some way based upon it. Do something different with your body and repeat that action until your body doesn't need to be told how to do it. For instance, have you learned that forgiveness is the best way? Speak your forgiveness to someone who has hurt you. Have you learned that God will provide for you as you care for others? With your body take some of what you have and give it to another person in need. Don't just think it over. Act. Put your body into motion because of it. This is how roots grow.

Jesus says that if one does not engage in such bodily practice based upon his moral teachings, when difficulties arise, one's moral purpose will be too weak to face them. We'll be shocked as if something were terribly wrong with the world and we will likely give up. But if we engage in disciplines and train our body to support our understanding, we'll find deeper strength to face those difficulties that inevitably come with ethical action.

Relations: The Role of Social Identity

The third type of soil has something else growing in it—thorns. When the seed falls into this soil, it can sprout a little. But the thorns compete for the nutrients of the soil and the seed is unable to grow into a fully functional plant that bears fruit.

> Other seeds fell upon the thorns, and when they came up the thorns choked them. (Matt 13:7)

> And the one sown in the thorns, he is the one who hears the word and the worries of the social order (lit. age) and the illusory lure of wealth choke the word and it becomes fruitless. (Matt 13:22)

The specific competition for our attention that Jesus mentions here is located in our social identity. He says the "worries of the age and the deception of wealth choke the word and it becomes unfruitful." In the New Testament, the first writings arising from the movement Jesus inspired, "age" typically refers to the social order—how things are generally expected to work in the current world. We might call them social habits.

A great deal of who a person is arises from how they interact with and relate to other people. Often people develop a variety of disparate personas—ways of interacting with and presenting themselves to other people. These can be mutually contradictory. For instance, I might have one way of behaving with people at the gym, and a very different way with my family, and yet another personality that comes out at work. Each of these personas, or ways of presenting myself, has an effect on who I actually become over time. If our way of interacting with people never changes because of the gospel, we will never grow into maturity.

For Jesus' word to complete the process of transformation within us, we need to renegotiate how we will live within our cultures or society.

Jesus' phrase "worries of the age" is packed with insight. Much of what holds an extended collection of people together—a society or culture—is a shared set of anxieties and aspirations.[44] In other words, cultures tend to share a sense of what things would make life unbearable, not worth living, tragic, etc. These are the anxieties or worries of that age or social order. Likewise, they share a range of aspirations, or a sense of what things are worth working, competing, striving, cooperating, or even dying for.

Wealth is viewed, across a great many human cultures, as one of the main things a person should strive to obtain. It's considered a primary good for many unreflective people. Jesus observes that this is simply an illusion or deception. Wealth routinely fails to give the satisfaction that its pursuers expect from it. Of course, possession of wealth in itself is neither a moral virtue nor a moral vice. Jesus is forthright about the particular moral challenges that possession of wealth presents to a person, but one would be mistaken to assume as a consequence that Jesus considered poverty, in itself, to be morally meritorious. The associated moral challenges are simply different for those who find themselves lacking basic material resources than for those who find themselves in possession of surplus resources.

Once we become students of Jesus, if we desire full transformation, our ways of interacting with others and with their cultural ideals must change. We must negotiate a new, consistent social identity for our personal change to be lasting. Personal change creates tensions because humans are so interconnected that when one person changes, everyone in proximity has to adjust to this new personal character. It's uncomfortable for a while and adjusting takes more energy than most people have available. So, they resist others' change. They don't want to let them become different—even if this difference is a vast improvement. Thus, social pressures are to be expected and must be successfully negotiated to attain a state of steady moral growth.

Your loved ones and everyday associates will resist your change too. They won't want to let you become different. Perhaps, as you initiated a positive life-change, you have heard an old friend say something like this. "You can fool other people, but I know who you really are." That friend does not want to revise his assessment of who you are, because he doesn't want to adjust to a new way of relating. He is resisting the change in you. If you haven't heard such dismissals, you probably will. It's best to take Jesus' advice and prepare for them now.

Achieving a stable, singular identity across one's various stations in life (family, school, work, recreational activities, citizenship, church, friends, etc.) takes substantial effort. There are a couple common pitfalls. One is to be too timid and continue trying to meld in with the crowd. This prevents real growth. The other is to become obsessed with correcting what one now sees is wrong in others. This too stymies personal growth and becomes its own harmful distraction. Between these extremes one might find a sweet spot—calmly pursuing what is good, joyfully withholding from what is wrong, and frankly speaking what is true without becoming agitated about trying to fix others who are not ready to change.

The Saint-Making Matrix

Jesus says that when these three elements—ideas, bodily practices, and social identity—work in harmony rather than against each other, individual change for the better accelerates and intensifies through a beneficial positive feedback loop of moral transformation.

> Yet other seeds fell on the good soil and produced fruit, one a hundred, another sixty, and another thirty times as much. He who has ears, let him hear. (Matt 13:9)

> The one sown on the good soil, however, is the one who hears and understands, who also bears fruit and produces one hundred, sixty, or thirty times as much. (Matt 13:23)

A positive feedback loop is when one alteration sets up the conditions for another to intensify it, which in turn sets up conditions for another alteration to repeat the process, and so on. The effect intensifies with each journey around the loop. For example, a very unpleasant type of positive feedback loop would be what happens when the sound of speakers gets picked up by the microphone that feeds into it. It picks up the sound, amplifies it, and sends the amplified sound out of the speakers. This sound gets picked up again, amplified again, and this twice amplified sound comes through the speakers. A few loops can result in an unbearably high-pitched squeal. In this case, intensification is undesirable and even harmful.

But there are beneficial positive feedback loops too. One virtuous change may set up the conditions for another. When alterations in one's ideas, bodily practices, and social identity all move in the same direction, each creating improved moral and spiritual conditions for the next to improve upon, Jesus describes the effect this way. "The one sown on the good soil, however, is the one who hears and understands, who also bears fruit and produces one hundred, sixty, or thirty times as much" (Matt 13:23).

To understand the significance of these numbers, a point of comparison is helpful. In the land of Israel, prior to modern agricultural technologies, the greatest return that one could expect for a crop of grain was seven to ten seeds for each seed sown.[45] Of course, there were no genetic engineering or synthetic fertilizers or advanced irrigation systems. So, the return on investment in a crop would not vary greatly from the average. As such, Jesus' numbers are dramatic.[46]

Through this metaphor, Jesus tells us that if all these elements work together—ideas, bodily practices, and social identity—the worst-case scenario would be that a person's moral transformation would be at least triple what anyone considers probable (i.e., thirty-fold). But then it can double and double again.

We really don't know just how transformed and thoroughly good a human being is capable of becoming. But the example of Jesus and of many of his notable followers through the centuries, sometimes called saints, indicates that the outer limit of human goodness is way beyond what we initially imagine. After embracing Jesus' moral message, in this specific manner, these persons came to look drastically different to the way they did when they started. And it is happening in our day as well. Not only in "the West," but in Asia and Africa and Latin America people who encounter Jesus' Way are changing in ways profound enough for their societies to take notice.

You really don't know just how wonderfully transformed and thoroughly glorious God could make you. But it is way beyond what you imagine.

Jesus' words can remake you into a being so glorious and good that it would take your breath away if you saw it now. It really is possible to become like Jesus.

Through the chapters below we will be examining this process of change.

CHAPTER TWO

Soul-Shaping in Jesus' Way

Key Parts of the Human Person and the Sequence
Imbedded in the Two Greatest Commandments
(Mark 12:28–34)

How We're Put Together: The Elements
or Parts of the Self

IN THE PARABLE OF the soils, we learned of three indispensable types of
activities for lasting personal change—incorporation and apprehension of
key ideas, tempering or toughening through bodily practices, and reordering one's social presentation and interactions. These activities will either
work together for one's transformation, or they will mutually frustrate
each other and stymie personal growth.

These activities work because of the nature of the human person—
the way we're put together. We have constitutive parts, each with intrinsic
characteristics, and those parts exist in mutual relation to the other constitutive parts.

Jesus, inheriting and developing prior Jewish understandings, sees the
human self as a differentiated—almost composite—entity. Specifically, he
distinguishes the human heart, soul, discursive thought, body, and social
relations (neighbor status) from each other. Each needs to be renovated
through the proper cultivation and focus of its love.

17

Experiential Entry Points: One Difficulty
in Understanding Jesus

We may find it difficult today to understand Jesus' account of the self. Part of our problem lies in accurately identifying, experientially, some element of ourselves as being the *same part* that Jesus is talking about. Without a specific experience that we can consistently name as an experience *of that part*, his distinctions remain opaque and mysterious to us.[47]

Talking about soul today presents a problem something like you would face if I were to ask you, "How is your pancreas feeling today?" You would probably be at a complete loss as to how to respond—unless you had been diagnosed with pancreatitis in the past and learned to connect the feeling with that part of yourself. You simply wouldn't know how to think about the question, let alone answer it. If I asked you, "How is your soul doing today?" you might be in a very similar situation.

Such terms as heart, soul, spirit, and mind are blurred together today and used in confused, ambiguous ways. This blocks us from grasping the specificity of Jesus' guidance for moral transformation. If the average church member did remember the litany of "heart, soul, mind, strength" from Jesus' teachings and were asked what it means, perhaps he or she would say it means something like "whatever it is that's inside me"—my "inner self" or maybe even "the real me."

But Jesus has something else in mind. He is working with sharply focused understandings not vague sentiments. For us to competently use his teachings in our life, we need to home in on this specificity—to employ Jesus' life-giving information.

We've already introduced the Hebrew notion of the heart that Jesus uses. It was central to his account of how his teaching initiates lasting change in a person. It's the first layer of how we consciously interact with the world. We'll briefly return to the heart below. But in this chapter, we need to focus on the soul.

Here's what we need to ask: *What is a soul and what is it good for?* To bring into focus the centrality of your soul for the transformation process, I'll start with clarifying the nature of the soul.

What's a Soul?

Scripture uses the term "soul" (that's *nephesh* in Hebrew, *psyche* in Greek and their cognates) to speak of the autonomic (self-regulating) depths of bodily life. The soul is *the life-force of a body*.[48]

I said soul is the life force of a body; I did not say of a *human* body.[49] In fact, soul is what connects us with the beasts (see Gen 1:20, 24; 2:7).[50] It's what we have in common with them—not what separates us. *All* the lower biological species are instances of soul—beginning with the goldfish in the bowl on your shelf, rising to your pet Labrador retriever at your foot, and going all the way up through the chimpanzee in the Rwenzori Mountains of Uganda. And, yes, the human body is also enlivened by soul. Our souls, which run our bodies, are kindred to the beasts. There is something within us that we share with the animals.

Within our bodily existence, soul experiences itself as an ever-connected flow.[51] Since we are identifying something in us that our dog might also approximate, we might begin by considering the experience of daydreaming or that nebulous zone between sleeping and being awake.[52] The "heart" or consciousness as alert, chosen engagement is not involved in these moments. Instead, images and feelings float through—sequenced but not rationally ordered—in a manner that does not differentiate what is "in me" and what is "out there." Inside and outside seem to have collapsed—or, perhaps, have yet to be distinguished. Time, as measured or even measurable, is not clearly experienced at this level of existence. The flow just *is*.

To illustrate, recall an experience you have had. You are dreaming as the alarm on your phone goes off. Within your soul experience—the dream—that noise gets incorporated into the story or image flow. It is inside you, just like everything else. As you come to consciousness, however, you differentiate and realize that the noise is actually outside you—blaring from your phone. This helps you recognize how the inner flow does not distinguish inside and outside—me from not me.

You may also recall the experience of hitting snooze and falling into another dream state. That dream—or rather what you are experiencing within it—is very long and involved. Your inner experience has immense duration. But then the alarm goes off again. Evidently, in terms of the external world only ten minutes have passed. The soul, however, was processing images that it felt to be long and involved. In these types of experiences, we notice that soul does not experience time in the way the heart—our conscious, engaged awareness—experiences time. From the inside, the flow just *is*. There is no reference, within it, to anything like measured time.

Moments of intense emotion also seem to surface the soul or suck us down into it. When anger or sexual desire or sadness exceed a certain threshold, I again find that what is in me and what's out there loses sharp distinction. Time awareness also warps or disappears. Again, the flow overwhelms. The depths envelope the surface of the self.

Once we've identified it, this elemental level of our experience is also recognizable on the periphery of our conscious life—haunting the edges of our heart-present moments. Here's one way to notice it. What are you pushing out of your awareness right now to read this chapter? Mental focus, such as that required when reading or attending to another's words in conversation, requires momentarily excluding other thoughts. But those other thoughts push against our concentrated attention. As you read, you are peripherally aware of those things that you are intentionally *not* focusing on.

For instance, in order to write I must hold some things to the side. The e-payment I forgot to make at my lunch break. The meaning of someone's unusual glance this morning. The discomfort and pressure in my lower back. A background sadness at the absence of a deceased friend, etc. You are probably negotiating some analogous prodding as you read. These are not thoughts I choose, nor do I allow them into my consciousness while I am working if I can manage to stay focused. But they are never really gone. They're just being held to the side, and that takes some energy.

Later, we will talk about the disciplines of solitude and silence in Jesus' Way. One therapeutic role of these disciplines is that they put one in touch with the experience of soul.[53] Even if you have not practiced that discipline, you can probably identify some period of solitude in your life—perhaps you experienced it once when weathering an illness? When we are alone, in silence, and not engaged in any work—soul more readily overwhelms our conscious experience. Without work at hand, it's very difficult to regulate the interaction between soul and heart—to maintain the mental wall between unconscious flow and intentional engagement. Whether we like it or not, prolonged time in solitude provides us with an inventory of what's in our basement. That's why most people avoid it. Soul isn't always pleasant to experience directly—for most of us it can be marked by deep pain, disappointment, and hopelessness.[54]

Experientially, soul shows itself in all the unconscious reflexes, appetites, habits, self-talk, imagining, and social locating of a person. Most of the stuff that contemporary neuroscientists would say is inscribed in the nervous system is what scripture refers to as soul. Soul runs largely beneath the level of conscious awareness. It constitutes what we are and what we want and experience before we know that we're doing anything.

What's a Soul Good For?

Soul is what runs your life when you're not actively deciding or choosing to do so. Like the autopilot program on a plane, your soul takes over when the pilot, that's your heart (or spirit), is just too tired, distracted, confused, or otherwise disinterested in governing life.

For *every person*, even in the most stable settings, this is a daily experience. Just think of mentally "checking out" at the end of a long workday or finding it's too early or late in the day to "think straight." Perhaps you discover odd urges taking over when you're hungry or exhausted or disappointed. Soul is running your life in those moments. The basement flow has risen into the living room.

Through the initial stages of apprenticeship to Jesus, and then in crisis seasons throughout life, these moments of overwhelm and reversion to soul-control become more frequent. There are a lot of decisions to make in these seasons. Each decision takes energy. The strain of breaking old habits and forming new ones, of adjusting to new kinds of social interactions, as well as the added demands of spiritual warfare—all these acts consume the limited energy available to the heart or spirit. Consequently, you must expect that even more of your day, in those trying periods, will be off-loaded to soul-guided living.

At the same time, however, the disruption of ordinary patterns means that your soul—the source of those unconscious, autopilot motions—will not yet be well adapted to this new life. All this amounts to a soul-quake and significant personal trial. We may find ourselves, for a season, with our heart consciously striving in one direction and our unconscious soul continuing to flow in another.[55]

The good news is that Jesus—the ultimate realist—knows how we're put together and teaches us how to live well. He knows that one simply cannot effectively and consistently love God and the guy next door without transforming this subterranean dimension—the soul.

But if soul is an element that I share with bull mastiffs, sea bass, and donkeys, how on earth could it ever be taught to love God and neighbor? What goes into training the soul?

Jesus and the Layers of the Self

To answer this question, we must consider the relation of soul to the other elements of the human self. Jesus does just that in Mark 12:28–34 when he's asked which is the first among the life-guidelines God has given. Here's the whole conversation:

> And one of the scribes, who had been listening to their discussion, approached Jesus. Seeing that Jesus answered them beautifully, he asked Jesus, "Which is the first command of them all?"

Jesus answered, "The first is 'Listen, Israel, the Lord is our God, the Lord is one. And you shall love the Lord your God out of all your heart and out of all your soul and out of all your discursive thought and out of all your strength.' The second is this: 'You shall love your neighbor as yourself.' There is no other commandment greater than these."

The scribe said to him, "Beautifully said, Teacher. You spoke in truth that 'He is one and there is no one else beside him' and 'to love him from all the heart and from all the understanding and from all the strength' and 'to love the neighbor as oneself' is more than all the whole burnt offerings and sacrifices."

Jesus, noticing that he had answered intellectually, told him, "You are not far from the kingdom of God."

Nobody dared to ask Jesus any more questions. (Mark 12:28–34)

Firstness: The Question of Order

The scribe asked Jesus about what is *first*. In other words, which of God's life-instructions forms a foundation from which the others can be seen as naturally following?[56]

Jesus replies, from scripture, that the first guideline—the prior basis for everything else—is the identity and unity of the LORD (or YHWH).[57] Jesus usually refers to him simply as our Father. As we focus on the peculiar unity of the Father's character, Jesus says, we will learn to order our love so it can be birthed from within each of the various layers of the self. In other words, as I get to know the Father, this starts a process that can bring the complexity of myself to love his unity. That unity is not simply mathematical—it's a matter of character.

We will return to the Father's matchless, unified character below. It is the first among the kingdom understandings that Jesus delivers, and we will give it our focus in a dedicated chapter. For the moment, however, we want to clarify these aspects of ourselves and how they can be attached in love to the Father.

Sequence: Which Part Follows Which?

Jesus' explanation of how our complex selves can love the Father's unity proceeds through a quotation of Deuteronomy 6:4–5, which lists key elements of the self. To understand the brilliance of Jesus' Way for personal transformation, we need to see that the order of the list is progressive. In other words, Jesus sees that Moses was not just giving a random catalog of some human elements. Rather, he was indicating the proper order or sequence in which those parts can be directed to love God. It begins with the heart, then moves to the soul, then to discursive thought, then finally to strength.

But we also should notice that the Deuteronomy quote is enhanced—added to. It is always instructive to pay attention to such alterations and to consider why Jesus modified the original statement. In this case, Jesus expands Moses' words about loving God with the whole self by adding into the order, between soul and strength, "out of all your discursive thought." As we consider Jesus' whole account in sequence, we'll see the importance of this element, as well as its order, in our transformation process.

i. Heart

According to Jesus, then, the effective sequence is to first love God "out of all your heart." We've already considered the biblical notion of the heart when we were attending to his parable of the soils. So, we'll be concise here.

The heart is *the actively engaged self*—the full range of my present, conscious awareness. My heart is what's functioning when I am aware and personally thinking or choosing.

Allow me also to connect a few dots that may otherwise be perplexing. I take the heart, in Jesus' teaching, to be roughly synonymous with the human spirit and with the human awareness or "conscience" (*syneidêsis*) in the rest of the New Testament writings. These other terms get used more by Jesus' followers, like Paul and the author of Hebrews, than by Jesus. They are operating in a different context. They are teaching in a Greco-Roman setting and need to translate the Hebrew notion of heart into conceptual terms more readily understood by Greek philosophers.[58] But Jesus' word for present, conscious awareness is heart.

So, to initiate the change, I must give God my conscious focus and *choose* to love him. There is no substitute for conscious, active choice. That's step one.

But it can only ever be the first of several steps. The heart—our conscious focus—just doesn't have sufficient energy to stay engaged all the time. God created it to oversee and superintend the human self, as choices needed to be made, but it was never supposed to micromanage human existence. There just isn't enough of it. God created other elements of the self to run most of the details of our everyday lives. Those other elements must also be trained to love God.

A life strategy that solely depends on actively choosing to love God, moment by moment, will fail. Inevitably. Every time. The heart simply lacks the energy to keep choosing without any pause. There are times when it must sleep or just check out to replenish its energy. That is why soul training is essential to successful apprenticeship in Jesus' Way (or, for that matter, in any other consistent way of life). Here's how it works.

ii. Soul

As central as the heart is, it isn't all that powerful. Compared to the soul it is tiny and easily fatigued. So, Jesus' wisdom tells us how to use our hearts to train our souls.

The heart's choice to love God can only become effective, long term, if it uses its limited energies to transfer its love of God into the soul. In other words, we must use what energy we have available for conscious evaluation and choice to engage in a process of training our unconscious habits, unreflective practices, and underlying dispositions. With this we enter the second level—the depths of soul.

Since we've identified our soul—both "out there" as something shared with the animals and experientially "in here" as an undifferentiated flow of unchosen images, feelings, thoughts, and impulses—we are now able to think more clearly about how it could be trained. Soul training would be something like redirecting the flow—realizing that the flow itself will have a momentum and tend to perpetuate itself even at those moments we are not directing it. Streams cut channels into the ground over which they flow. This creates its own set of challenges for redirecting them.

Moreover, soul is not the most literate or cerebral part of us. This means that we must approach the training of our souls in a manner more like how we build loving rapport with our pet dog and help her live well as a member of the household. We learn her body language, so to speak—use belly-rubs and tones and gestures of delight to show her she's loved. We use stern tones and sharp gestures to alert her to a behavior that is not appropriate and must not be repeated. Thus, we train our dog to "sit and stay" on command or not to beg at the table. We connect and we direct by adapting our guidance to what our cherished pet can understand.

Soul training is similar. There is a part of me that does not respond well to reason—it cannot be *talked* into new habits; it must be wooed and drilled and habituated over time. Bodily actions and repeated images or signals, over a sustained period of time, at first disrupt old patterns of flow and then carve new channels for soul's flow.

In contemporary, neuropsychological terms, these regular actions produce brain alterations at the basal ganglia level of procedural, as distinguished from prefrontal and hippocampal episodic, memories. Even a person whose brain has been damaged in regions needed for verbal recall can still develop new motor skills and habits. This underlying layer of us, which operates largely without the need for verbal expression or spoken command, has a life of its own that can be altered and transformed.

This is what spiritual disciplines, if used wisely, do. The regular bodily practices, which Jesus has already called "roots" in his parable of the soils, establish an unconscious flow towards what is good for God and God's project. In other words, they help us move from loving God with all our *heart* to loving God with all our *soul*.

We will devote space later in this book, to Jesus' big-picture (or theoretical) account of how the disciplines work (chapters 8 and 9). But here's a sneak preview. In Matthew 6:1–18 and 25:1–13, Jesus offers a coherent theory of how such practices transform our unconscious habits, dispositions, reflexes, etc.

If you can, quickly read the parable of the wise and foolish virgins in Matthew 25:1–13. Jesus tells us that our capacity to co-work with God (kingdom of the heavens) *in crisis moments* will largely depend on what has become autonomic—in other words, what we do without conscious deliberation or choice. Everyone in the parable "sleeps" or runs out of a capacity for conscious engagement. This is true of both the wise and foolish. Limited heart energy is not a feature only of the foolish person. Every human has such limits. What makes the difference at the crisis moment is the "oil" of character stored up beforehand. In other words, habits and unconscious reactions play an irreplaceable, vital role in enabling us to co-work with God.

We simply won't be able to join in with what God is doing, at least on some important occasions, if we need to be fully awake and engaged to do so. Fully awake choice is the level of heart engagement with which we begin. But, in the course of a *life*, those moments of full alertness are too few to sustain. Therefore, the oil of *transformed habits*—subterranean soul change—or its absence will determine our capacity to step into God's activity in those moments.

Regular practices—or disciplines—gradually alter the soul. Not only do they work on creating habits, which are soul phenomena, but they change the type of images and stimulations the soul incorporates. Since the soul's flow consists largely of the after-effect of the images, words, and bodily motions it has experienced recently, taking on a structured life discipline may even change what happens in your dreams. (Do you remember skiing through the night in your dreams after a day on the slopes?) What goes in changes the content of the flow over time.

Soul training is essential. The wise strategy is to use our heart to leverage our soul, but that's not the end either. After descending to the primordial layer of soul, we find that the flow also produces a *talk* of its own. Jesus calls upon us to change that next.

iii. Discursive Thought

The third level of progress is the one Jesus adds to the words of Deuteronomy 6:5—*discursive thought*, or we might say, churning thoughts. In most translations this will simply appear as the command to love God "with all your mind." But mind is not an adequate translation. Greeks talking about mind are like Eskimos naming snow. They have lots of distinctions we don't find in English.

The term *dianoia*, which Jesus adds here to Deuteronomy 6:5, means specifically discursive thought. *Dianoia* is all the stuff turning over inside when you are mentally chewing on something, or when you're trying to figure out what you think.

Discursive thought includes both conscious and semiconscious talk—but one has a way of flowing into the other. You engage discursive thought to think through something when focused, say, on planning an event or figuring out a math problem. But you experience discursive thought even more frequently as that running commentary in your mind when you're focusing on doing something else.

We might call it "self-talk." In the Texas hill country, we'd say, we're "noodling." It's that voice in the back of your mind that rarely shuts up—the sound track we don't actively choose but that accompanies us through most of our life.

We've all had the experience of getting the words of a song stuck in our mind. Those of us who had small children when Disney's *Frozen* was released can remember how agitating the line "Let it go! Let it go!" became. It stuck, first in our children's minds and then, through their repetition of the song, in ours. What was supposed to be a moving line symbolizing felt release for a character in the cartoon, became an interior torment for the rest of us. It replayed relentlessly in the back of our minds while we were trying to complete our everyday business.

That experience of a refrain you cannot shake tells you something about *dianoia*. It happens *in* us, to be sure. But we often experience it more as something that *shows up* within us than as something we actively do.

This illustrates how the content of *dianoia* or self-talk is largely supplied by the subterranean soul. To leverage our self-talk for love of God, disciplines that put such words into the soul must be practiced. When your soul is realigned through practices like memorization of and meditation upon scripture, prayer, praise, and gratitude, then the script that runs in the back of your mind will gradually change.

If what is unconscious in us is adjusted to routinely act in the best interests of the Father and to adore his character (i.e., loving God), this will alter the thoughts that bubble up unbidden. The churning thoughts in the background of our lives will begin to carry phrases and images that lean into God instead of away from him. At this point we are loving God from all our discursive thought, and we will find new capacities for action.

iv. Bodily Strength

Fourth, as the subterranean elements of your personality fall into line, your strength—your concerted action in the world—will become an effective overflow of your love for God. I take Jesus' words "out of all your strength" to refer to those things we do with our body in the world. This is our capacity for action.

Effective action depends, among other things, on what occurs to a person to do. You cannot act on something that never crosses your mind. Very often our "strength" or capacity for action is limited by a lack of imaginative possibilities. To take a trivial example, perhaps someone has never tried juggling or baking her own bread or learning Spanish. It's not because she thinks she cannot do it; it's just that the very thought of trying never occurred to her.

Having the idea occur is the most essential element of any non-habitual action. One cannot initiate without it. Often the physical capacity can be acquired once the guiding thought has been embraced.

One way that Jesus infuses us with transformative strength to co-work with God is simply by introducing the idea that it can happen. He passes this role on to his students too. He sends them out to announce that God's project is available for each person to step into. Then they show people how to do it. Lots of new actions follow.

But this initiation of kingdom action is not all externally occasioned. We don't always need to be told by someone else. It begins to bubble up from within us when our self-talk is transformed. Words of gratitude and wonder and love for the Father spark new ideas for action. Different things seem obvious possibilities within a mind occupied by such inner speech.

Giving to a neighbor in need or praying with someone you find in distress becomes the natural thing to do. Through the remaking of habits and self-talk, Jesus' student finds new capacities and resources for co-working with God in everyday life.

Social Relations

The most notable change in our action, which this potentiates, is a move away from anger, distorted desires, and deceit and toward active love of our neighbor. Jesus says this care for the person who happens to be physically near us is the second life-guideline that the Father gives.

The new ideas and impulses for action, which are received in this transformation process, enable us to love the person next door or whoever walks across my threshold.

The web of relationships within which I live—family, friends, colleagues, institutional memberships, citizenship, etc.—is also an irreducible element of myself. The same is true of you.

Humans by nature live in social relations with others. There is no exception. Social relations are not primarily contracted, as moderns tend to imagine. Rather, many of the most important relations are already there when we enter this world. If a baby is born but nobody ever relates to it—bonds with him or her—that baby will simply die. It will not grow into adulthood. Attachment is a necessity, even at a biological level, for human existence.

These particular relations are part of what make you unique and irreplaceable in God's world. Each of you are, as Jesus notes, salt of the earth and light of the world (Matt 5:13–14). You occupy an unrepeatable place in a complex web of personal relations—parents, siblings or not, extended family, friendships and acquaintances, coworkers, bosses, teammates, and such like—and *only you* can shine light there. If you are not salt and light in the place you alone occupy, there will simply be no salt and no light in that place. God made you irreplaceable in relation.

This also means that those relationships are not really outside you. Our relationships shape our insides. Who we manage to become over time will depend to a large degree on how that is made to fit into our relationships. Jesus provides significant guidance, which we will consider in chapters 10 and 11 below, concerning how to renegotiate our social relations. As students of Jesus, we will need to establish new social habits and help those in close relation to us to understand them.

This solidifies our new existence and enhances the change of heart, soul, discursive thought, and bodily strength.

A Common Failure in the Process

Jesus has outlined a viable trajectory for sequential change through five connected levels of the self. It really works if we take them all in sequence.

In my experience, however, we often fail because we try to take a short cut. Many church traditions tend to think a lot about getting people to decide on Jesus. That's level one—the heart. But then we immediately seek to engage people in the observable work of mission or ministry. That's levels four and five—bodily strength and neighbor love. Unfortunately, without following Jesus' teaching through the soul and churning-thought levels in between, personal collapse and moral failure become fairly predictable. The stats on this score are pretty discouraging; if one could not see Jesus' more realistic way of shaping people, they would be despairing.

As it happens, this neglect of soul and self-talk cultivation isn't just a problem of our day. In fact, Jesus' conversation partner in this passage has some of the same tendencies.

The Scribe's Intellectualism

The scribe with whom Jesus is conversing echoes back most of Jesus' answer. But there are some crucial alterations that betray a sort of intellectualism in the scribe.

The scribe abstracts the commands, which in Moses' and Jesus' words are personalized. "You shall love the LORD your God out of all *your* heart, . . ." becomes "to love from all *the* heart." It's not *my* heart. It's one's heart.

More importantly, the scribe collapses what Jesus differentiates. Soul and discursive thought are conflated into something else—"understanding" or even "erudition." The word that the scribe substitutes (*synesis*) means a joining together or connecting. It is used for the mental faculty of understanding and also for the process of "cross-referencing" typical of rabbinic and scribal explanations of scripture. The erudite or understanding person is the one who can quote one scripture passage to explain another, place one rabbinic pronouncement within the context of other similar ones. It's an important ability, but it does not exhaust all that goes into the soul and discursive thought that Jesus wants to transform.

In short, the scribe has a tendency to keep the locus of inner change between his ears. Jesus notices it.

A Hair's Breadth from Co-working with God

"Jesus, seeing that he had answered intellectually (*nounechōs*), told him, 'You are not far from the kingdom of God'" (Mark 12:34). Jesus is as gentle and complimentary as he can be with the scribe. But what he offers is a left-handed compliment. The scribe is not quite in a position yet to co-work with God. He's too exclusively cerebral. A full life of co-working will require dropping below the level of intellect to work on the other parts of the self too. He'll have to plunge into the soul and deal with the kind of self-talk that isn't fully conscious.

There are parts of the self that simply do not respond to quoted texts. It's significant that these are the parts the scribe collapses and intellectualizes. But soul is more like a golden retriever. Perhaps, in my case, it's more like a donkey—less eager to please. It must be negotiated and reshaped in ways that are not purely intellectual.

Full transformation, indeed, real *knowledge* of the Father too, will take something more. It requires stepping into a yoke—strapping our beast-like lifeforce next to Jesus—and training our less-intellectual elements too within the kingdom of God. To this we'll turn in the next chapter.

CHAPTER THREE

Obediential Knowledge in Jesus' Way

(Matthew 11:25–30)

Summary

LET'S REMIND OURSELVES OF where we've come thus far. Jesus, unlike Socrates, offers humanity life-giving information—the seed to structure a new form of human existence. This teaching interacts with human beings at several levels.

The primary material on which it works—the first layer—is our attention or heart. But our attention floats upon and must use underlying living stuff that is neither focused nor clearly purposive, at least not in the sense of answering to *our* purposes. This secondary layer, in some ways deeper than the first, is the soul, followed by the automatic self-talk rising from it.

These bottom-up elements of the self are less directly accessible by intellectual argument. They are renovated in ways akin to how we tame and train animals. That process is more like horse-whispering or the process of drilling a new trick with your pet dog than it is like proving a theorem. Rather than guide the animal through a syllogism, we interact in scripted and consistent ways to introduce visceral urges and inhibitions, to craft unconscious experiences of comfort or unease in specific situations, that result in new automatic behaviors in the animal. The automatic, habitual depths of the human soul operate much like an animal. Only, whereas the animal needs a human to guide it through the drills for a new habit, we are given a heart that can guide the process of soul-formation.

Since these layers are irreducible and essential elements of the human person, full transformation will include transformation of the content and direction of soul, self-talk, bodily action, and social relations. In so far as that is the case, we must ask a new question.

A New Question

The new question is how, and in what form, might the seed—Jesus' life-giving information—make its way into these layers of the self? How can Jesus' teaching shape what, by its nature, lies outside our direct attention most of the time? Is that even possible? Is there such thing as a *soul* whisperer?

Perhaps we should point out that soul, not to mention self-talk, certainly does contain information—whether or not it is accurate information. Dreams and images and cravings are more than just amorphous blurs. They have specificity and reference. We dream *about* things and have cravings *for* things. Likewise, we think and argue *about* things. So, we should not glibly ask for "transformation not information" as we're often told today. Rather, we need to ask how the relevant, transformative information can get to the parts that need it but cannot receive it directly. Is there an effective, *in*direct way for these layers to receive it?

To extend Jesus' metaphor complex, if the heart is soil, then the soul is a subterranean water[59] spring, which when adequately present to the soil enables fertility. Both good soil and compatible moisture levels are needed for the seed to grow. How can we bring our soul—that unconscious flow—to work together with our heart's attentive choice for God?

Jesus intimates the way in Matthew 11:25–30. The general topic of his teaching there is a question: What bestows knowledge of God? We will consider this passage closely below. But it is important to first put it in context—both in its life context for Jesus' ministry (as indicated by the literary context in Matthew), and in the broader context of the general nature of knowledge.

The Life Context

Jesus, in Matthew 11, must deal with a failure of education, which he observes generally in the Israel of his day. The specific failure is this. Despite an abundance of miracles—deeds of power—these wonders have not brought people to rethink the character of God and of God's proper representative.

Jesus observes that even good people have this problem. John the Baptist was the best. Yet, in prison, when he hears of Jesus' mighty deeds, he does not reconsider God's project in light of the specific types of power that Jesus wields. John still wants to know when Jesus will get on with slaughtering some Romans. "Are you the Coming One, or should we look for someone else?" (Matt 11:3) Jesus sends back a report to John connecting his deeds with the promises of YHWH[60] in Isaiah 35:1–5 and 61:1–3. If God's concerted action in the world looks like this, maybe John needs to rethink YHWH's character?

Then Jesus reflects that although God's activity—kingdom—has broken into the world in unexpected and powerful ways (Matt 11:11–12), his generation's self-contradictory response to him and to John amounts to pouting over not getting to control the game being played (Matt 11:16–19). In a pagan context, Jesus muses, the same miracles might have produced a rethinking (or "repentance"), but in Israel assumptions about YHWH's character are too deeply fixed (Matt 11:20–24). Even miracles have not helped them rethink these deep images and assumptions. The wake-up calls that Jesus performs cannot reach deep enough on their own.[61]

Evidently, real knowledge of the Father's character—the kind of knowledge that transforms us—must reshape not only our explicit concepts but also the unreflective images and desires and reactions of our souls. Deep repentance—or rethinking—will remake not only the ideas I explain and endorse when fully attentive, but also how I experience God and myself and the world when I'm not paying attention.

When those layers all line up and correspond to how things really are—including who God is—then I have genuine knowledge of God. That's a tall order. But nothing less will really transform us. Nothing less is real knowledge of the Father.

The General Nature of Knowledge

It's important to connect this issue to a second, broader context. This is the broader consideration of what, generally speaking, constitutes knowledge and how it is acquired. In the philosophical traditions streaming from the Greeks through our own day this general issue is called epistemology—the theory of knowledge.

I'll start by stating a general principle. Knowledge is only possible for those who *put themselves in a position* to know. Very few forms of knowledge are compulsory—and those are generally immoral to impose.[62] Most forms of knowledge require that we seek them out in appropriate ways.

Since knowledge is the capacity to represent something as it is on an appropriate basis of thought and/or experience, to acquire knowledge one must take the steps needed to obtain an appropriate foundation—a reliable basis for guaranteeing the truth of what one is representing.

If you want to learn mathematics, for example, you will have to apply your attention over time. Maybe you hire a tutor or pick up a textbook. You trust that your guide is generally reliable for the task at hand and, based upon a disposition to assent, you try to make sense of specific formulae and to solve problems.[63] You do the work. This leads eventually to personal insight into the mathematical relations, which we would call knowledge of math. Knowledge emerges through personal engagement with its object.

Something similar must occur for me to acquire deep knowledge of God.[64] But that's getting a little ahead of ourselves.

Why the Knowledge Question Is Important

The "knowledge question" is terribly important—and not just regarding Jesus' teachings. Here's why: human beings cannot sustain a consistent way of life without some answer to it. The basic human problem for every age and every place is how do we find a knowledge base adequate for life.

Try thinking about the issue this way: Truth is a kind of match or close approximation between what one thinks about something and the way that thing really is. The Hebrew concept of truth (*emet*) has the underlying notion of reliability, stability, and dependability. It is used to describe a quality not only of speech and thought, but also of physical objects. A true thing can be counted on—it matches up with what it purports to be. As such, truth gives people access to reality. It allows us to integrate our plans and actions with what's really there—or what *will be* there when the time comes.[65] Otherwise, we would be continually plagued by frustrations, failures, and unexpected results. Only truth enables a person to live with confidence and to choose effectively.

Knowledge guarantees truth. A guess or a leap of faith might land on the truth occasionally. But we cannot *rely* on them to do so—acquiring truth in those ways is accidental. When someone has knowledge, however, he has a way of reliably and consistently speaking or otherwise indicating the truth on some matter about which he knows. He doesn't just happen to be accurate at the moment in his claim. He has good reason to guarantee that he is right about it.

In any significant area of life, we want knowledge. If I'm on a gurney, being wheeled into surgery, I don't want to hear the anesthesiologist say that he's "got a hunch about the right dosage." At that point I would fight my way off the bed and check myself out of the hospital. Likewise, I don't want an airline pilot to "take a stab at" the proper amount of fuel for a transatlantic flight that I'm boarding. And, frankly, I don't care in the slightest if she feels confident in her guess or has a really good feeling about the upcoming flight. With the stakes so high, only *knowledge* can be trusted. There must be reliable information that is adequately understood by those in charge.

The truth is just too precious, and the consequences of misunderstanding are too dire to trust anything less than knowledge. Strong opinions and heartfelt beliefs won't do. We need *knowledge*—an adequate basis for guaranteeing truth.

Does that mean only "researchers" and people with letters after their names can know? In some matters, maybe so. (In yet other cases, knowledge may be currently or permanently inaccessible for human beings.) But *that is not the case when it comes to knowledge of God.*

We should also note that even in those cases where it is likely that only someone with a PhD would possess a particular bit of knowledge, the letters after her name would not be the source of that knowledge. The letters would only be an indication that she had successfully gone through a process to acquire knowledge.

So let's talk about the knowledge-acquisition process.

The Nature of Knowledge and Methods

Knowledge is an ability to represent something as it really is on an appropriate basis of thought and/or experience.[66] At this point we need to reflect on that phrase "on an appropriate basis."

What constitutes an adequate basis is peculiar to each area of life. In philosophic terms, "method is relative to subject matter." It changes depending on the kind of thing you want to know.

To illustrate, good certified public accountants (CPAs) and anesthesiologists possess an adequate basis for saying how things are *in their field*, but not in some other field. Knowledge of biochemistry would not help the CPA fill out my tax return, and additional familiarity with the tax code would not keep the anesthesiologist from frying my brain during surgery. These activities require different knowledge bases with different methods for their acquisition.

God created this world with such wonderful diversity and nuance and specificity that knowledge will always be something particular, not universal. In other words, just because I come to know something in one field does not mean that I will have any knowledge or competence in another field. I can only have knowledge about distinct things. Universal, absolute knowledge does not exist among humans. There simply is no such thing as a human person who knows everything.

Moreover, by nature, there are as many methods for discovering truth as there are areas of life in which truth is needed. Humanity's constant challenge is to discover the proper method for each subject matter. That's what we need in order to expand our knowledge base.

So, I want to ask the obvious, but crucial question: How can I come to *know God?*

Scripture, from its opening pages, provides profound answers to this question.[67] In clarification of the prior teachings, Jesus tells us that God, the distinct person of the Father, is active all around us. What, then, constitutes an adequate basis for knowing this active, ever-near God? Does Jesus provide us with the proper method?

In Matthew 11:25–30 Jesus provides his answer. It comes in two waves—11:25–27 and 28–30. Usually, the two waves of this passage are disconnected, and popular explanations and encouragements tend to go directly to the second wave ("Come to me all you who are worn out and weighed down . . ."). However, we are bound to miss some of its meaning unless we let the first wave carry us into the second. Here's why: the first wave tells us that Jesus is talking about knowledge *of a particular kind.* So, let's begin with Jesus' statement of the underlying question.

Who Really Knows the Father?

In Matthew 11:25–27, Jesus implicitly evokes and answers the following question: "Who can really know what God the Father is like?" In the background, you will remember, is the related question of why miracles did not enable his generation generally to repent or reconceptualize their view of God. If wonderworking does not produce knowledge of the Father, who or what can guide us to authentic, knowledge-producing interaction with the Father?

Jesus provides both a positive and a negative answer.

> On that occasion, Jesus responded, "I thank you, Father, Lord of heaven and earth, that you have hidden these things from the wise and understanding and revealed them to speechless

children. Yes, Father, for this manner of revealing was well
pleasing in your sight. All things have been handed over to me
by my Father. No one knows the Son except the Father, and no
one knows the Father except the Son, and anyone to whom the
Son chooses to reveal him." (Matt 11:25–27)

The Negative Answer

Negatively, Jesus clarifies what is *not* a sufficient basis for knowing the
Father. Neither the sages nor the understanding (or erudite) really know
God—not in the deepest sense.

When Jesus speaks of the "sages," we should think of the wisdom
tradition in Israel stretching from the book of Proverbs in the Bible up to
the writer, a generation or two before Jesus, of the Wisdom of Ben Sirach.
The tradition is filled with astute observations of natural and human regu-
larities distilled into memorable sayings. We'll compare and contrast Jesus'
Way with this tradition below.

"The understanding" ("erudite" is another good translation) probably
refers to those who can quote not only the scriptures but also the various
rabbis' pronouncements (the "oral Torah") so as to balance each statement
against another. Later rabbinic texts (especially the Mishnah, Tosefta, and
the two Talmudim) amply express this approach. Rabbinic oral tradition, as
a whole not in parts, claimed to offer understanding of the Torah.

Jesus says that neither the wisdom tradition nor the rabbi's frictional
cross-referencing of texts[68] is sufficient by itself. To be clear, Jesus does not
say these are bad. Both the wisdom tradition and the rabbis' erudition offer beautiful insights and present many truths. They contain a great deal of
truth and goodness. They're just not sufficient to really know the Father.[69]
Something more in needed.

The Positive Answer

Positively, Jesus tells us who is capable of knowing the Father's character.
On his own, only the Son knows the Father. In the same way, only the
Father has interacted enough with the Son to really understand him. Nev-
ertheless, the "infants" or "speechless children," to whom Jesus chooses to
reveal the Father, will be in a position to know God. They have a capacity
to know God *through the Son's help.*

Study plays an important role for Jesus (note Matthew 13:52 on "scribes trained for the kingdom . . ."), but one cannot achieve knowledge of the Father's character through study alone. Books can only take a person so far. Perhaps an abundance of study, in the absence of Jesus' way of life, could even hinder reception of his revelation.

The capacity of infants to receive revelation stems from *their awareness that they do not know*. Infants don't presume to have the answers yet. "But why?" and "how?" fall easily from their lips—too frequently, in fact, for their parent's comfort. Because "infants" acknowledge their dependence and ignorance, Jesus is able to reveal God's character to them.[70]

This is where the first wave of Jesus' explanation crests.

A Method for Knowing the Father

As we roll into the second wave of Jesus' explanation (Matt 11:28–30), an obvious question hangs over his words. *How* does the Son reveal the Father's character? This well-beloved passage describes the *means* by which Jesus provides knowledge of the Father's character.

When recognized as such, Jesus' words both shock and inspire.

> Come to me, all you who are worn out and weighed down, and I will give you rest. Take my yoke upon you, and learn from me, for I am gentle and humble in heart, and you will find rest for your souls. For my yoke is kind, and my burden is light. (Matt 11:28–30)

The most thorough knowledge of God can neither be spoken nor heard. It is not something one could simply memorize and repeat. Rather, Jesus leads his apprentices into this knowledge through a distinct way of life—a "yoke."

Obedience as Method for Knowledge

I'm tempted to say the deepest knowledge of God is discovered experientially. That's true as far as it goes. But it is much truer to say that Jesus *reveals* this knowledge through our obedience in his way of life. According to Jesus, the proper method for obtaining knowledge of God is *obedience*. Nothing else will provide an adequate basis for guaranteeing its truth.

The word "obedience," given its connotations today, is scary. Images flash to mind of dictators and totalitarian regimes demanding minute conformity to arbitrary rules. Many also suffer from personal memories of religious leaders—whether well intentioned or with perverse purpose—who used an expectation of obedience in manipulative and harmful ways. In fact, such misuse in both secular and religious contexts often demanded blanket and groundless control of people's thoughts as well as their actions. "Obedience" has been coopted in demonic ways. The word makes us cringe now, and for good reason.

Obedience, however, is a concept and practice better chastened and repaired than replaced. Understood properly, it names a life-giving form of interaction that other words don't quite convey.

First, obedience in the original Hebrew and Greek (as well as in the Latin that gives us our word) simply means to listen to or to hear—something like embodied attentiveness. There is no connotation of mindlessness or automaticity. Rather, obedience is *a responsive form of interaction with a guide one trusts*. So, for instance, there is no coach–athlete or teacher–student relation apart from obedience in this proper sense.

Second, obedience—rooted in the metaphor of using ears and appropriately responding with one's body—implies active, embodied partnership in some larger task. Obedience means *bodily inhabiting or performing instructions*. And the boundaries of the task set the perimeters of proper obedience. I listen to my weight-lifting coach when he corrects my form in the clean and jerk and embody his instructions as best I can. However, I rightly ignore his comments about politics and listen to more informed guides. I seek to embody the prescriptions of my language instructor, drilling the paradigms and repeating key phrases aloud to get my tongue around them, but he teaches me how to say something in the new language, not *what* I should seek to communicate. The bodily drills are essential for obedience, but so is the clarity about what is and is not the shared task at hand.

Obedience is Jesus' method for guiding us into knowledge of the Father's character—that's the shared task. Embodied responsiveness and consistency are needed because the kind of knowledge that Jesus wants to pass on needs to penetrate deeper than that produced only by our conscious thought and choice (i.e., "heart"). We're aiming to know at the soul level. Of course, the process starts in the heart, as we've already noticed in other contexts. But Jesus will show us how to acquire such deep familiarity with the Father that it reorders and refreshes the *soul*—that bestial basis for bodily life and experience.

Long-term obedience requires more than our heart's attention because that's inevitably a quickly diminishing affair. We can only strain our attention for so long. Eventually we find that the sustained effort is just impossible to maintain. We become "worn out and weighed down"—there's no more energy for focused choice and mental presence. The heart can only travel so far. Something else will have to take over. Is there any way for that other, deeper part—the soul—to continue in a process that familiarizes us with the Father and his true character? Jesus claims so.

The Yoke

In Jesus' world, the yoke was a common metaphor for a prescribed, overall way of life. A number of different "yokes" were offered. The Rabbis routinely exhorted people to take on the "yoke of the Torah" for it would deliver its devotees from other "yokes" of political oppression and worldly anxieties.[71] By the yoke of the Torah, they meant the life ordered in entirety by obedience to the legal specifications that the Rabbis collated and taught. It was a total way of life—but it was heart-intensive and required one to constantly make distinctions. All focus, little flow.

Within the wisdom tradition, Ben Sirach offers the "yoke of Wisdom" (Sir 6:30). This refers to a disciplined life. Under the "yoke of Wisdom" one memorized the sayings of the sages and approached life in a posture of discernment to know which saying applied best for the situation. Again, wisdom provided a total-life package—but it too was more cerebral. One embraced the vast repertoire of sayings and used them to talk oneself into a new life.

Amid the market of "yokes," Jesus offers a distinctive way of life. No one else in Israel offered *their own* "yoke." Jesus does. Here he invites us to take up his own practices. "Take *my yoke* upon you and learn from me. . . ."

We should draw to mind, for example, the Sermon on the Mount at this point. Of course, there is conceptual content there too. And it is derived from the Torah and Prophets. But it is readily understood because it is sufficiently distilled and presented in a principled order. There are important insights conveyed. But to follow them you don't have to keep the whole corpus of the wisdom literature or the whole history of rabbinic pronouncements in mind. Jesus' yoke is doable by ordinary people. It can pass into and through our heart level.

By adopting a handful of central practices (such as regularly seeking reconciliation, habitually refusing to indulge a lustful gaze, speaking unadorned truth, turning the other cheek, and blessing those who curse us) we can place our neck beneath Jesus' yoke. Obedience—embodied responsiveness—in Jesus' Way is eminently doable for ordinary people.

Soul Refreshment

Jesus' Way *starts* with choices, but here's the secret. Over time, obedience to Jesus' way of life is simple enough to sink into the soul level of habit, unconscious responses, spontaneous internal images, and even dreams. As Jesus' Way sinks into those depths of the self, the soul begins to experience a calm and refreshment it had never known.

One source of the soul's rest is simply the abiding, though usually peripheral, awareness of neither being alone nor unaided. For some, this experience of soul connection and assistance in one's activities has never entered their adult experience. Perhaps not since the bonding of early child-hood have they felt in their unconscious depths that they are supported and empowered by the constant presence of another.

The soul begins to experience this aid and accompaniment, because the yoke into which we bow our necks attaches us to Jesus within the Father's work. The metaphor of a two-necked yoke as the instrument for learning is rich.

Remember, a yoke is a connecting device used for combining and shar-ing power in a common project. The yoke attaches two beasts of burden (the power source) both to each other and to the instrument they are pulling. The idea is that through this way of life we are connected *with* Jesus and *to* the Father's larger project—his kingdom and specific tasks within it.[72]

Imagine something like this. Jesus is an old ox engaged in plowing the furrow—expertly living in line with how his Father would tend his field. As young oxen we are invited to slip in beside Jesus. This is an age-old strategy for training a young beast of burden—attach it to a veteran in the yoke. When we make missteps or find our attention wandering, Jesus will simply continue in the correct direction. We'll be pulled along, . . . tugged back into line.

We discover that there is an added source of direction and momentum within this life of co-working. And it eases the strain of pulling. Pairing with Jesus is restful. This yoke (overall life-pattern) is kind and light. In chapter 6 below we will learn more about the Father's action in this paired, synergistic activity called the kingdom. For now we can simply note that we will not be the only one at work—our labors are folded into a larger project with many hands, visible and invisible, engaged for its completion.

This deep attunement with Jesus as he instructs us in co-working with God both refreshes the soul and guides us toward true knowledge of the Father's character. What, at first, may feel difficult and awkward becomes second nature and easy through practice. As we continue in this overall life, we become familiar, experientially, with the Father and his ways. We learn who he is.

The Father's Character: Content of Knowledge

In Matthew 11:28, Jesus gestures toward the *content* of the knowledge, which he passes on through his yoke. Through obedience to his teaching and example, we learn Jesus' character. By learning Jesus' character, we are, implicitly, learning the Father's character. To know the Son's character *is* to know the Father's character. In the context, that's unmistakable.

So, what does the soul-sating yoke teach us about the Father? Jesus' words are startling. I doubt any of us would have guessed this about God, but the Father is gentle and humble in heart. That's his personal character. When we take on Jesus' overall way of life, we will learn this by experience—not just by rumor or report—and it sinks not only into our conscious thoughts but into the unconscious flow beneath them.

Gentleness and humility rarely come to mind when humans describe God. In fact, I know of no such description in the history of human thought before Jesus. There have been a lot of descriptions: Is he "Holy"? Yes. "Distant and other?" For most. "Powerful?" Of course. "Angry?" All too often. But *"gentle and humble?"* That's new! However, now that Jesus has lived and spoken, how could we imagine the Father any other way?

The Gentle Father

Perhaps a contemporary thought experiment will help us put the Father's character in perspective. The Father is the Creator of heaven and earth. Jesus, with the rest of scripture, affirms this.

Let's think about that in our own terms.[73] Consider, for a moment, the immense power of a being who can initiate the space-time universe with a word. In order to think about such power, allow me to offer a point of comparison. We now know that energy and matter are convertible—that's the point of Einstein's famous $E=mc^2$ formula. So, imagine for a moment that I had a small ball of uranium in my hand, it would be very heavy because of its density—a baseball-sized portion would be over thirty-five kilograms in weight. The energy within the matter of that uranium baseball, however, would be so great that, if released, it would transform the geography of the part of Greece in which I live. The whole city would be gone and much of the countryside. That's how much energy is in just a baseball-sized bit of matter.

If there's that much power inside a piece I could hold in my palm, try to fathom how much energy or power it took to create the whole space-time cosmos. There are about 100 billion galaxies in our universe. Our galaxy, the Milky Way, is only one of those created. Our solar system circles only one of 150–250 billion stars in our galaxy. But that star, which is our sun and which is small by cosmic standards, could contain 1.3 million planets of our earth's size inside it. Our entire planet, in cosmic scale, is a mere speck of dust. You and me? We are like microbes crawling around upon that speck.

Got the picture? That's the true scale from which to think of our Creator's power.

Now with that scale in mind, consider this. How is it possible for the Creator to interact with us at all without crushing us? Given such immense power, only a character of unimaginable gentleness could speak to us and not destroy us in the process.[74] His interactions are tender, and he is careful to preserve us. If there's any being in this universe who is gentle, God must be the gentlest of all. We learn this intimately as we interact with him, alongside Jesus, in everyday activities.

The Humble Father

But not only does the Father interact with us gently, he sent his Son to become one of us. Since the Son too is Creator,[75] we can say that the Creator of all located himself in one human body—one of those microbes crawling around on the speck of cosmic dust. Only one filled with unfathomable humility would stoop to become one of us and teach us the way for which we were created.

But he descended even further. From within that human existence, he took the form of a servant. He walked our streets and washed the dust from our feet. He spoke words of life into our great need, yet when we rejected him, he was willing to receive death at our hands in order to make a way for us to return to him. In so doing the Son, as the image of the invisible God, reveals to us the character of the Father. In other words, in the humility of the Son we see the humility of the Father made manifest. If any being in the universe is humble, the Creator is humblest of all.

Soul Knowledge and Its Availability in the Easy Yoke

Jesus knew all this about the Father from the inside. He knew the Father's character because he shared it. By taking on Jesus' way of life, we too can interact with the Father enough to know him in this way.

Jesus' invitation stands yet today. You really can know God. These claims are as testable as any other form of knowledge. Also, as with any other form of knowledge, it isn't coercive. If you want to know chemistry or tax law, you have to put yourself in a position to know it. Life choices and regular practices are required. Generally speaking, knowledge does not run over you or force itself upon you. The same is true of knowledge of God.

Anyone can know God—anyone, that is, prepared to put him- or herself in a position to know him. Jesus has provided the method. Try taking up his overall manner of life, within God's kingdom, and see if you don't come to know this God experientially.

INTERLUDE

Jesus' Philosophical Teachings

Three primary questions concerned the ancient philosophers. Each of the various schools of ancient philosophy focused on three big questions, formulating their problem a bit differently, and arrived at different conclusions:

- *What is really there?* Answers to this inquiry were known as physics. (Among the ancients, this inquiry was broader than modern physics and included issues we would describe as metaphysics.) Therein they offered various theories of nature explaining the structure of the world, of God or the gods, and of human beings.

- *How does one know?* The name for this category varied from school to school. Theoretical answers to this basic question were known as logic (Aristotle and the Stoics), or canonics (Epicureans), or dialectic (most Platonists).

- Given what is really there (i.e., what kind of world we inhabit and what sort of beings humans really are), *what is the best way to live?* Answers to this question constituted the ethic of a given school.[76]

Jesus addresses all three of these big questions in distinctive ways. Of course, he lives and teaches within the (mostly) Aramaic speaking world of Second Temple Jewish life. So, he does not explicitly label his teachings with these three categories found in Greco-Roman philosophies. Nonetheless, if one approaches Jesus' teachings with bi-focal lenses—attentive both to Second Temple Jewish thought and to the Greco-Roman philosophical thought of his day—the claim of his earliest followers proves quite reasonable. Jesus provides a coherent philosophy. It is a broadly *Jewish* philosophy to be sure, yet it is more, not less, coherent for its Jewishness.

In section 1, above, we have already touched on elements of all three big questions. We began with Jesus' teaching about the makeup of human persons (an element of "physics" or an explanation of what's real) and how this leads to a process by which we come to lead the best human life (a bit of ethics). The section ended with Jesus connecting this account of human beings with how they come to know—in a deep and transformative manner—the character of God. So, we're already in the thick of Jesus' philosophy.

A Practical Philosophy

Since we are focusing, like Jesus, on a practical or lived philosophy, we want to touch on those elements most needful for everyday life. As we saw in our first chapter, in his parable of the soils Jesus describes three key actions, that humans must engage in to grow morally and spiritually.

First, each person must grasp the meaning of key ideas in Jesus' teaching. There is no substitute for understanding. Second, key regular practices must be employed to give more of our heart to this view of the world. Disciplines toughen Jesus' students to successfully face the difficulties of life. Third, key elements of our social identity must be renegotiated. As we present ourselves and interact with other people and groups in a manner that harmonizes with the life we are learning from Jesus, we find ourselves increasingly liberated to grow.

In the subsequent sections we will take as our guide Jesus' account of these three essential, interrelated activities.

The Sections to Follow

In section 2 we will think closely about the two primary ideas that Jesus introduces:

- the Father's unique character
- the kingdom

In ancient terms, these are "physics" because they tell us what is most real in the world. Jesus' most basic answer to the reality question is *God*, his character and his actions.

Next, in section 3, we'll look at Jesus' explanation of a few key practices or disciplines. Jesus introduces these three disciplines (giving in secret, fasting in secret, and praying in secret) within a broader explanation of how disciplines work within the transformation process (Matt 6:1–18). In this book, we'll focus on Jesus' general explanation. Toward that end, we'll consider a further explanation of why our capacity to co-work with God, particularly in crisis moments, will ultimately depend on the residual effect of having followed these disciplines long before there was a crisis.

In the fourth and final section, we'll examine Jesus' most general depiction of what we must avoid and what we should aspire to in terms of social identity. In other words, how should we understand the boundaries of our natural community? And what types of personal interactions will enable us to effectively grow into this life that Jesus offers?

SECTION II

Kingdom Ideas

CHAPTER FOUR

—Prelude—

Background Understandings

Or, What Jesus' Students Already Knew

The Background Understandings
Assumed by Jesus

IF WE ARE GOING to grasp the key ideas that Jesus introduced, we will need to first know something about those understandings he could assume were already held by his first students. When Jesus spoke to his students in the Gospels, they already inhabited a shared web of understandings concerning what and who God is.

We will refer to their cultural context as Second Temple Judaism. In other words, they are situated within Jewish life and thought in the period stretching from the reconstruction of the Jerusalem temple under Zerubbabel in the 500s BC until the destruction of that temple by the Roman general Titus in AD 70. Despite the great diversity of Second Temple Jewish thought and life, a broadly shared set of background stories, categories, and traditional practices provided enough in common for meaningful disagreement between the various groups.

No doubt the conceptual web was not in equal repair among them all—some were more or less informed than others, and each had appropriated the inheritance differently. As every teacher, counselor, or thoughtful listener knows, there is always a peculiar relation between any collective

51

worldview and the "mazeways" of individuals finding their way within those cultures. Every person is distinct and unpredictable in some way. Moreover, there were significant tensions and internal contradictions between certain elements of this Second Temple Jewish inheritance. Nonetheless, there was a culturally available catalog of attributes, images, and claims about Israel's God that had emerged over the course of the preceding centuries. It had been largely (though not exclusively) inscribed in the text of the Hebrew Bible and its popular translations into Greek and Aramaic.

The Folk Ontology of Israel and Her God

Since Jesus' teachings assume many of these shared understandings as a platform for further refinements, it's important for us to begin with these inherited conceptions of what kind of being God is.

In the language of Greek and subsequent philosophy, the answer to the question "What is it?" is an account of a thing's *being* or *essence*. An account of what different sorts of things there are in the world, usually with some indication of how they relate to each other, is called an ontology. While most ontologies only exist in the minds of a few intellectuals, one that is broadly shared by a culture or people group may be called a folk ontology. This is what we want to clarify for Jesus' world.

Embedded in the shared understandings of Second Temple Jews was a more or less explicit ontology, the most distinctive feature of which was an account of YHWH, usually rendered in English as "the LORD," who is the incomparable God of Israel and also the Creator of all.[77] But before we speak of the LORD, we should say a word about Israel herself.

Basic Components of Israel's Ontology

In order to prepare ourselves for Jesus' teachings, let's briefly delineate the contours of Israel's ontology—or her basic list of what kinds of things exist—and the place of YHWH within it.

Adam's Seed: Israel and the Nations

Israel's ontology of God and the world cannot be described without placing Israel within it. One thing that every Jew knew, and most people of other nations were also aware of it,[78] was that the Jews owed their existence to their special, exclusive relation to their God, YHWH. The LORD chose Israel, and the Jews (those descended from or otherwise aligned with the southern tribe of Judah) were a key subset of Israel.[79] The LORD had brought them out of Egypt millennia before. The Jews knew that Israel, of which they were a part, had been chosen by this particular God and, like it or not, it was their duty to maintain loyalty and service to this God alone. The "Shema" (or "Hear!") prayer from Deuteronomy 6:4–9, recited daily, maintained this in their awareness.

Of course, there were other nations and the LORD had created them too and "scattered" them throughout the world. However, while the LORD had entrusted other nations to intermediary spiritual beings ("angels" or "sons of God"), he initially chose an unmediated relation with his people Israel (Deut 32:7–12, 15–18 and 4:15–40, esp. vv. 19–20 and 37).[80] Beginning with Abraham, the LORD chose to personally journey in relation to one family in order to develop a distinct people through whom he could effectively bring the blessing of his way to all peoples (Gen 12:1–4). Humanity was one, Adam's seed one and all, but Israel knew that by God's choice they were to play a special role within the one human race.

YHWH's Educational Project

In a very basic sense, the LORD's selection of Abraham's family was the start of an educational project of cosmic scope.[81] He chose a particular people with very distinct *dis*advantages in order to introduce them to features of reality—of this world—that humans could not easily see otherwise (see Deut 4:32–40; 7:7–8; 9:1–8, etc.). The LORD, YHWH, intended, through a long and patient relationship with Abraham and his descendants, to teach a segment of humanity about himself and about the nature of this world he made.

As an intergenerational educational project, YHWH's self-revelation was layered and sequential (or progressive). He patiently worked with humanity as it was in order to establish base understandings, which would enable them to rethink and achieve new insights into the nature of God and the world. Thus, they would attain a new level of comprehension. The process would continue by taking their new mixture of misunderstandings and true insights as the starting point for YHWH's work in the next generation. This is how competent educators work—it's simply adapted to an intergenerational people group as the student being developed.

Throughout her history, Israel's prophets reminded her that her received insights into YHWH, his ways, and the best ordering of human life would eventually be passed to the nations. Sometimes this process of enlightening the nations was anticipated as a great, voluntary pilgrimage of the nations to Jerusalem to worship and learn (e.g., Isa 2:1–4; Mic 4:1–5, etc.). At other times it was imagined as the aftermath of a military and political subjugation of the nations by Israel's king (see Pss 2:4–12; 72:8–11; Pss. Sol. 17:21–32, etc.). Despite the conflicting imaginations, Israel largely shared the understanding that her journey of learning from YHWH would someday shape all the people-groups of the world. Her distinct destiny would be formative for the whole world.

This long transformation of persons within a community, which would eventually be instrumental in the transformation of humanity as a whole, *is* God's purpose in human history. In fact, it is his primary purpose in creating the universe. Within this universe and within humanity as a whole, YHWH has a special role for Israel to play as the first witness to YHWH's own unique kind of existence. Israel herself, by Jesus' day, had come to see an essential element of her witness to be contained in a special collection of writings produced among her people over the centuries.

The Sacred Writings

The Hebrew Bible, in an important sense, is a secondary, intermediary product of YHWH's primary aim to produce a transformed people whom he would use to transform the other peoples or nations. God's intentions were bigger than just creating a "perfect book" imagined in abstraction from the people it would serve to develop. (In this sense, the Bible occupies a very different place in the life of Israel and, later, of Jesus' followers than the Qur'an does in Islam. For Islam, the Qur'an is Allah's primary aim.) Rather, the LORD oversaw the production of many writings that both individually (at the time of their original production) and collectively (as a gradually assembled canon or normative library) would be especially serviceable to his end of producing transformed people. As such, the library (a better term than "book" for this collection) needed to be thoroughly truthful. But the library could usefully contain points of tension or even contradiction, at least to the extent that the questions raised by such tensions furthered the process of growth within his people.

One could almost call the writings of the Old and New Testaments *by-products* of God's choice to journey with humanity in order to reveal himself. Almost. Except that the production of these writings is both a result of his interactions and something he intentionally uses to further that educational process.

By Jesus' day, there were differences over the relative authority found in the various books of this library, as well as the overall extent of the collection.[82] The Sadducees, who controlled the temple in Jerusalem, only accepted the first five books—the Torah, often translated as "law." That was also true of the non-Jewish Israelites called Samaritans. A Jewish movement of popular piety called the Pharisees, or "Separatists," accepted the Torah, the Prophets (which included the historical books and those books named after particular prophets), and the Writings (which includes the Psalms and all the other texts not included in the Torah and Prophets). The "Yahad" or community at Qumran seems to possess a somewhat different selection of the Writings. But all saw this collection—however large or small they deemed it to be—as essential to Israel's witness to the one God.

No Meta-Divine Realm: How Israel's God Is Distinct from Pagan Gods

Israel's God, the LORD, is incomparable in a very specific way. The uniqueness of Israel's God may be grasped by contrast with a shared assumption among all the non-Israelite nations' understandings of their gods. Strung through all the dazzling diversity of paganisms in the world, the Israelite sees a common thread. The essence of paganism, as it manifests in myriads of cultures over time, is a belief in some realm that stretches beyond God or the gods and from which those deities derive their powers.

In Israel alone do we find a distinctive insight: there is no meta-divine realm—nothing over, behind, or beneath the Creator God. There is just God . . . all the way down.[83] This is the essence of Israelite monotheism.[84]

Every form of paganism postulates some realm behind the deities. The gods are local expressions of power that must be rooted in something bigger and more comprehensive. The world, though not necessarily the cosmos or ordered world, is older than the gods. It has always been there. The gods are born, live, die. Sometimes they are reconstituted after death and dismemberment. But the world just is. And with it is some background power.

The gods' dependence upon this background power, or meta-divine realm, may be illustrated by pointing to some basic accounts in which this power is referenced.

Consider the source of moral order, for instance. In the ancient Near East, the Sumerians thought of law as having two components. The particular dos and don'ts that produce an approximation of equity and justice in society are called *mesharum.* These particular laws are issued by the king. But the king does not hold the immutable truth and right that are the deep basis for these laws—the *kinatu*. These are held by the sun god, Shamash. Yet even Shamash does not make these deep truths, he only receives them and guards them from something beyond the gods. Deep morality, for the pagan, is meta-divine.[85]

Fate, or destiny-controlling luck, also explicitly issues from the meta-divine realm. For the Greeks, Zeus himself, reputed to be the most powerful of the pantheon, remains under the ultimate control of fate—helpless to alter it. Life and death. Weal and woe. Honor or dishonor. Wealth and poverty. These all are determined by something, in most accounts, impersonal and always deeper than the gods.[86] For this reason, even Zeus is powerless to raise the dead, because life and death emerges from this background realm which the gods do not control. Deep causality, for the pagan, is meta-divine.[87]

Or consider the role of magic within pagan worldviews. It is telltale that pagan pantheons include magician gods. Magic, for the ancients, is rooted in this realm beyond the gods. The human magician seeks to tap into the same power source from which the gods live and to use it without having to depend on their fickle choices. Pagan gods also require sustenance from this deeper realm—special foods or elixirs to provide ongoing youth and immortality, spells and potions to bestow superhuman abilities, or closer derivations of birth from something within this meta-divine realm.[88] Most pagan pantheons include magician gods who specialize in accessing this background realm. In Israel, the LORD has no such need. Deep power, for the pagan, is meta-divine.

Even when pagan intellectuals in Greece and Rome, or earlier in India, move towards a concept of the unity of the divine realm, really what they are describing is this meta-divine realm. Because all the personal character of their particular divinities must be removed to think it. For Plato, the forms are beyond the gods. The gods receive immortality by gazing upon them, they possess no immortality on their own. For the Indian sages of the Upanishads, Brahman is the sacred power that pervades all things and makes them one. It is before, behind, and beyond the gods.

> Whence was it produced? Whence is this creation? The gods came afterwards, with the creation of this universe. Who then knows whence it has arisen? Which this creation has arisen—perhaps it formed itself, or perhaps it did not. . . . (*Rig Veda* 10.129.6–7)[89]

Deep being, for the pagan, is meta-divine.

For Israel, the unique being of the Creator anchors everything without any need or possibility of a meta-divine realm. Deep being, deep power, deep morality, deep causality—it's all found in the LORD. There is nothing behind, beneath, or before him. How is this possible? To understand we must consider the distinctive existence of YHWH, the LORD.

The Ontology of God: YHWH's Non-Contingent Existence

What kind of existence does God enjoy? What sort of being is God?[90] The answer takes us all the way back to Exodus 3. Our aim is to get a fairly workable understanding of God's being. God reveals to Moses in Exodus 3 that he lives a type of existence unlike any creature in that his existence is not dependent on anything else. He exists in an unconditioned way. Everything else we interact with, or experience, is conditioned by all sorts of other things. But God isn't.

That's the gist of the passage, but to understand its significance let's look at the passage in context. Recall that, as a child, Moses was rescued through God's providence. In a most unlikely turn of events, Moses is raised in the house of the Pharaoh as one adopted by the Pharaoh's daughter. Decades later, as a man, he comes out to see the plight of his kinsmen, the Hebrews. Moses sees an Egyptian abusing a Hebrew, intervenes and kills the Egyptian. The next day he tries to intervene again, this time to mediate between two Hebrews in conflict. When one of the Hebrews rebuffs Moses, he becomes aware that his killing of the Egyptian is public knowledge, and he flees to the wilderness of Midian. There he marries and settles as a simple shepherd (thus far is a summary of Exodus 2).

Forty more years pass. Now Moses is shepherding his father-in-law's sheep and comes across this paradoxical sight.

> Moses was pasturing the flock of Jethro his father-in-law, the priest of Midian; and he led the flock to the backside of the wilderness [in American idiom we might say he was "in the middle of nowhere"] and came to Horeb, the mountain of God. And the angel of YHWH appeared to him in a blazing fire from the midst of a bush; and he looked and behold the bush was burning with fire, yet the bush was not consumed. (Exod 3:1–2)

This interaction employs a teaching strategy that the Lord frequently utilizes. Very often, in scripture, the Lord will give us implicit conceptual content in imagery, which he will then unpack in words. Try to think about this image in that way. What information is implicit within it?

Unfed Fire: The Conceptual Image

The LORD first appears to Moses through a fire that is occupying a bush, but it's not behaving like other fires. What happens when you see a bush on fire? *How* does that fire exist? For any ordinary, material fire to exist, it has to be consuming something in order to last.

Ordinary fire releases the energy from a pile of wood, or if we're unfortunate a house or something like that. It always releases energy *from something else* and is thus dependent, for its existence, on the energy in that other thing. If you deprive a fire of fuel—either oxygen or the wood its consuming—it dies. Why? Because the fire we experience in this world is a type of energy that is dependent on other things—on matter.

On this mountainside, however, Moses sees a fire, which is in the midst of a bush, but it is not consuming the bush. The fire is not dependent upon the matter in that bush for its energy. Here is a form of energy, witnessed by Moses, that does not rely on anything else.

Of course, Moses wants to get a closer look. You would too. As he approaches, God speaks to him from the bush and begins the process of commissioning Moses. Moses must return to Egypt and issue an undesirable command to Pharaoh. "Let my people go!" Understandably, Moses is very hesitant to accept the task. By all human standards, it is an incredibly dangerous task to undertake. Moses resists God's call.

As part of his resistance to the commission, Moses asks God for a name (Exod 3:13). It's important to consider the function of a name in ancient religions. When you read pagan prayers, of which we possess many written records from the ancient world, you find extensive litanies of names, titles, and honorifics at the start of the prayers.[91] The reason for those litanies is the idea that if you had the name, which holds something of the essence of that deity, then you would have power over that being.[92] The power of a name taps into something behind any particular divinity—it's an order of the meta-divine realm. If you get the name right, they're required to show up. Now you have some control. Therefore, Moses asks for a name.

What Moses is really doing is asking for a guarantee. If he has God's name, then Moses thinks that he can ensure access. He will know that he can make God show up. So, he asks the fire-garbed voice for a name.

The LORD responds by giving him a name that is not really a name. It's very strange. "And God said to Moses, 'I am that I am'" (Exod 3:14). Now, what does *that* mean?!

Non-Dependent Existence:
The Conceptual Word

Consider that God alone can say this. Here's why: when the LORD says, "I am that I am," he is saying that his being is dependent on nothing but himself. He says that he exists simply because he exists—he is incapable of not existing.

To grasp its significance, you will need to contrast this claim with anything and everything else you have interacted with.

Start personally. For example, I, Daniel Napier, am because there was a school principal named Fred Napier who took a shining to one of his teachers, named Meredith. She reciprocated, they got married, and here I am. I am one result of that union. But, really, that's just one of an innumerable host of conditions for my existence. There are thousands upon thousands of possible scenarios in which I would not be here to write this sentence—conditions wherein my parents never met, or wherein any one of their ancestors never met to produce them. Or, even given my birth, there is a comparably vast number of scenarios where my life might have ended before reaching this point.

My being—my existence—is *radically dependent*. It's dependent upon literally millions of contingencies. That is not just true of me. That is true of you and everyone else.

It is also true of every item that you encounter. Something as simple as the coffee cup on my desk, or the desk itself, or this laptop on which I'm typing, or the house—there are untold thousands of ways that they might not have been here. They're all dependent on many other things for their existence. That is the nature of everything we interact with, with one exception. God is the sole exception.

God alone exists in a way that his existence is not derivative from anything else. There is no meta-divine realm from which God receives existence and power. He simply *is* by his own power. It's not an accident that the LORD reveals this to Moses at this point in the story. He's sending Moses to carry out a very dangerous job under precarious circumstances. The LORD is not being cruel in sending him, but Moses needs to know that God has his back.

It's important to notice that, in a sense, YHWH really is answering Moses' question—or, at least, the orienting concern behind it. Remember, Moses' question about a name is a way of saying, "Give me a guarantee that you'll be there when I call out your name." The LORD's response to Moses is, essentially, "I'll tell you who I am. I'm the only being that is not dependent upon anything else. Because of that, I could never be manipulated. If you're asking for a lever to pull that will force me to show up, that lever simply doesn't exist. I'm not the type of being that could ever be forced or manipulated into anything."

Insight: Connecting the Image and the Word

In your mind, connect this statement about God's mode of existence with the image, which was given at the beginning of Exodus 3. The fire Moses encountered occupied the bush without burning the bush. In preparation for this conversation, God spoke to Moses from a fire that needs no fuel to burn—a fire that is not dependent on anything. Having given the counterintuitive idea in an image, the LORD proceeds to give its equivalent in words. The union of image and word, things and explanations, enables Moses to understand something so profound that it is difficult to get our minds around it.

YHWH's Character: The Assurance beyond Control

Moses now knows that YHWH is not a God that he could ever control, because of YHWH's unique existence. That could be really good news or really bad news, depending on God's interest in his plight. However, this is not the end of the LORD's self-revelation. In the next verse, as it were in the same breath, the LORD tells Moses,

> Thus you shall say to the sons of Israel, "YHWH, the God of your fathers, the God of Abraham, the God of Isaac, and the God of Jacob, has sent me to you." This is my name forever and this is my memorial-name to all generations. Go and gather the elders of Israel together and say to them, "YHWH, the God of your fathers, the God of Abraham, Isaac, and Jacob, has appeared to me, saying, 'I've paid close attention to you and seen what has been done to you in Egypt. . . .'" (Exod 3:15–16)

As soon as he reveals that his mode of existence makes him unmanipulable, the LORD immediately evokes the promises to Abraham, Isaac, and Jacob. Why? God's free covenant, which he makes with his people, and his personal character are the only true assurance any human can have.

In effect, this is the LORD saying, "You cannot manipulate me. But you'll never need to. Because I'm willingly binding myself to you. I've already committed myself to be present when my people cry out. I'll be there when you call upon me. You can count upon it, not because you will have any power over me but because my own character and promises will bring me there." And that's better than a lever any day. After all, levers can break. It happens all the time. But the consistent character of the truly existing One—now, that's real reliability![93]

This unique, non-contingent power is the God who calls to Moses. That's the "what" of God that passes into Israel's shared understanding. This shared understanding not only tells them about God's distinctive being, but it also tells them about their own distinctive being. The two are linked.

Witnessing to God's Non-Dependent Existence: Israel's Reason for Existing

Slowly it begins to dawn on Israel—or at least on insightful, prophetic individuals within her midst: her primary reason for existing is *to bear witness to the one God whose existence and power is utterly non-dependent.* That's why God chose a people with so many natural and circumstantial disadvantages. They were a suitable medium through which he could invite the world to notice his actions and reflect upon the implications of his being.

Consider Isaiah's understanding of the matter:

> Bring out the people who are blind, even though they have eyes, and deaf, even though they have ears. All the nations have gathered together in order that the peoples may be assembled. Who among them can declare this and proclaim to us the former things? Let them present their witnesses that they may be justified. Or let them hear and say, "It is true."
>
> "You are my witnesses," declares the LORD. "And my servant whom I have chosen, in order that you may know and believe me, and understand that I am He. Before me there was no God formed, and there will be none after me. I, even I, am the LORD; and there is no savior besides me. It is I who have declared and saved and proclaimed, and there was no strange god among you; so you are my witnesses," declares the LORD. "And I am God. Even from eternity I am he; and there is none who can deliver out of my hand; I act and who can reverse it?" (Isa 43:8–13)

Israel's call, although they were often blind to the matter, is to bear witness to YHWH's unique being. They are given the opportunity to interact with (i.e., to "know"), to trust, and to understand this singular, self-sufficient divine nature. Moreover, they would bear witness to the significance and impact of this singularly divine being on human life. "I act and who can reverse it?" (Isa 43:13). Because God, unlike any other type of thing, has no dependencies or external constraints on his power, the nature of his action in the world is unlike any other.

In the exilic and post-exilic periods, Israel deepens her appreciation for the fact that her very existence depends upon an inexplicable power, not bound by human or other material means, which continues to sustain her. "The God of Heaven" needs no temple, no priestly curator, no human king or mortal army to decisively guide events and provide for his people. Glancing back over YHWH's journey with her, Israel can see that this was his recurrent lesson. For instance, why in Judges 7 does YHWH tell Gideon "The people who are with you are too many for me to give Midian into their hands"? Further back, why does Abraham refuse to take anything from the king of Sodom—not even a thread or sandal thong? (Gen 14:21ff.).

The very existence of Abraham and his people is a witness to a power source that cannot be reduced to material possessions, human resources, or natural means. The depth of humanity's resistance to the reality of God necessitates such a stark, persistent witness to YHWH's distinctive essence. Israel is created and called to be that witness.

This background ontology of YHWH and Israel forms the context within which Jesus articulates the most central idea of his entire philosophy—the Father's matchless name.

CHAPTER FIVE

The Father's Matchless Name

"Father Sanctify Your Name": Jesus' Most Basic Request and Its Import

THE CORE OF JESUS' philosophy flows from his conception of the Father and the Father's name—we might say, his character. Although Jesus returns repeatedly to the Father's character, the opening words in the prayer, which Jesus teaches his students, provide a helpful, concise entry point.

> Therefore, pray in this way:
> Our Father in the heavens, sanctify your name.
> Your kingdom come, your will be done as in heaven so on earth.
> Give us today our daily bread.
> And forgive us our debts as we also have forgiven our debtors.
> And don't lead us into testing but rescue us from evil.
> (Matt 6:9–13)

When Jesus instructs his students on how to speak with God, the most basic request is "Father, sanctify your name" (Luke 11:2/Matt 6:9). The whole life of conversation and co-working with God, so distinctive of Jesus' Way, flows seamlessly from this fundamental understanding that Jesus teaches his students to seek.

But what does it mean? What are we asking for when we ask the Father to make his name holy—sanctified?

To begin with, the sanctity of the Father's name is an *understanding*. In fact, once its meaning is grasped, you will recognize it is also the basis of Jesus' account of the *first* among God's life-instructions and the sequence by which they transform human lives. "Listen, Israel. The Lord is your God, The Lord is one" (Mark 12:29, quoting Deut 6:4). In chapter 2, we looked closely at Jesus' teaching concerning the effective sequence of foci for human transformation. Here we consider Jesus' understanding of the one LORD.

Holiness as Uncommon, Uniqueness

In the simplest possible terms, when we ask the Father to make his name holy, we are asking him to make his true character known to ourselves and to the world. "*Make people to know you as you truly are—as holy.*" That's the substance of the request.

Two words, "sanctify" and "name," are important to consider if we are going to make sense of this request. Let's start with "sanctify" and its cognate "holy."

What does the world "holy" mean? A good way to get to the basic meaning of "holy" in scripture is to consider its opposite. In scripture, the opposite of holy is not wicked or sinful or even dirty. The opposite of holy is common.[94] That's it. Common. Common means that it is not distinctive to or possessed by anyone in particular. It's not unique.

To illustrate, I have a coffee mug on my desk right now as I am writing. It's a good mug and I'm grateful for the mid-afternoon coffee boost inside it. But, if you considered this mug, you would see that it is *exactly* like several others in my cupboard. Moreover, I could go down to IKEA and find about eighty more on their shelf that would each be completely identical. It's a good enough mug, but it is common. If I broke it, it wouldn't be any big deal. There would be no reason for tears because it is easily replaceable. Moreover, the replacement would lack nothing—it would be completely indistinguishable from the one now on my desk. Commonness—that's the opposite of holiness. An interchangeable unit is not holy.

By way of contrast, I'm guessing that somewhere in your home you have a special cup. And it is something irreplaceable. Maybe it's a teacup passed down from your grandmother. Or, perhaps, it's your great-grandfather's beer stein. That drinking vessel is completely irreplaceable. If it's broken, there is no way to replace it, because at this point it has become something unique. It is utterly distinct—not like any other—and special. It is holy. That is fundamentally what holiness is.[95]

When we talk about the holiness of the Father, we are talking about how the Father is unlike anyone or anything else. Jesus' philosophy does not begin from a generic idea of a God—a concept of some supreme being, as significant as that concept may be. Rather, Jesus is talking about one specific personality—the irreplaceable uniqueness of YHWH *as Father*. He teaches us, his students, to pray for the Father's name to be sanctified. When we do that, we're asking that the Father's utterly unique personality become known in our hearts and sink into the depths of our souls. To sanctify means to make completely unique.[96] We don't make God's name unique, of course, but we do ask for God to make his name unique *to* and *among* us.

What's in a Name?

What's in a name? In scripture, names are not just sounds nor are they handles for easy reference to a person. Rather, names reveal a person's real character.

Often, in scripture, when a person goes through a significant transformation process that person will be given a new name. For example, Jacob (whose name means "cheater") has his name changed to Israel ("overcoming with or for God") when he finally learns to speak forthrightly in his nocturnal wrestling match. Here's the story.

Jacob is born, the second of twins, to Rebecca and Isaac. A conflict, Rebecca felt, was already underway in the womb and at birth Jacob was grasping his brother Esau's heel. It was as if he were trying to overtake him and cheat him out of his birthright. So, the infant is given the name "Cheater"—Jacob. And Jacob lived up to his name. Every relationship was a chess game. He maneuvered and tricked his way into advantageous positions. But his maneuvering had consequences. By the time he had tricked both his brother into giving away his birthright for a bowl of beans and his father into blessing him as firstborn in Esau's place, Jacob had made an enemy of his brother. Esau planned to kill Jacob once their father was gone. So, Jacob escaped to Mesopotamia where, for a couple decades, he engaged in a battle of wits and tricks with his uncle Laban. Again, he comes out richer but also with enemies.

In Genesis 32, Jacob is finally traveling back to Canaan land, back to the brother who had decided to kill him. The old cheater crosses the river Jabbok and sends his family and flocks in companies ahead of him. They're buffers to give him, and perhaps some of the later companies, a chance to escape if Esau attacks. And Jacob? He crosses back over the Jabbok to give himself a running start. But that night Jacob finds himself wrestling with "a man" until daybreak (Gen 32:24). The man, who turns out to be a manifestation of God, cannot defeat Jacob outright, so he "touched the socket of his thigh" at the hip and dislocated it (Gen 32:25). Despite his injury, Jacob refuses to release his hold. He demands a blessing of his nameless wrestling partner. The "man" extracts a confession from Jacob. "What's your name?," he asks. "My name is cheater—Jacob." Now God gives him a new name. "Your name shall no longer be cheater but Israel for you have striven with God and with men and have prevailed" (Gen 32:28). From now on he will be *Israel*—the one who struggles or overcomes with God. In other words, God overcomes, and the former cheater will be in on God's victory.

Israel has a new name. Notice what happens next. In Genesis 33:3, Israel—the one attached to God overcoming—walks out ahead of his family to meet Esau first. The cowardly cheater doesn't make it across the Jabbok. A new man emerges. *Israel* now risks himself instead of his family. New name. New character.

Similarly, in the New Testament, Jesus' student Simon becomes Peter (the Rock) when he receives insight from the Father concerning Jesus' identity as Messiah. New character. New name. But his character is not stable yet. When he again acts like a knucklehead, Jesus again addresses him as "Simon, Simon" (e.g., Luke 22:31–32). Name and character coincide. Names reveal the deep reality of a person.

The Name Sanctified

So, what do we want to happen when we ask the Father to sanctify his name? We are asking God to move us and the world beyond a generic, empty concept of some God out there.[97] Even grasping that he exists without any background realm behind or beyond him, while good, is not yet enough. In this prayer, "Sanctify your name," we are requesting that the Father help us grasp his specific, unique character. We want to know his personality, we might say, in the sort of way we cherish the peculiarities of our close family members. This isn't just some highest being above and beyond everything. He is our Father. We're learning all the peculiarities of what he's like. And we're asking for the world to know him this way too.

Jesus' vision and prayer, in part, goes back to a passage in Ezekiel 36:16ff. The people of Israel were in exile because, by corrupting their way of life, they had given the world a false picture of the character of YHWH. They profaned, or made common, YHWH's matchless name. They made YHWH look like an interchangeable unit—just another god of a nation like all the other local gods out there. They had created misunderstandings of YHWH's unique moral character.

Now that Israel is in exile, however, YHWH's character is again being misunderstood because of the situation. People have begun to think that he isn't strong enough to provide for and protect his people in their own land. "These are the LORD's people, yet they have come out of his land" (Ezek 36:20). Their current state created misunderstanding of YHWH's power.

So, to reveal his unique, matchless character, YHWH says he'll act—he will "sanctify his name" by changing their rebellious heart and restoring them to the land. In other words, he will correct the misunderstandings people have of him by showing his true character and power. This is the backdrop to Jesus' request, which illuminates the core of his philosophy.

The Father's Personality and the Kingdom Prayer

The request that the Father's true personality would become obvious to everyone—this is the foundation for joining in the Father's kingdom. Everything flows from it. If just this one request were made and answered, universally, humanity would instantly live in a different world. It would change most of the details of everyday life.

A Diagnostic Question

Here is a diagnostic question to help you know if the Father's name has been sanctified in your heart. Ask this: "Do I believe that God is as good as Jesus is?"

When I think of the Father, does he have that beautiful attractive character we see in Jesus? Gentleness. Tenderness. Humility. A capacity to do and bring about what is right without just running over people but bringing them along. Is the Father as good as Jesus?

Ultimately, what it means to sanctify the Father's name is to know that if you see Jesus you've seen the Father. That's precisely the distinct character or personality of God the Father—the personality that we've seen in Jesus (see John 14:8–11).

Once we come to think of the Father—YHWH, the Creator of heaven and earth—as being just like Jesus, possessing the same personality, the second request flows effortlessly. "May your kingdom come, your will be done as in heaven so on earth." In other words, we begin to ask for God's project to succeed right here where we live. We'll return to this central teaching in the next chapter.

The Disaster of God-Centered Projects without the Sanctified Name

At this point, however, I would like to ask you to reflect on a very simple question. Why would it make sense to ask for the Father's project to succeed? Why *his project*, even when that may entail my own choices and projects not being realized? How could one intelligently desire the Father's plans to hold, even if they override one's own plans?

This too flows from really seeing who the Father is—from sanctifying his name.

Only once the Father's name is sanctified is it safe to pursue a God-centered project. Any attempt to create a God-centered society, which is not rooted in genuine knowledge of the Father's matchless, unique character, leads to ruin. Inevitably.

For the last four years, I've lived and worked among Middle Eastern refugees who have sought protection against the abuses of their own governments. They are hoping for a new start in Greece or, perhaps, further West in Europe. They are fleeing God-centered political systems. Their very presence in Europe, along with their detailed testimony of conditions in their lands of origin, bear grim witness to a fact. When someone who does not know that the Father's character is just like Jesus' tries to fashion a God-centered society, the human carnage and the damage to everyday life can be unspeakable. It is not safe to put "God" at the center if you do not know the Father's unique character. After all, if one doesn't understand the Father's character, then the "God" at the center will just be a twisted human idea of God.

The Disaster of Human-Centered Projects

That said, the solution is not to attempt to put human beings at the center instead. We've tried that too and we've seen how it turned out in human history. I could just give you names, and you would shudder to think of what they've done. Stalin. Hitler. Mao. Pol Pot. We could go on. Each name represents a human will and a human vision of how the world ought to be put together, which humans tried to enact without God. And we've seen just as much terror as in a "God"-centred vision—perhaps more—coming from their deeds.

So, humanity is on the horns of a dilemma. Those who try to put God at the center end up destroying human life. Those who try to put humans at the center also destroy human life. Where do we go from here?

What is it about the Father that makes Jesus think that his kingdom, the Father's project, would be a good idea for us? Why is the Father's kingdom any different from other societies that have tried to put God at the center?

A Glimpse of the Father's Matchless Character

In the Gospels, Jesus repeatedly foregrounds the Father's distinctive character. In Luke 6:35–36, for example, Jesus describes the Father as both "merciful" and "kind to the ungrateful and to the evil." In case this clear statement about the Father's character passed by too quickly, Jesus expounds on the description in the parable of the prodigal son. There we find a father not only forgiving, but preemptively extending unprecedented kindness to his two different, but equally evil and ungrateful, sons. (I encourage you to read the parable in Luke 15:11–32.)

In Matthew 5:45, Jesus again describes the Father's undiminished generosity and goodness toward not only the good but also the evil. The Father's character is marked by a capacity to love even enemies and those set against him. His love is "perfect"—fully functional.

And, in case this description was too terse, Matthew returns to emphasize and expound on the Father's character later in his gospel. In Matthew 12:18–21 he opens to us a special and ancient window into the Father's heart. In this passage, Matthew uses a quotation from the prophet Isaiah to link the Father's project with the Father's distinctive character. I would like to connect some dots.

In context, Jesus is under criticism, even attack, precisely because of the way he interprets the Torah—the instructions that the Father has revealed for life in Israel.

Compassion in Reading Torah

Certain members of a group in Jesus' day called the Pharisees or "Separatists" think that Jesus is too soft in his application of the Torah.[98] For righteousness to be real, they think, it must be pitiless—must be enacted without much compassion for human beings and their weaknesses. Although this notion found a home among some of the Pharisees in the Judea of Jesus' day, it's not a distinctively Jewish thought or trait. It's a *human* thought pattern and a *human* trait. Perhaps you've entertained this approach or had intimate interactions with someone who did?

Many of my Middle Eastern friends lived in places where this was the dominant assumption. People thought that to take submitting to God seriously they had to be prepared to do without any human being. But I've also lived and worked among Christian churches with the same basic assumption. So, this mentality is not Jewish, Christian, or Islamic—it's just *human*. But it had indeed found a home among some members of the Pharisees in Jesus' day.

In context, Jesus has been interpreting specific commandments in the Torah. In every case, Jesus advocates on the side of compassion. The Pharisees are upset about it. In fact, they decide they must remove Jesus from the religious-social scene and plot to kill him (Matt 12:14). This is ruthless righteousness, as an ideal, put into action. The context is first-century Judea. The problem is human.

Isaiah's Vision of YHWH's Servant

So in Matthew 12 Jesus reminds his audience that many years beforehand God had spoken a word through the prophet Isaiah (Isa 42:1–4). Isaiah related something of the Father's character and a strategy that the Father has for changing the world. It's the type of strategy that no one unfamiliar with the Father's distinct personality would ever dream up as a potentially successful strategy for changing the world. Nobody would have guessed this.

> Behold my servant (or child), whom I've chosen, my beloved in whom my soul is well pleased. I will place my spirit upon him, and he will announce justice to the nations. He will not argue or quarrel, nor will he cry out. No one will hear his voice in the open square. A crushed reed he will not snap off and a smoking wick he will not snuff out, until he brings justice to success. And in his name the nations will hope. (Matt 12:18–21)

This is the Father's plan for how to bring about broad-based social change so that his project succeeds among the nations. It's all built upon gentleness and care-filled compassion for the people whom he is approaching. The servant through whom God's Spirit will work is not going to argue.

He's not going to be found shouting in the streets or the squares. He's not going to be making a big public scene.

How the Father Changes the World

Pause there for a moment. You might ask yourself: Have I ever seen an attempt to change a regime, a society, in which such strategies were not employed? This really looks like the generic formula for *every* human attempt to change a society—without regard to the particular political persuasion of the activists.

The revolutionary argues with people. Fights. Gets a bunch of people to make a scene. Marches. It's the formula. This is the world's way of changing the world. But it doesn't really *change* the world—not deeply. It only stirs it. Temporary power changes hands, but the same things happen again, just to different people. The revolutionary's character and strategy ensure it.

The Father, by contrast, says, "I'll do something different. I'll change things through my servant without such methods."

You might wonder: How is it possible that there would be any success in transforming a society without those basic political tools? Hundreds of years before Jesus embodies it so completely, the Father answers in the oracle from Isaiah 42. He says, in effect, it will look like this: the *character* of my servant will show *my* character to the world. That's my strategy for individual and social change.

The Matchless Character: Gentleness

The Father's character is marked by a type of gentleness. "A bruised reed he won't snap" (Isa 42:3)—what does that mean? It's the Father's way that he will not simply dispense with those who are bearing the wounds of their past.[99] If you think of a crushed reed, it's got a weak spot in it. You cannot lean on it or build with it because it might break. There's nothing you can do with it, so you might just snap it in half and toss it on the fire. You dispense with it. It's weak. It's unusable. But that's not the Father's way.

The Father's character cares about each of the persons involved. He will not dispense with a *person* because of weakness. He never discards an individual in order to reach a "larger" end goal. Did you know that about the Father—about God?

We all come deeply, deeply broken. There's not a reed to be found that is not bruised and ready to break if too much pressure comes upon it. We're all that way. The Father will not, in the process of transforming the world, dispense with you in your weakness in order to get the society he wants.

If I may point out the obvious; this is not how revolutionaries typically pursue their work. Revolutionaries dispense with people all the time because they do not fit the picture of society they want. They think of people as tools to be used to achieve the end result of a particular kind of society.

That is *not* the Father's way—it's not his personality or character. He's distinct, holy, different.

Matchless Character: Nurturing What's Still Living

"A smoldering wick he will not stuff out." The smallest spark of light still at work within you the Father will nurture to bring back to flame—to be at work in this world. Again, he does not dispense with any person to get the society he wants.

This is really basic. So many attempts to change the world turn on the idea that what matters is the final macro-product (whether that is an institution, company, nation, political system, or economic or cultural outcome). People are to be used or gotten rid of in service to that end. Unfortunately, even church leaders are sometimes possessed by this worldly picture of leadership. But not Jesus and not the Father.

The Father created each of you with the intention that you would live forever. Societies come and go. But you will live forever. So, the Father would not have a just society *instead of* each of us broken people. That is not sentimental irresponsibility on the Father's part. His choice is rooted in reality. You, despite your current brokenness, will live for untold millennia beyond the inevitable end of any earthly social order that one may be seeking to change.

So, the Father uses a different strategy. He works in our lives with incredible gentleness that actually inspires each person with the capacity to change. He arouses within us the positive conditions for change. Through this gentleness, we're told, "he will bring right living to success."

Matchless Character: What Succeeds

It's interesting to notice when Hebrew Bible quotations are enhanced by the New Testament writers. Jesus' quote from Isaiah adds two words to what is in the original Isaiah passage: "unto victory" or "into success" (Matt 12:20). Why?

Jesus, and then Matthew, wants to point out that the Father's character and strategy for changing the world *will succeed.* It will overcome. This gentleness effects an alteration in persons that allows us to actively change ourselves and, through our self-change, to incrementally transform the societies to which we belong.[100]

It's a simple process whereby the balance shifts. The balance of a society that once tilted toward those who, under appropriate conditions, were willing to do wrong gradually shifts. A preponderance emerges of those who, because of what they've seen of the Father's character and his love in Jesus, have come to where they could not imagine doing something wrong. It's just not who they are. They've changed.

These new people are enraptured with the Father's character—it has so captured their hearts that it changed them. As the balance of people moves in that direction, the society will change.

It's worth pointing out that this is not just wishful thinking—something that "ought to work." Two thousand years later, it's historical fact. It's been seen in countries, nations, and cultures where enough people have turned that the entire society changed for the better. No, those societies did not become perfect and there were still pockets of darkness with which to contend—but they became *sooo* much better.[101] And the kingdom continues to come.

Hope: The Active Ingredient of Change

We're also told about how this gentleness effects the change. How does the Father's gentleness bring justice to victory—right living to success? What's the active ingredient? It works by bringing people to hope in his character or name. "In his name the nations will hope." Hope is what changes people—gives the moral courage and energy to persevere in doing right.

You already know this, at least negatively, by experience. At some point, you've probably shared with somebody a vision that stirred you as right and personally beckoning. You were ready to bear the difficulties to do what you saw as right. But that person then convinced you that it was impossible for this approach to succeed. Suddenly, your resources for personal change vanished. Hopelessness crushes moral aspiration. All that is needed to deplete a person's moral drive and to induce apathy is to convince him or her that it cannot succeed.

The inverse is also true. Solid hope motivates. Hope transforms families and organizations and societies. Hope is what will change cities and nations. As hope takes over, change occurs. But hope requires a basis. Such assurance of eventual success is founded simply on who the Father is and the proximity of his action to each person.[102]

Here's the Father's strategy, which is rooted in his unique character: through Jesus, the Father approaches each person with uncommon respect, with care-filled compassion, and with self-giving love. As he does so, he strengthens the places that were broken in the person and fans into flame the smoldering wicks. A new life of possibility and hope opens before the person. He or she just can't help but act differently. And as she interacts with other people, new hope is inflamed in those others. There is no limit to the change that can take place in this manner—one person at a time, one family at a time, one group at a time—as each comes to see the distinct character of the Father.

So, why does it make sense to pray, "May your kingdom come" rather than focus on my own project? Once we see who the Father is—how beautiful and caring and loving and good his character is—once we grasp that the Father really is just as good as Jesus, who wouldn't want to pray this prayer? Because even when his choice is different from mine, the Father's choice will be better. It will even be better *for me*. And so, I come to long for the particular, personal will of the Father to be done.

That leads us to the next key concept in Jesus' philosophy, which is the subject of our next chapter: the kingdom of God and the experiential texture of life within it.

CHAPTER SIX

The Kingdom, or God in Action

Recalling the Foundation

THE GOD WHO IS dependent upon nothing else for his energy and existence is also utterly unique in character. With gentle care for each person, he moves the world toward what he intends for it to become. This picture of the nature and character of the Father—as the source of all that is—forms the foundation for the key ideas in Jesus' philosophy.

Transformation of human life requires a basic cognitive grasp of the Father's reality. Only then can we begin to choose to love him with our heart, retrain our souls to love him, fill our background self-talk with what is good for him, and thus act in the world and toward our neighbors in love. The Father is foundational.

The Father Acts

But the second truth we need to understand is that the Father *acts*. In fact, when the Gospel writers summarize what Jesus teaches publicly, they boil it down to an announcement of God's present action and its accessibility to each of us in our everyday lives. This is Jesus' "gospel."

Jesus' gospel introduces us to a world that is saturated in God's activity. Consider this summary of Jesus' core message as found in Mark 1:14–15:

> And after John had been taken into custody, Jesus came into
> Galilee, preaching the gospel of God, and saying, "The time is
> fulfilled, and the kingdom of God is at hand; repent and believe
> in the gospel." (Mark 1:14–15)

It only takes a sentence to articulate, but the words are so full that they
each need to be unpacked or they'll burst open. Of what, exactly, is Jesus
informing us?

In this chapter, I want to give a basic explanation of this element of Jesus' teaching, show how we know its meaning historically, and then unpack
what it means in terms of our own experience today.

The Kingdom—Jesus' Physics

In the simplest possible terms, the "kingdom of God" refers to *what God
is doing*—how the Father, as King, is acting to reshape the world. Jesus
clues us in to the fact that the Father is in action right where we live. His
project is unfolding right under our noses. And we're invited to join in—to
participate with the Father in his project.

Now, I am aware that many read this phrase "kingdom of God" or
"kingdom of heaven" as referring to a place or condition after death. Below
we'll consider why this cannot be the case. Others take it primarily as a new
social order. Again, that is not a sufficient reading—though the kingdom
does bring profound social implications.

Instead, Jesus is making a reality claim about the world we currently
live in and the present moment, not only about what might happen after
death or in a future age. Like all ancient philosophers, Jesus has an account
of a deep structure in the world, which forms the core concept around
which the rest of his philosophy is built.

In this case, Jesus is making a claim about what's really out there. If
you recall the three big questions among the ancient philosophers, Jesus'
teaching on the kingdom is addressing "physics." In other words, it answers a
series of concerns about what is real? How is the world put together and how
does it work? What place do human beings have within the world? What
sorts of things can we count on being there whether we like it or not?

For Jesus, the deepest layer of reality is simply the Father at work
in the world. Beneath and behind both what we would call the "natural
world" (the turning of seasons, the budding of trees, the growth, flowering,
and decaying or burning of grass) and what we recognize as the human
world (conversations, governments, meals, fights, and reconciliations) is
the Father's constant action.[103]

Within the Father's action Jesus also notices a propensity. The Father delights to incorporate into his actions any human being who is willing to pay attention to them and add his or her little efforts and resources to them.

This is the reality principle we encounter in Jesus' philosophy. Now, like all big-picture accounts of the world, Jesus' claim can only be evaluated by thinking carefully and experimentally testing it. Living in it will show whether it is true or not. It's known in the yoke. Jesus gives us enough clarification on the experience to run the experiment. We'll turn to this below.

But, first, let's examine the historical sources from which I can make such a claim about the meaning of Jesus' words. We'll have to step out of the Greek world and into the world of Second Temple Jewish life. I want to give you enough historical detail to be confident that the phrase "kingdom of God" already meant, among the Jews, something like "God at work in the world to dramatically change things."

If you find this historical section difficult, however, and are already confident about the meaning, feel free to skip to the subheading: How Jesus Modifies Prior "Kingdom" Understandings.

How We Know What the Words Mean in Second Temple Jewish Life

The kingdom of God was a readily understandable and frequently used phrase in Jesus' day. While the robust statements of YHWH as King in the Hebrew Bible provide a conceptual backdrop, the precise phrase "kingdom of God" was absent from earlier sections of scripture.[104]

To be clear, a word or phrase may be absent when its reality is present. Things are sometimes called by different names. The kingdom of God, as God in action, is a reality from everlasting to everlasting. The *phrase* "kingdom of God" emerges in Jesus' era, but the *reality* it names had been there all along and can be seen at work in Israel's history. In this section we're primarily talking about the phrase. Our best access to the range of meanings this specific phrase carried for Jesus' ordinary hearers comes by considering its occurrences in the Targums for Isaiah and the Minor Prophets.

A Targum is an Aramaic gloss on the Hebrew Bible. By Jesus' day most Jews in the land of Israel could not understand classical Hebrew and needed a translation into their spoken tongue, Aramaic. Hundreds of years prior, the Jews had gone into exile in Babylon speaking Hebrew, but they returned to their land mostly speaking Aramaic. The ordinary people needed a translation. So Targums were originally presented orally in the synagogue following a reading of the corresponding section in Hebrew.[105] Later, these traditional interpretations were committed to writing.[106]

Some Targums—especially those on the prophets—tended toward paraphrase and interpretive expansions. (If you are comparing these Targums to English Bibles, think of *The Message* not the *New American Standard*.) These free expansions of the scriptures are helpful because they allow us to overhear key ideas as they circulated at the popular, grassroots level in Jesus' day. They give us a window into what Jesus' first students would have already thought when Jesus started teaching them.

A Method of Comparison

Our method is simple. We can learn what Jesus' first hearers associated with the phrase "kingdom of God" by comparing its appearance in a Targum to the corresponding passage in the original Hebrew. Even for those who cannot read Aramaic or Hebrew, today one can easily do this by comparing the English translation of the Targumic passage to a literal English translation of the corresponding Hebrew text. (The NASB is good for this purpose.)

For the reader's convenience, I've provided a representative set of five parallel passages one may compare. Those words italicized in the Targum translations below have no corresponding word in the Masoretic text of the Hebrew Bible. The italics are provided in the translations cited.

Key Targum References Compared with the Hebrew Bible:

Isaiah 31:4 (NASB): "For thus says the LORD to me, 'As the lion or the young lion growls over his prey, against which a band of shepherds is called out, will not be terrified at their voice, nor disturbed at their noise, so will the LORD of hosts come down to wage war on Mount Zion and on its hill.'"

Isaiah Targum 31.4: "For the LORD said to me, As *a* lion or *a* young lion *roars* over its prey, and, when a band of shepherds *are appointed* against it, it is not *broken up* at their shouting or *checked* at their *tumult* so *the kingdom of* the LORD of hosts will *be revealed* to *settle* upon *the* Mount *of* Zion and upon its hill."[107]

Isaiah 40:9–10 (NASB): "Get yourself up on a high mountain, O Zion, bearer of good news, lift up your voice mightily, O Jerusalem, bearer of good news; lift it up, do not fear. Say to the cities of Judah, 'Here is your God!' Behold, the LORD God will come with might, with His arm ruling for Him. Behold, His reward is with Him, and His recompense before Him."

Isaiah Targum 40.9–10: "Get you up to a high mountain, *prophets who* herald good tidings *to* Zion; lift up your voice with *force, you who* herald good tidings *to* Jerusalem, lift up, fear not; say to the cities *of the house* of Judah, '*The kingdom of* your *God is revealed!*' Behold, the LORD *God is revealed* with *strength,* and *the strength* of his *mighty* arm rules *before* him; behold *the* reward *of those who perform his Memra*[108] is with him, *all those whose deeds are disclosed* before him."[109]

Obadiah 20 (NASB): "The deliverers will ascend Mount Zion to judge the mountain of Esau, and the kingdom will be the LORD's."

Obadiah Targum 20: "Liberators shall go up to Mount Zion to judge the *citadel* of Esau, and *the kingdom of the LORD shall be revealed over all the inhabitants of the earth.*"[110]

Micah 4:6–7 (NASB): "'In that day,' declares the LORD, 'I will assemble the lame, and gather the outcasts, even those whom I have afflicted. I will make the lame a remnant, and the outcasts a strong nation, and the LORD will reign over them in Mount Zion from now on and forever.'"

Micah Targum 4.6–7: "At that *time,* says the LORD *God,* I will assemble together the *exiled,* and I will gather together *the scattered,* and those *who were* treated harshly *on account of the sins of my people.* I will make *the exiled* a remnant, and *the scattered* a mighty nation. *The kingdom of* the LORD *shall be revealed* upon them on Mount Zion from now on and forever."[111]

Zechariah 14:9 (NASB): "And the LORD will be king over all the earth; in that day the LORD will be the only one, and His name the only one."

Zechariah Targum 14.9: "*And the kingdom of the LORD shall be revealed* upon all *the inhabitants of* the earth; at that *time they shall serve before the LORD with one accord, for* his name *is established in the world; there is none apart from him.*"[112]

A general picture emerges as you notice the alterations. The phrase "kingdom of God" carries a double connotation in the Targums—which indicates the meaning it held in the minds of ordinary Jews of Jesus' day.

First, the kingdom of God is an active concept. It refers to *God acting in strength.*[113] Whenever God, through mighty deeds, changes things in this world, the Targum will gloss it as "kingdom of God." In the Targums, this especially occurs when battle is waged, and wars are won, through divine power. So, despite the grammatical form, try to think "verb" rather than "noun": when you hear Jesus say "kingdom" it means that God is *doing* something. God's kingdom is not a location but is rather God's *active reign*—God's exercise of his rule in creation. We might say it is the *kingship* of God.

Second, in Second Temple Jewish thought, God's kingdom still awaits *revelation or unveiling*. In other words, it has existed since before the creation of the world but will not be accessible to humans until God unveils it.[114] The verb most often attached to the kingdom of God is "will be revealed" and, in the Targums it is almost always future.[115] In other words, *God will show himself* and his overarching sway whenever he finally acts with power. A person's character becomes visible in his or her activity. Likewise, the Lord's character will be disclosed through prodigious feats when he acts.

Those were the connotations in the peoples' understanding when Jesus began teaching about the kingdom of God.

How Jesus Modifies Prior "Kingdom" Understandings

Jesus assumes and retains the kernel of both these connotations, but he also modifies them in important ways. For Jesus, the kingdom of God refers to God's *activity* and God does make himself known by his actions—it is a matter of revelation. However, Jesus also understands two key differences that were lost to the composers of the Targums.

First, for Jesus the kingdom of God is *here and now*.[116] In the Targums, the revelation of the kingdom is almost exclusively future. Jesus also acknowledges more to come of God's kingdom—how could it be otherwise since it means that God is pursuing his project?

But Jesus' emphasis is on the close proximity of God's work to you and me in our everyday activities. God is doing something right where ordinary people live. His kingdom, which is from everlasting to everlasting, has moved into our neighborhoods. It is being revealed today. Jesus even pointed to his own compassionate works—healing and exorcism—as an indicator of God's kingdom already active (Matt 12:28). This claim also gestures toward another key difference.

Second, Jesus redefines power. The Targum's messiah does not suffer. But Jesus' vision of effectiveness, like Isaiah's, involves suffering.[117] When God acts, a very different sort of effectiveness marks his action. We will consider this carefully in the next chapter. For the moment, let it suffice to say that Jesus emphasizes God's character as gentle and humble (Matt 11:25–30), generous and merciful (Matt 5:44–45), forgiving (Matt 18:21–35), good (Matt 19:17; 20:1–16), and seeking the well-being of others (Matt 5:43–48). These also are the marks of God's activity in this world. God's power comes girded in a towel, not clad with battle armor. It wields washbasins rather than swords.

So, Jesus' core message amounted to this claim. "God—the rightful king—is acting here and now to remake this world. Given God's character of compassion and love, his way of making things happen could easily be missed if you expect power as humans usually wield it."

The Existential Significance of "Kingdom" as God in Action

It might help us conceptualize God's kingdom if we consider that each of us also has a kingdom.[118] In the language of scripture, we were created with a "dominion."

That word, "dominion," if read with contemporary connotations, may leave a bad taste in one's mouth—as if exploitation and arbitrary privilege were humanity's birthright. Nothing could be further from the original meaning. Rather, Genesis sees humans as possessing moral responsibility and genuine agency in the world. Moreover, our moral responsibility and agency mirror God's responsibility and agency. That's the key point of "dominion."

Recall the creation account in Genesis:

> "Let us make man in our image, after our likeness. *And let them have dominion* over the fish of the sea and over the birds of the heavens and over the livestock and over all the earth and over every creeping thing that creeps on the earth." So, God created man in his own image, in the image of God he created him; male and female he created them. And God blessed them. And God said to them, "Be fruitful and multiply and fill the earth and subdue it and *have dominion* over the fish of the sea and over the birds of the heavens and over every living thing that moves on the earth." (Gen 1:26–28 ESV, emphasis added)

Human beings reflect God, according to Genesis, through exercising dominion. In fact, this theme runs from the beginning to the end of scripture (see, e.g., Ps 8; Dan 7:13–14; Mark 2:23–28; Heb 2:5ff.; 1 Cor 6:2–3; Rev 22:5). Jewish biblical interpreters in Jesus' day, notably in the community at Qumran, also emphasized "rule" as essential to humanity's creation and destiny as image of God.[119] The background idea is that just as God exercises dominion over the heavenly court, so human beings in partnership with God are designed to exercise dominion over this part of the created order.[120]

What's a Person?

However, this is not just an ancient metaphor. Nor is it something one ought to believe simply because it is in this book. Rather, dominion is a fundamental experience we have all had as persons.[121]

Persons are created with dominion—a built-in impulse to make things happen as we see fit. This agency, aimed at the good, is so essential to human personality that we cannot imagine a person without it. Just try.

Start by reflecting on yourself. Would *you* like to spend your whole life without having ever made any difference? Could you imagine anyone else really being a person if they had no impulse to effect things around them? When some catastrophe reduces a human being to such a state, we talk about her or him being reduced to a "vegetative" state. Dominion, or agency for the good, seems to be hardwired into human beings. To be a person is to be given say over some (big or small) portion of reality.

Perhaps we see this impulse in its most stark and unrefined form in little children.[122] When we are born, our dominion encompasses only our bodies—and that is more of a project than a possession. A little baby has not yet mastered her own body, but she pushes herself to gain dominion over it. So, she always wants to do for herself. Sitting in her highchair, my infant daughter would grab the spoon and try feeding herself. Of course, since she lacked sufficient control, the food ended up in all the wrong openings. Our scrapbooks contain some delightful, and now nostalgic, pictures of her first attempts at exercising dominion.

As she grew, this impulse to effect things expanded outward from her body. We would try to tie her shoes, but she insisted, "*I* do it!" She entered into her "terrible twos" and readily exercised those favorite kingdom words—"No!" and "Mine!" Both words highlight the built-in human need to affect the world around us.

Over time her dominion has expanded in concentric circles from her body outward. Now she makes things happen in the house and (when properly stimulated by rewards and punishments) in the backyard. She contributes to the world of a circle of friends, our local church, and her school. Lord willing, in time her dominion will enlarge to encompass cognitive mastery of deeper subject matters, responsible work, a family, neighbors, and much more.

Dominion is not just something we read about in Genesis. It is something we see around us and personally feel moved to exercise every day. However, despite being hardwired into us, not all dominion is used well.

The Human Problem and Dominion

The human problem may be described as a choice to use my dominion or agency while disregarding God's dominion. As a result, I also find my dominion not only set against God but also in hurtful competition with other's dominions. The opening chapters of Genesis recount how as a race we chose to annex our little kingdoms from God's great kingdom. Interpersonal blame and hostility, personal shame and exposure, and ultimately death followed from our choice to go it alone in this world. So, Adam blames Eve. Cain kills Abel. Soon every thought of the human heart is "always evil all the time" (Gen 6:5).

Human dominion simply does not function well apart from God. We were never designed to live—to make things happen—without any reference to God. It is built into the metaphor of "God's *image*." Try it out. Stand in front of a mirror and gesture. What does your image do? Images act in concert with their source, not independently. We were created to exercise agency for the good *in partnership with God.*

Jesus' good news is that God has a special place for each of us in his project. His great offer is to enable us to work with God. One may yield his or her little dominion to God's greater dominion. When I do so, I learn to do what God is doing. Jesus' preferred language for co-working with God is "entering into the kingdom of God" or the "kingdom of the heavens" (see Matt 5:20; 7:21; 18:1–4; 19:23–26 // Mark 10:23–25 // Luke 18:25; John 3:5).

Supple Collaboration: The Experiential Texture of Life in the Kingdom

Life in step with God's activity or kingdom possesses a distinctive experiential texture. I like to describe that texture as supple collaboration or submissive synergy. In other words, it's a form of co-working—coordinated effectiveness. Thus, the word synergy or collaboration (from Greek or Latin roots, respectively). But I am not the primary actor in this joint enterprise. God is guiding. God is the primary actor. I join in. Hence, the adjectives supple and submissive. I become effective by flexibly adjusting my efforts and movements to God's ongoing action in the world. In this dance, the Father leads. Let's attend to some of Jesus' depictions of this life.

To help his apprentices gauge whether they are aligning their dominion with God's activity, Jesus supplies thick descriptions of life in the kingdom—largely through parables or comparisons. Please consider a couple examples from the Gospel of Mark.

In Mark 4:26–29, Jesus uses the image of a farmer to describe the experience of coordinating one's activity with an unseen power. This power is beyond one's control, yet reliable. Certain intrinsic challenges arise when working with an invisible, yet living, God. One is the question, how can I know if I'm doing it? Here's Jesus' answer:

> And Jesus was saying, "The kingdom of God is [gloss: When God is at work, it is] like a man who casts seed upon the soil; and he goes to bed at night and gets up by day, and the seed sprouts and grows—how, he himself does not know. The soil produces crops by itself; first the blade, then the head, then the mature grain in the head. But when the crop permits, he immediately puts in the sickle, because the harvest has come." (Mark 4:26–29)

In this case, Jesus describes the kingdom of God—God's action—as like a man throwing seed on the ground. The farmer does not understand how the seed grows (4:27). He does, however, recognize how to time or coordinate his interactions with those of the unseen power. So, he does his initial part by throwing the seed. Then he sleeps. He waits as other factors work. Jesus is explicit that these other factors are mysterious to the farmer. He doesn't know *how* they work; all he knows is *that* they work. When the harvest arrives, those other factors have done their part, the farmer acts again. Co-working with God requires timing our actions with his interventions in our world.[123]

In Mark 4:30–32, Jesus expands on this experiential description. The emphasis in this comparison falls upon the incongruity between visible cause and effect. There's a mismatch between what humans contribute to an action or event, and the outcomes we see from it.

> And Jesus said, "How shall we picture the kingdom of God, or by what parable shall we present it? It is like a mustard seed, which, when sown upon the soil, though it is smaller than all the seeds that are upon the soil, yet when it is sown, it grows up and becomes larger than all the garden plants and forms large branches; so that the birds of the air can nest under its shade." (Mark 4:30–32)

The kingdom of God—God's activity—is like sowing a mustard seed. What goes into the ground is the smallest of seeds. Yet, what emerges is the largest of the garden plants. When one works with God, there is a routine disproportion between one's own talents, efforts, and resources, on the one hand, and the effect of one's activity on the other.

The phrase Jesus uses in Mark 4:32, "the birds of the air can find shelter [or, take refuge] in its shade," uses a stock image from Israel's literature. The "birds of the air" are the multitude of nations or "gentiles"—people very different from his hearers.

By surveying the way this image is used within Jewish literature, we can appreciate Jesus' message. In some of Israel's texts, the birds fight against those who rightfully dwell under the tree (Mid. Ps. 104:12), in other stories they are simply driven off (Dan 4:12, 14; Ezek 31:6ff.). The mutual hostility between Israel and the nations of this period was well known.[124] Jesus' disciples would have been ready for that sort of story about the birds.

One could, for instance, imagine a very different parable in which the mustard tree grows up and the planter drives the birds away to protect his comfortable garden. Many in Jesus' day would have expected that sort of story. Unfortunately, there are churches today who think that is their job too.

However, Jesus chooses to quote a different verse that casts a different vision—a goal of welcome and help to the outsider. Psalm 104:12 speaks of birds that are given shelter or who take refuge in what YHWH provides (see also Ezek 17:23). To take refuge or find shelter is a known metaphor for conversion in Second Temple Jewish literature.[125] It speaks of how one comes to be at home among God's people.

Here is Jesus' point: *when we co-work with God, God restores our dominion or created agency.* As he makes us effective like we were created to be, our Father increasingly does things with us that we could never manage alone. The effect of our seed planting far outstrips our own talents. But God will also use us to help people whom we might not have selected on our own. The disproportionate effect of his followers' labors will be *for the benefit of the nations*—not simply a special advantage for the individual worker or his natural community.

Kingdom Reconsideration

Let's return, at last, to Jesus' second phrase in the passage with which we began this chapter. "Repent and believe in the gospel" (Mark 1:15). "Repent" is a poor translation even though it is standard. The underlying word (*metanoeo*) simply means to "think again," "reconsider," or even "think about how you've been thinking." This is the philosopher's task—to reconsider all of life based on what he has discovered to be real.

In other words, Jesus calls us to reconsider everything in the light of God's activity here and now. Rethink what is real and illusory, what is possible or impossible. Revisit what you have considered worthwhile or a waste of time, an intelligent move or hopelessly foolish. Since God is doing something right where you are, think again!

The Meaning of Life

We've covered a lot of territory in this chapter—from ancient physics to Targums and from the God's image as dominion to Jesus' existential descriptions of co-working with God. Allow me to boil it down and state the essence of this understanding. What, in the simplest terms, does it mean that you and I reflect God's image through dominion or agency for the good? What is the significance of being given restored agency by being invited into a life of supple collaboration with God?

Well, it tells us the meaning of life. No, really. That's not a joke. This vision tells us how to lead a life that is meaningful, which is what people really mean when they ask about the "meaning of life." So, would you like to know the meaning of human life?

Here it comes in one sentence: *your life is an unfinished act of God's love for God's world.* That's the meaning of human existence. If you were created to effectively steward or care for the world under God, then that's *what you are.*

The statement is dense and pregnant with significance, so I'll unpack it a bit. You and I are uncompleted acts of God's love. His acts, which we are, are incomplete because our life is still unfolding. But from birth to death to resurrected existence in a world to come, you and I are acts of God's own love seeking completion.

We are unfinished acts of God's love *for God's world*—his love is not just for us, but for his world. That's entailed in creating us to be agents or to exercise reign over this world. Of course, God is loving you and me too. But the important, horizon-righting point is that God is loving you *through* me and he's loving me *through* you and the fullness of his creation *through* us. Our very existence, and the agency that enables us to exercise dominion, is an expression of his love for the rest of his creation.

This is why submissive synergy or supple collaboration with God—in Jesus' language that's "entering the kingdom"—is such a wonderful life possibility. Here's the existential import of being unfinished acts of God's love for God's world. To the degree that I resist pouring myself into producing good for others and seek to live for my own selfish ends, God's act of love, which I am, will be frustrated and unfruitful. I'll be miserable. To the degree that I join with God in deliberately giving myself for others and caring for God's world—to that degree God's love in me will be fruitful and joyous and effective and overflowing with significance.

CHAPTER SEVEN

Power Under

Understanding Kingdom
Effectiveness

OUR LAST CHAPTER UNPACKED Jesus' basic message or gospel. We've seen that the "kingdom of God" was a phrase commonly used in Jesus' day to refer to God acting *in power or strength* and thereby revealing who he is. Jesus employed this phrase in ways that largely assumed its popular meaning—largely but not completely.

The Question of Power

In particular, Jesus' teaching about God's way of acting problematizes the sort of power expected.[126] God's action is more like leaven working through dough (Matt 13:33) or a tiny mustard seed sown in a field (Matt 13:31) than like a firestorm neutralizing an army (see 2 Kgs 1:9–16 and Luke 9:51–56). Likewise, the sorts of activity whereby Jesus invites us to co-work with God often seem rather mundane. Ordinary kindnesses, service, healing, kingdom-focused teaching, hospitality, and providing cups of cold water to others—these acts lack the expected flare. Why?

The Father's character circumscribes how he makes things happen. Thus, Jesus radically, and brilliantly, re-conceptualizes the very nature of power. Let's start from the bottom.

Power and Character

In the simplest possible terms, power refers to the capacity to perform work—any ability to make things happen. Effectiveness might be a rough equivalent. There is nothing *necessarily* sinister about power as such—the morality of power depends on the *type* of power and *how* it is wielded.

Jesus has a distinct vision of how God makes things happen—his power. Moreover, Jesus invites us to wield the same sort of effectiveness as we co-work with God. To co-work with God, we must make peace with the Father's character and his way of changing things. We cannot willingly fit our little efforts into God's great project unless our twisted instincts concerning effectiveness are righted. Unless we grasp what sorts of things God might do, we will find it difficult to recognize the opportunities for collaboration when they arise.

Recognizing the Father's character—his matchless name—enables us to see his action. Without this understanding we would be blind to God's movement among us—constantly looking in the wrong direction or focused too far off to notice his deed right where we are. God's character redefines power. Jesus offers us a window into God's sort of effectiveness in the world.

To grasp the significance of Jesus' understanding of power, we need to return to the biblical picture of humanity created in the image of God. This time we will place the Genesis account in proximity to a counter-story in antiquity—the Prometheus myth. The juxtaposition helps to illuminate something distinctive about the biblical picture.

We noticed, in the previous chapter, that agency plays a central role in human life as created by God. Humans are given a peculiar sort of agency. We are supposed to be effective—having say and shaping this world below—but only through a divine synergy. Humanity would enact, or play a particular and partial role, within the larger project of God. Thus, we would reign, under God and by his power, here below. That was God's plan.

Creation as Collaborative Finite Goodness

It is worth pausing to ask what God was doing in creating such a creature. Remember, from chapter 4, the baseline understanding of God in Israelite monotheism? There is nothing over, beneath, or behind the Creator God. Apart from creation, there is nothing but this particular God. There is no meta-divine realm.

Therefore, creation means that this God chooses to make room for beings that are not-God—in other words, creatures—to exist and to act.

By calling agents—people who can decide and act—into existence, God is delegating. He grants initiative and effectiveness, within measure, to humans and other creatures. Because God created us, there will be things that happen in this world that God does not personally choose. Since God does not create by necessity, we must ask why God does it.

The answer seems to be something like this: creation is God's experiment in producing limited forms of collaborative goodness. God simply delights in enabling finite creatures to enjoy authentic goodness and genuine effectiveness through collaboration with him.

By limited or finite I am just referring to the fact that creatures begin and end. They occupy some space and span of time but not others. They can do some things and other things are completely beyond their powers. They have a horizon within which they can comprehend a measure of reality, but the whole forever escapes their grasp. That's us. We're finite. We were created with distinct edges.[127]

Evidently, God wants there to be small, limited beings like us who receive their created edges or existential limits not as a tragic flaw to be overcome but as a gift. He wants us to play a real role in how this world unfolds. By entering into the kingdom, we learn that our created edges— our distinctive traits, energies, moments, and places—enable us to fit into the Father's overarching project. This created world, and God's kingdom or project within it, make it possible for us to become truly effective even though we're small, and truly good even though we're easily broken. God relishes empowering dinky, fragile beings like us to live in ways that are cosmically significant, genuinely effective, and morally good.

That's the significance of creation, at least in part.

The Superadded: Adam's Co-Dominion vs. Prometheus' Provision

God delights in human agency within his world. He gave us a real capacity to act—to initiate and direct events. However, human action was never enough—never *intended* to be enough—on its own. Rather, humans were initially fashioned to be effective when something more was added to their action. We were created to be collaborators, not solo agents. God's creative project, his kingdom, would frame and infuse human deeds so that humanity could be effective. Human agency, by nature, required superaddition. As an image, human action would only work in concert with its divine prototype. It needed something else—a something more that came from God.

When human beings decided to secede their little dominions from God's great project, futility followed. Thorns and thistles marred the ground. Food would now be scraped out with sweated brow. Death ultimately conquered. Human agency by itself just isn't enough to match the task of ordering this world. In that solo project, our striving is losing. That's the story of Genesis 3.

This basic intuition, that human agency *by nature* requires something additional to complete it, also resounds through a counter-story of human origins. In that story, the something added is different, but it's founded on the same basic intuition.

Among the Greeks, the tale was told of how Zeus fashioned beasts and men out of the clay and then had Prometheus arrange for their various provisions. Our primary source for the story is Plato's *Protagoras*.[128] The dialogue presumes, however, the earlier tales of Hesiod in the *Works and Days*[129] and *Theogony*[130] and perhaps also Aeschylus' *Prometheus Bound*. Let's consider the gist of the story.[131]

Prometheus' Provisions

Once upon a time, there were gods but no mortals. When the fated day came for mortals to emerge, the gods mixed clay and fire to produce them. Then they charged two Titan-born brothers, Prometheus and Epimetheus, to distribute equipment to each mortal.

The names of both brothers are significant. Prometheus means forethought or consideration. Epimetheus means after-thought or hindsight. They embody their names.

Prometheus is cunning and constantly maneuvering in view of some hidden goal or other. He strategizes. Epimetheus is entirely immersed in the moment—bumbling into outcomes that he never anticipated. He specializes in oops and uh-ohs. Together Prometheus and Epimetheus are a pair—respectively exemplifying two purified traits that usually come mixed up in ordinary mortal characters.

Now, Epimetheus is enthralled by the idea of providing equipment—critical resources for life—to all these creatures. He begs Prometheus to let him do the apportioning. He'll give it his best. And then Prometheus, he says, can inspect the work when he's finished.

Prometheus agrees.

Epimetheus gets absorbed in the project, seeking to preserve each creature through its gifts. To one he gives great size as a protection, to another strength without speed, to others meager strength but great speed.

POWER UNDER   91

To those who can fight or fly he gives a low birth rate, to those who are hunted he gives the capacity to reproduce rapidly. Some he wraps with armored hides and others with furs to protect them from the heat and cold. Epimetheus is so entranced by the work before him that he fails to notice his supplies running low. He apportions all the gifts before coming to the last creature—man.

About this time Prometheus arrives to inspect. He sees that all the materials are used up; all the resources spent. But there is no more time. Fate presses in. Man is about to be released into the world as he is—naked, defenseless, unequipped for survival.

In perplexity over how to save human beings, Prometheus steals provisions from the gods. From Hephaestus and Athena, he takes technical skill—the wisdom of craft-production. Then he steals fire from Zeus, smuggling it down from Olympus in a hollow reed. These will be the gifts of humanity and allow their survival without the built-in capacities that other creatures enjoy. The beasts get suitable natures. Humans get technology. That's Prometheus' "salvation" or *sotēria*.[132]

Technology, in other words, provides what is lacking in human agency.[133] However, technology by itself is not quite enough. Tools and weapons help. They make up for intrinsic lacks in the human frame. But humans will still need the protection of collectives—cities and combined efforts. Eventually, Zeus arranges for Hermes to supply politics to give technology-furnished humans a fighting chance of survival. And such is it today, or so the story goes.

Shared Hunch, Opposing Solutions

Reading Plato and Genesis together is instructive. The shared intuition—humanity's deep hunch—is that human agency by itself is insufficient. We need more for effectiveness in this world. Something must be added on top of our own deeds. Both Genesis and the Greek myths assume that much. But, in these stories, that hunch gets evaluated from opposing angles.

The Greek picture, submerged in the myth of Prometheus and Epimetheus, is that technology and politics add what is inherently missing to human agency. Fire-fashioned tools and persuasive maneuvering within groups supply that extra something. They enable human beings to make their way in the world. Technologically extended action and political guidance of collectives can make human life viable and significant in an otherwise inhospitable world. That's Promethean salvation in a nutshell.

The biblical picture, implicit in Genesis and articulated afresh by Jesus' gospel of the kingdom, sees human agency as fashioned to complement divine agency. *God* is the something more that makes human action viable and significant. But it's not so much that God's action is added to human agency as that human agency is invited into God's project. By "entering the kingdom," our personal edges and limited resources come into focus as gifts. Through submissive synergy, we discover that the edges of our agency are actually puzzle pieces fitting snuggly into the great good thing that God is doing.

Technology in the Bible

Technology, in the biblical story, comes later—after sin and exile from the Garden. First, Abel develops pastoral life (Gen 4:2). It's an innovation. He allows the sheep to work the cursed soil in his place. Then Abel uses what they produce. Later, Cain's line develops cities and metallurgy and epic song (Gen 4:16–24). That's closer to what we think of as technologies.

There's certainly a suspicious element to how technology is first depicted in scripture. But technology is not all bad in the biblical view. God finds uses for it too. When God desires to rescue Noah from the flood, he doesn't snatch him up to the heavens to wait until it has passed. God guides Noah to develop yet another technology—the ark (Gen 6:13–22).

So, technology is not intrinsically set against God. But it can be idolized—imagined as if it were the ultimate answer to humanity's plight apart from God. When that happens, humanity begins to imagine effectiveness primarily in terms of compulsive force and manipulative political coercion. The Babel story shows the end of that path (Gen 11:1–9). Along this path lies the imperial impulse. By slave labor, which in context is implied by the use of bricks to build the tower, human collectives may try to make a name for themselves, preclude a diversity of people groups, and achieve quasi-divine significance for their projects. Even in the Bible, something like Promethean salvation—technical and political coercion—presents itself as a primordial alternative to the submissive synergy with God for which we were created.

These stories are in the primordial history of Genesis 1–11 not because they're long past but because they depict things ever present. Primordial events not only happened then but are still happening in a thousand ways today. That's why they're primordial and not just ancient. The human folly they describe is archetypical.

It should be no surprise, then, to learn that Jesus' own students had Promethean, or Babel-leaning, instincts too. Jesus labored to help them see beyond such instincts into God's primary way of making things happen.

The Nature of Power

Mark 10:35–45 relates a crucial teaching moment in this regard. Let's try to follow Jesus' insight as he clarifies what constitutes true power for his disciples. Our section opens with his disciples attempting a classic "power move."

James and John want to secure a privileged position within Jesus' coming government, because they think of power in terms of position.

> James and John, sons of Zebedee, approached him and said to him, "Teacher, we want you to do for us whatever we ask." He said to them, "What do you want me to do for you?" They said to him, "Grant us to sit, one on your right and one on your left, in your glory." (Mark 10:35–37)

Their move makes perfect sense within the ordinary human understanding of power. Humans regularly confuse power with social position and the control it provides. We tend to think that power emanates from the top of an organization. The closer one gets to the top of the organization, the more control one wields. And, to the Promethean mind, control is power. It's so obvious that we don't bother saying it out loud. It is also a grossly distorted picture of power.

Of course, there is a grain of truth behind the confusion. Within specific social configurations, position can provide power as a byproduct. When other persons have decided to compete for position within a group, occupying a higher rung does seize a scarce resource. The scarcity is artificial, but real. Controlling scarce resources gives one a *certain measure* of power in relation to those who need them. The Zebedee boys are making their move based on the assumption that the kingdom of God functions like a social competition with control found on top.

At this point, Jesus begins to reframe, for the Zebedee brothers, what goes into true power and glory. Curiously, Jesus does this by offering two images of *suffering*.

> Jesus said to them, "You don't know what you are requesting. Are you able to drink the cup which I drink or to be baptized with the baptism with which I am baptized?" They said to him, "We're able." So, Jesus said to them, "the cup which I drink you

will drink, and with the baptism with which I am baptized you
will also be baptized, however, to sit on my right and on my
left is not mine to give but is for those for whom it has been
prepared." (Mark 10:38–40)

To understand this passage, one needs to understand the significance of
the images of "drinking the cup" and that of "baptism" or immersion. Let's
consider them in turn.

Cup of Iniquity

The "cup of iniquity" is a common image, both in the scriptures and in
Second Temple Jewish literature (cf. Gen 15:16; 18:20; Dan 8:19–23; 9:24;
11:36; Jub. 14:16; 2 Macc 2:12–17). The cup tells us both that sin or error
eventually self-destructs and that there is an organic connection between
the error involved and the destruction.

While sin brings destruction, judgment rarely falls *immediately* upon
the sinner. There's a time lag. For a period of time, it appears as if there
were no penalty for the evil committed. They got away with it, or so it
seems. But then, often when least expected, the person or the society simply collapses under a vast array of problems. The pattern recurs throughout history. Why?

According to scripture, wrongdoing and error is like strong drink
gradually filling a cup. It accumulates a drop at a time as we act with aban-
don. Consequently, wrongdoers do not *immediately* reap the consequences
of their misdeeds. But the cup only holds so much. There is a limit. Reality is not infinitely malleable. If one does not rethink and change course,
iniquity eventually splashes over the lip of the cup. Then the person or
culture is obliged to drink what he or they have mixed for themselves.
Sin eventually destroys the sinner. Persons and societies can only bear so
much wrongdoing before they implode.

Jesus uses the image, but with a significant twist. *He* is drinking the
cup, though he didn't mix it. Jesus is absorbing the wrongdoing of others.

Baptism of Fire

Likewise, a baptism of fire is coming upon Jesus' generation. John proph-
esied it (Matt 3:11; Luke 3:16–17). Most people, then and now, associ-
ate baptism with water. John too baptized with water, but he also spoke
of two other baptisms or immersions. The one coming after him would

overwhelm each segment of his generation either with the Spirit or with fire. For those who repent, the Spirit would flood their lives with good. For those who refuse, however, there would be the fire of judgment to consume them. John wasn't one to mince words.

Jesus also employs the metaphor of judgment as fire. However, he has revised it considerably. Jesus calls the fiery baptism *his own* to suffer (Luke 12:49–50). Jesus intends to take the judgment of others upon himself. Already he is being baptized—absorbing the judgment due to his generation's errors and rebellion. He didn't create their problem, but he is accepting the hardship and absorbing the blows to correct it.

Here's the question: Why might Jesus respond to a request for power and glory—think of glory here as manifest effectiveness—by inquiring after one's capacity to suffer? Is Jesus randomly changing the subject, or might there be a deeper connection between one's readiness to suffer and true power? For the moment I'll let that question hang in your mind. We'll loop back to it soon.

Overreactions

Back to the story. The other disciples see the Zebedees' move and are irritated. What bothers them most is that they hadn't worked up the nerve to try it first.

"When the ten heard, they came unglued at James and John" (Mark 10:41). Most translations render the main verb as "became indignant." That's correct too. This verb is primarily used for anger. But the verb behind "became indignant," which I've glossed as "came unglued," has a particular connotation. It's built on a particle, *agan*, meaning "too much." The Greek word is simply a verbal form of that particle (*aganaktein*). Their response is excessive. The ten are "too-muching" toward James and John. In colloquial English we might say they're over-reacting. They've come unglued.

Evidently, the Zebedees' request struck a nerve in the ten. The other disciples genuinely fear being outmaneuvered in their pursuit of power. They think of effectiveness as something that could be lost or negated through another's preemptive scheming.

Two Types of Power

So, Jesus gathers the disciples together and explains power to them. He supplies a simple contrast between the sort of power known to the gentiles (or nations) and a very different kind of power exercised within God's project.

> Jesus called them to himself and said to them, "You know that those presumed to rule the nations lord over them, and their big men exercise authority over them. It's not that way among you. Rather, whoever wants to become great among you will be your servant, and whoever wants to be first among you will be slave of all. For even the Son of Man did not come to be served but to serve and to give his life as a ransom for many." (Mark 10:42–45)

The nations know only of power *over* others. They imagine efficacy in terms of compulsion and force. Their "leaders" and "big men" wield a sort of effectiveness that others must suffer.[134]

The power of the nations' rulers is characteristically Promethean. Technical extensions of physical ability and maneuvering to coerce groups sum up their playbook. But one man's Promethean salvation is another person's victimization. Power over is always a zero-sum game.

In contemporary discussions of politics, we commonly contrast "hard power" and "soft power."[135] While that distinction is understandable, both are forms of Promethean power over others. Hard power is simply the power of force and physical, or at least threatened, coercion. It corresponds to one use of technical skill to enhance and extend our bodily capacities in the world. But "soft power" is, often, another word for manipulation and political maneuvering to bring about particular goals. In Matthew's version of the story, the initial request to Jesus does not come directly from James and John but indirectly through their mother (Matt 20:20–21). There's the "soft power" strategy. All things being equal, of course, "soft power" is better than its "hard" alternative. Point taken. But it is still Promethean. It just uses the political more than the technical element.

The Illusion

Jesus subtly hints that this type of power over others is ultimately illusory—more about what seems to be than what really is. Promethean effectiveness is more limited than it likes to admit. Notice his words in verse 42. Here are a range of legitimate translations: "Those who *seem to be* leaders," or "those *thought of as* princes," or "those *considered to be* rulers" of the nations lord it over them. Power over others is not yet true power.

Jesus understands something that could only be learned by reflecting upon God's use of power. Here it is: power over others is not only damaging to others, but also always *limited*, finite. Remember, power simply means effectiveness—the capacity to perform work or make something happen. There is no such thing as absolute power or boundless effectiveness in this sense of power *over* others. I realize that claim runs counter to every human impulse, but it's true. You will see so yourself if you reflect with me.

A Thought Experiment

What are the primary forms of power over others? Brainstorm for a moment. I'm guessing one or more of the following came to mind: Money. Sex appeal. Social Position. Fame. Physical intimidation. The ability to shame or threat of shame. Most forms of power over others can reduce to these. And all of them are limited. Every last one.

In each case, what would limit one's power over others? Answer: the *goodness* of the person one would control.

Power over is inherently limited by the goodness of others. In each case, the improvement of others (either morally or by acquiring the specific quality, position, or possession lacked) will reduce the amount of power I can wield over them. Let's consider some specific forms of power.

Take money as a power source. Imagine that I had a great deal of cash at my disposal—say one hundred million dollars. The cash would give me a certain amount of power over another person. People are willing to do and relinquish many things for money. Some are prepared to do unspeakable things for money. But my capacity to control or exert power over a person through money will be limited by her goodness. If she improves financially—no longer needing the stack of money in my hand, then I lose power. Likewise, if she improves morally, becoming content with what she has, I lose power over her. My power over her is always limited by her goodness.

Consider physical intimidation as a power source. If I were physically intimidating, then threats of violence would grant me a measure of power over another person. People dislike pain and humiliation. They are willing to do many things to avoid it. But my capacity to control another person through intimidation would be limited by his goodness. If he improved physically—say hitting the weights and taking MMA instruction—I would lose power over him. Likewise, his moral improvement would strip me of power. If he grew in character to the point where he could say, "You can break my bones and kill me, but you cannot make me do that," then my power over him would evaporate.

Analogous improvements would dissipate my capacity to make things happen through sex appeal, social position, shame, and fame. Power over others is inherently limited. That's just the nature of it. Jesus knows it even when the rest of the world can't see it.

The Reality Principle

Jesus then describes true effectiveness as service—a kind of power under and alongside others (Mark 10:43–45). Jesus' choice of words is weighty with significance. The gentiles' illusory power is invested in "rulers" and "big men"—specific socially acknowledged positions. (We find these words, especially *archontes* or "rulers," everywhere in the ancient world—on statues, inscriptions, and in literary records.)

But Jesus then shifts to speak of how to become "great."

What do you think? Is Jesus talking about who gets to put the phrase "the great" behind his name? (Perhaps, in our day, one would use it as a title under one's name in an email signature line.) Maybe something else is behind Jesus' choice of words. What if Jesus is describing what goes into *actual* greatness? If I know anything about Jesus, it's that he's focused on reality.

Jesus is talking about *true* greatness—genuine effectiveness with reach. A group may vote to call someone a "prince" or "leader," but no one can be voted into greatness. Greatness is inherent. It's a quality of the person's character and action expressed in a particular circumstance. So, what makes for true greatness? Where are the deepest effectiveness and truest power to be found?

Power Under

While power *over* can only reach so far, Jesus sees that power *under* and alongside others—through service—is potentially unlimited in its effectiveness. When I give myself to make another person better—to elevate and ennoble him or her—there is no external limit to the good that I can produce. Again, this sounds counter-intuitive, but its truth will be readily grasped upon reflection. Consider the forms of service and how they actually make things happen in this world.

Another Thought Experiment

Let's run this through another thought experiment. For instance, imagine that you were going through a low point in life. Someone comes to you there and, in Jesus' spirit, enables you to find new direction and hope. She gives of her means. She devotes her time and energy and her best thought to instruct you. All of this changes the direction of your life. You have a way forward now—a new life in Jesus. She has exercised power under you. She made something happen in this world. There's a real effect. That's power.

Now, imaginatively, try adding back all the improvements and enhancements that limited my power over others. See if they would diminish her effect in your life. Imagine that after her service, you gain significant financial resources. Your business takes off or you inherit from a long lost relative. Has her work been diminished? No. Imagine you study diligently to gain knowledge and earn formal degrees. A new social status follows. Has her service lost effectiveness because of your improvements of knowledge and status? No. Could moral growth and spiritual insights undo her power? If anything, all these improvements to your life would only extend the reach of the effect she initiated. They would enhance, not negate, her efficacy.

Power under can continue to grow in effectiveness as others improve. It is fitted for collaboration. While power over is a zero-sum competition, power under is capable of synergizing—combining with and enhancing others' influence for the good. It alone is unlimited in the range of its effects.

The Creator's Power

Indeed, this is the sort of power the Creator wields, and that Jesus consistently chose. Think for a moment about the effectiveness of Jesus' power under others. For only a few decades, over two thousand years ago, he walked the hills of Israel. That's seven thousand miles and an ocean away from my hometown. He held no official position in the social orders of his day. He had no wealth of his own, refused military force, and made no use of sex appeal. Yet, by unswervingly choosing to pour himself into service of others, Jesus' life effected more change on planet earth than any other single person. That is just historical fact. No exaggeration.[136]

From social institutions like the orphanage and hospital, which came into existence because of his teachings and example, to legal reforms, ethical insights, philosophical doctrines, people movements, and even your birth date on your driver's license—more things have been affected by Jesus than anyone else. His life simply is the most powerful in human history and its effects are still growing around the world. Power under is potentially unlimited.

The Internal Limit to Power Under

If "power under" is the most God-like form of effectiveness, what will limit my exercise of it? Jesus begins and ends with the answer. When the question of obtaining true power is raised, he asks, "Can you drink the cup? Endure the baptism?" Now we know why. So, after contrasting the gentiles' way of "power over" with his way of "power under," Jesus tells us that "even the Son of Man did not come to be served but to serve and to give his life to liberate others" (Mark 10:45).

My effectiveness will ultimately be determined by the degree to which I expend my life *for* others. My willingness to suffer, not due to selfish ambition but *in service of others*, will ultimately be the limiting factor in my effect upon this world.

So, Jesus assured the Zebedee boys that they would have their opportunity to absorb others' wrongdoing. There would be cups and baptisms for them too. But the right and left hand of Christ's glory—to be situated on either side of him at his most effective moment—that had already been reserved for others.

Of course, James and John imagined that moment to be in a palace or, perhaps, on a field triumphantly surveying the aftermath of a cataclysmic battle. They could not fathom what Jesus' most powerful act would look like. But we are not left to guess.

The Right and Left Hand of Glory

Only once more does Mark's Gospel speak of persons placed at Jesus' right and left hand. In fact, it occurs at the point when Jesus exercises his greatest power under others and irrevocably changes this world for good:

> They brought him to the place called Golgotha, which is translated Place of a Skull. And they gave him wine mixed with myrrh, but he wouldn't take it. And they crucified him and divided his garments, casting lots over them to decide what each should take. Now, it was the third hour when they crucified him. And the inscription of his charge was inscribed: "The King of the Jews."
> And they crucified two brigands with him—one on his right and one on his left. (Mark 15:22–27)

Factually, this is the moment when Jesus exerted the greatest influence over the course of human history.

By giving himself completely to God and for others, undeterred by the specter of the cross, Jesus carries this power to its limit. The Father completes—superadds—to Jesus' self-giving action in the resurrection. The cross and resurrection, together, simply are the most pivotal moment in human history—the most powerful act ever performed. This is kingdom power at its purest.

Translating the Gospel of the Kingdom

In concluding this section, I want to briefly connect some dots between Jesus' gospel of the kingdom and some equivalences in the language of his earliest followers—particularly Paul and John. Perhaps translation is a better word for the needed connections. Because after Jesus' teachings in the Gospels, the language of the kingdom largely—though never completely—fades away. The *reality* of the kingdom does not disappear, nor does the experience of entering into the kingdom cease. But the most frequent *language* used to describe these realities and experiences does change.

Walking by the Spirit

The first translation needed concerns the Holy Spirit, or the Spirit of God. I'd imagine that some of you have started wondering: Where does the Holy Spirit fit into all this talk of human agency and transformation and God's project? Actually, we've been talking about the Spirit's work all along.

Already in Jesus' teaching, the kingdom of God is explicitly identified as mediated by or instantiated through the movement of the Spirit. "But if, by the Spirit of God, I cast out demons, then the kingdom of God has reached you" (Matt 12:28; cf. "by the finger of God" in Luke 11:20). While Jesus, and the Spirit, delight in emphasizing the Father as the initiator of this work, the kingdom is forever suffused with the Spirit's activity.

When Paul describes submissive synergy with God—what Jesus refers to as "entering the kingdom"—he usually talks about walking by the Spirit, sowing to the Spirit, or being led by the Spirit. (See, for instance, Romans 8 and Galatians 5.) In the church's memory, an important shift takes place following Jesus' resurrection and ascension. On the day of Pentecost, the Spirit of God was poured out—became palpably present in and among Jesus' followers (Acts 2). The invisible force within the kingdom, by which Jesus acted, became generally available to the internal experience and common life of Jesus' community. The book of Acts tells this story. The indwelling Spirit is an extension and enhancement of the kingdom—not its replacement or competitor.

Dying and Rising with Christ

The second translation concerns the character of kingdom effectiveness and the term gospel. While it is comparatively rare for Paul to speak directly of the kingdom, he routinely describes the gospel as centering on Christ's death and resurrection—a dying and rising in which we are invited to share.[137]

Paul has not abandoned Jesus' gospel of the kingdom as God's action in the world with which we are invited to collaborate. Rather, Paul focuses on the epitomizing moment of human-divine collaboration—the cross and resurrection. The kingdom comes to its clearest expression in Jesus' self-giving and his subsequent resurrection. So, Paul foregrounds this event as the gospel—what it looks like when God acts.

In so doing, Paul is highlighting the nature of effective action with God. Jesus' faithful obedience and resurrection is the paradigmatic moment of the kingdom. He expends the last of his own agency in going to the cross. Then he is raised by power from above. Thus, he completes what no human life could do alone. This is kingdom agency. The experiential texture of kingdom effectiveness is always dying and rising with Christ.

In other words, to co-work with God involves us pouring ourselves into a God-given opportunity, the outcome of which we are personally insufficient to ensure. We expend our resources, talents, energy, time, and effort. But we cannot, on our own, guarantee their return. The effect needed is beyond us. That's dying with Christ.

But God, having opened the door for us to collaborate in this piece of his project, adds to the overall situation what we cannot. At the right moment, God adds to the enterprise resources, relevant actions of others, uncanny timing, renewed energies, and meaningful connections. Our inadequate actions nonetheless prove truly effective within God's project. We rely upon these enhancements and reversals but can never control them. The success, therefore, of each venture of faith is an experience of rising with Christ. Paul describes it in different words. But the reality and its experience are the same as Jesus taught.

Eternal Life

Finally, in John's Gospel, the kingdom is translated into the language of life or eternal life. Near the end of the book, eternal life is defined as a kind of knowledge. "This is eternal life—that they may know you, the only true God, and Jesus Christ whom you have sent" (John 17:3). Knowledge, in biblical parlance, is a type of interactive relation. For instance, Adam *knew* Eve, and she bore him a son (Gen 4:1, 25). Personal interaction with God and Jesus Christ constitutes eternal life.

But another equivalency had already been established at the beginning of John's Gospel. In John 3, when speaking with Nicodemus, Jesus speaks of the necessary conditions for one to "see" and to "enter the kingdom of God" (John 3:3, 5). Once this phrase, remembered as Jesus' most characteristic talking point, is introduced it never appears again in John's Gospel. But in his words to Nicodemus, Jesus explains that entering "the kingdom of God"—in other words, co-working with God—only becomes possible through being generated from above by the Spirit. By the end of his explanation, Jesus has replaced "kingdom of God" with the language of "eternal life" (John 3:15–16). Spirit-enabled personal interaction with the one true God and Jesus Christ whom he has sent—that's eternal life and that's the experience of entering into the kingdom. The language has changed but the reality hasn't.

INTERLUDE

Daily Practice and the Authentic Philosopher

The Philosopher and the Charlatan

IN THE ANCIENT WORLD two figures, or types of people, were often distinguished from each other—the philosopher and the charlatan. Ancient literature, especially in satirists like Lucian, delighted in exposing pretenders to philosophy as mere charlatans.

The two figures had a fair bit in common. Both taught in public settings, and often received payment for their services. Both claimed to really understand how things were put together and the best way for humans to live. Both acted in ways that were unconventional and raised questions of propriety, while claiming the role of moral educator for their society.

Their differences were a matter of authenticity. The philosopher was the real thing. The charlatan was merely aping the philosopher in certain settings to get some associated benefits (money, public attention, special concessions, deference, etc.).

So, what are the key marks of this authenticity difference? How can you tell when you are confronted with a genuine lover of wisdom, whose words are worth considering, or if you are being worked by a trickster—someone using big, deep-sounding words and public postures just to run a scheme? You look at his or her life.

Training or Spiritual Exercise

The key difference is the practice of *askesis*—which is translated most literally as "training" and most frequently as "spiritual exercise."[138] Genuine philosophy—the love-stirred pursuit of wisdom—is nothing but the everyday training for wisdom. In other words, philosophy in essence simply is spiritual exercise. The Greco-Roman philosophers agreed on this much. Studying and talking about philosophical ideas, regardless of one's school of philosophy, were not sufficient to make one a philosopher. The philosopher practiced what he spoke; and practiced it everywhere always. The charlatan just spoke.

Jesus' account of lasting personal change, which we considered in his parable of the sower and soils, includes a distinct role for training or the production of "roots." His early followers continued to insist on the centrality of training. In fact, training was essential to their self-understanding as adherents of "the Way." So, before we examine Jesus' initiatory account of spiritual exercise, let's take a quick detour to consider his earliest followers self-understanding.

What Is "the Way"? Unpacking Paul's Description

Jesus' followers simply referred to themselves as adherents of "the Way." To highlight this life, we will travel into two unfamiliar worlds—the world of Hellenistic and Roman philosophy and the world of Hebrew experience lived out before the LORD's face. The second, Hebraic aspect must await our chapters on Jesus, but the Greco-Roman aspect we'll consider now. These two worlds come to us already intertwined in the most expansive early summary of "the Way."

The Acts of the Apostles is speckled with references to the early Jesus movement as the Way. But the most expansive and helpful account comes in Acts 24:14–16.

> But this I do confess to you. In keeping with the Way, which they call a sect, I worship the Ancestral God believing everything written in the Law and the Prophets and having a hope in God (a hope that these men also expect) that a resurrection of the righteous and of the unrighteous is coming. Because of this conviction, I myself train to maintain a blameless conscience before God and before men at all times.

In context, Paul's opening words would bring people to the edge of their seats. Paul is standing before Felix, the Roman governor. He has been forced to defend himself against wrongful allegations brought by Judea's temple elites. A series of denials fill his opening statement. Suddenly Paul offers a confession. He's about to cop to something.

As his hearers lean forward, Paul confesses and describes the life pattern shared by Jesus' earliest followers. But he does so by using, in part, the language of Greco-Roman philosophy. We could easily miss it. But Paul's vocabulary and emphases would be unmistakable in his own world.

The Way as a Philosophy

Paul's adversaries have already started the process of translation. They referred to him as a ringleader of the "sect of the Nazarenes" (Acts 24:5). Paul repeats the term "sect" (*hairesis*) and simply connects it to Jesus' followers' own self-description as "the Way" (Acts 24:14).

Here's why that's important. The term translated "sect" is the standard way of referring to any specific philosophic school in distinction from the other philosophic schools. The Stoics could be referred to as a *hairesis* and so could the Epicureans, academics, and others.[139] We get our word "heresy" from the term, but the basic meaning is simply "choice." Philosophic schools were designated by this term because they demanded a choice of a way of life.

Philosophic Conversion

Philosophy was a way of life to which one converted. That's right. Conversion is the language of philosophy, not religion, in the ancient world. In other words, every philosophy required fundamentally re-describing one's life in terms of before and after—the life lived prior to embarking on the philosophic journey and everything else that followed from that choice. The philosopher was the one who had converted—taken on a new form of life marked by continual spiritual exercise.

Conversion was the paradigm because any philosophy worth the name offered a holistic life orientation. As a lived pursuit of wisdom, the philosophic school claimed to offer an integrated, consistent way of life shaped according to "nature" as distinguished from mere "custom" or "convention." In other words, the philosopher sought to bring every detail of his or her life into conformity with the way things really are ("nature"). He would no longer simply keep step with what had come to be affirmed and expected within his human society ("convention"). As such, philosophy was an all-or-nothing life option. One converted and became, say, a Stoic or Epicurean, or one did not. Dabbling with the ideas of a school and being able to speak lucidly about them did not make one a philosopher. That, without a consistent life of askesis, just made one a charlatan.

The *Askesis* of the Way

Paul quite intentionally evoked this category of philosophy in the minds of his Roman listeners. Grammatically, Paul links his adherence to "the Way" with two principal actions in this passage—worship (with a set of very Hebraic sub-activities which we will consider in the following chapters) and "spiritual exercise" or "training" (*askesis*). This second principal focus names the acknowledged core of any philosophic regime in the ancient world.

As an adherent of the Way, Paul says, he engages in *askesis*—spiritual exercise or character training—to a specific end. His training consists of maintaining a blameless conscience in the presence of God and men. Conscience seems to be Paul's standard way of translating the Hebrew Bible notion of the heart for gentile audiences. He routinely glosses the more Hebraic language of a pure heart with the more Greek-tinged "good conscience" or "clean conscience."

"Conscience," both in Greek and in the Latin from which our word is derived, literally means something tucked away within or accompanying any act of knowing. It is what you *also know*, whether you want to or not. But here simply note that Paul describes the Way's fundamental spiritual exercise—the training designed to reshape one's character. It consists in consciously living, even in secret, as if one's every action were performed before the face of God and other persons. The distinctive *askesis* of "the Way" means that whatever else I'm doing, God is there. First, I'm living attentively in the presence of God and, second, I'm engaging in the activity of the moment. Though certainly distinguishable from any of the specific character exercises described by Stoic and Epicurean philosophers, this activity holds all the distinctive marks of a philosopher's exercise.[140] It's an *askesis* centered on one's relation to Israel's God.

But Paul did not invent this most central form of spiritual exercise. *Jesus* introduces it—prescribes and explains it to his students. Such a practice is very much an extension of the kingdom of God and of Jesus' teaching about the proper use of disciplines within it, as we'll see in this section. So, in the next chapter, let's consider Jesus' understanding of spiritual exercise.

SECTION III

Kingdom Practices

CHAPTER EIGHT

How the Disciplines Work, Pt. 1

From the Top Down (Matthew 6:1–5)

Rooting Disciplines in the Way

ACCORDING TO JESUS, DISCIPLINES or training regimes strengthen key elements of the self. They penetrate through the soil of conscious attention, connect with something deeper, and through this strange conjunction enable the person to accumulate new strength. They are roots. Their strength will be needed in moments of difficulty and trial. Without such practice, when the person encounters difficulties, he is prone to feel that something is terribly wrong with the world and simply give up.

What are these exercises and how do they produce such personal growth? In this chapter, we will consider Jesus' big-picture account of spiritual exercise and the disciplines.[141]

In Jesus' Way, spiritual exercise is a life-pursuit. Spiritual exercise aims not simply at doing what one ought to do, but at *becoming the kind of person who could routinely and reliably do it*. The distinction is important. It is one thing to know what one *ought* to do and to muster one's resolve to do it. It is a very different matter to become a person for whom the good and right deed regularly happens even without the need to actively choose it. Spiritual exercise is aimed at producing the second state—the personally transformed and habitual type of goodness. It produces a kind of goodness that you've already chosen and now can enact without making another choice.

Spiritual exercise—or "rooting"—as a life-pursuit uses a series of dis-creet disciplines or practices. A discipline is simply a set of regular actions that is within my power, and that over time enables me to do what I cannot presently do by effort alone.[142] Over time, we become what we do. Jesus knows that daily rhythms shape us—physically and mentally. Nervous systems are a one-per-customer item. Long hours of work at a computer seated in a chair, if never counterbalanced by exercise, produces chair-shaped bodies that find it difficult to stand erect and move freely. Likewise, one's habits of attention channel varying forms of content (or information) into the depths of the self. Over time the deep flow—soul—in its momen-tum and direction gives back what was put in.

So, how can we remake the daily rhythms that shape us? The answer is central to Jesus' account of lasting personal change.[143]

How Do Disciplines (*Askesis*) Work?

Disciplines leverage what I will call the "principle of progression" within the human being. Progress is inevitable for persons in this sense.[144] Over an extended period, whatever a person does repetitively becomes easier and easier to repeat again. This is as true of eating potato chips and watch-ing Netflix through the afternoon, as it is of solving mathematical formu-las, or fighting with your spouse, or praying for your enemy. If you do it regularly, it becomes easier.

Much of human life is a process of gradually transferring actions and skills from one's mind to one's body—from active thought to the habits of one's nervous system. We can restate this in terms native to Jesus' account of the human person. Learning starts in the heart—or focal awareness—and gradually gets deposited in the soul.

Consider any case of skill acquisition. For the sake of clarity, start with something simple, say dribbling a basketball. The youngster who first attempts it will require rapt attention to keep time, judge how hard to thrust the ball into the ground and where to position his hand to receive it without catching it, etc. . . . In fact, at the beginning the considerations are usually too complex to dribble and walk at the same time. All his attention (or heart) is required for the new motions. But gradually the movements smooth out and speed up as the child's nervous system adapts—the soul acquires the skill initiated in the heart. At a certain point, much of this new action has become automatic. Now the child can dribble without looking and can move simultaneously. He can devote more of his attention to scan-ning the court for teammates and openings, because the skill is in his soul and body, not just his heart or mind.

The same type of progression happens with any skill acquisition—whether that be a scholarly, athletic, social, or some other skill. Those actions we repeat tend to become easier, each time, to repeat again. Whether we are learning to perform brain surgery, or to decorate a wedding cake, to look a person in the eye when conversing, or to meditatively read the scriptures—whatever we do more than once becomes increasingly a tendency within our unconscious soul and thus easier to repeat.

Footprints in the snow gradually accumulate and become paths. Streams of water produce ravines. This is just the nature of the type of beings we are. We cannot choose to live without habits and a patterned inner flow of tendencies. They are necessary for our type of life. Human existence is impossible without them. What we can choose, however, is *which* tendencies to practice henceforward—which actions to make automatic.

The use of choice for repetitive practice, so as to make Jesus' Way automatic within us, constitutes the remedial work of discipleship. Disciplines do crucial work, which cannot be done by other forms of training.

Disciplines: The Soul-Shaping Level of Training

The Gospels depict Jesus as engaged in personal training by means of specific exercises, which he also instructs his students to employ. Some are well-known and, in our day, have been used by Jesus' followers for centuries. Others are less often recognized as disciplines at all.

Among those readily known as disciplines, consider a few. Jesus spends significant time in solitude and silence—frequenting lonely places apart from social circles—and teaches his students to do the same (see for instance Mark 6:31, 45–46). Jesus routinely performs acts of merciful healing without calling attention to himself—even requesting secrecy from those who receive his benefits (e.g., Matt 8:4; 9:30; Mark 1:44; 5:43; Luke 5:14; 8:56). Likewise, Jesus teaches his students to perform their acts of mercy in secret (Matt 6:1ff.). Prayer, by Jesus' practice and teaching, involves a discipline, which I will call "positioning" before the Father. This is an open awareness of God's nearness and is a preparation both for prayer and for a life of intentional (and later habitual) alignment with God's will. Jesus engages in a rhythm of fasting and feasting—again, instructing his student on the appropriate moments for each.

Among those practices in the Gospels that are less commonly understood as disciplines, consider this one. Jesus, in training his students for the subsequent mission, calls them to a temporary discipline of intentional vulnerability. In Luke 10, for instance, Jesus sends a group of his students (the Seventy or Seventy-Two) ahead of him to the villages of Israel. They will announce God's present action and show signs of it. But here's the disciplinary element: on this trip they will travel without food, extra clothing, or money. Moreover, they are to be silent while on the road—they cannot use that time to ingratiate fellow travelers and to make arrangements beforehand for lodging and meals. They must enter a village without prior announcement and without any backup plan for their provision. When his students announce God's action there to others, the students will also *see* God's action for them through the hospitality they will receive. This discipline, judiciously timed, provides his students a powerful experiential basis for life within the kingdom.

This exercise of intentional vulnerability is just that—a training exercise or discipline. It was not Jesus' prescription for all mission all the time. In fact, Jesus explicitly tells his students during his last meal with them to take extra supplies and even a sword (Luke 22:35–36). But the memory of the intentionally vulnerable experience will last. As they go out, even if they have brought extra supplies, they will know that God's attentive action on their behalf already awaits them wherever they go.

These are some examples of rooting exercises. As regular though time-bounded practices, they transfer more and more of the soil, which is my heart-attention, to that new kind of life being formed from the seed of the word of God. In so doing, they pass through my attention into something underneath. They reshape the soul.

Jesus' General Theory of Training

Now that we have a general idea of what discipline or training is and have some identifiable cases of training before us, let's ask another question. It will occupy us for the remainder of this section.

How does Jesus conceptualize the effect of these disciplines? Does he supply a big-picture—a theory—of how they work to produce beneficial effects?

Jesus, in two passages (Matt 6:1–6, 16–18 and 25:1–13), does provide such a description of the disciplines' benefits. Both attend to the *transition* from intentional choices to unconscious or habitual actions. The first emphasizes the role of intention while forming the unconscious habit, the second emphasizes the needfulness of the resulting unconscious responses for a full life of co-working with God.

Attention Determines Benefit

In Matthew 6:1–6, 16–18, Jesus invites his students to consider the manner in which they exercise their deeds of right living (*diakaiosyne*). More specifically, he warns them to consider before whom or in whose presence they are situated when they perform standard, publicly recognized deeds of right living. The publicly recognized deeds are, in Jesus' world, primarily mercy-giving, prayer, and fasting. Jesus approaches each of them as disciplines.

Since Jesus' theoretical description remains the same for each discipline, we will quote and consider only the first of them—mercy-giving. Here are Jesus' words:

> Be attentive to not practice your right-living in the presence of human beings for the purpose of being observed by them. Otherwise, you do not have a wage from your Father in the heavens. Therefore, when you practice mercy-giving, do not blow trumpets before you, like the actors do in the synagogues and streets so that they may be esteemed by people. Truly I tell you, they have received their wage. But when you practice mercy-giving do not let your left hand know what your right hand is doing, in such a manner let your mercy-giving be in secret. And your Father who sees in secret will pay you. (Matt 6:1–4)

Jesus has both prescribed a specific exercise and described how it works, or otherwise would be prevented from working, properly within the human person.

We can use this discipline as a lens to peer into all of them. Jesus' patterned repetition, in describing practices of prayer and fasting as well, implies that he is focusing on the general features of disciplinary practices *as disciplinary practices*.[145] He is offering a general theory of the disciplines.

What Is the "Wage"?

To understand Jesus' account of how the disciplines work, we need to think about the significance of a key metaphor he uses—the metaphor of payment or wages and from whom one receives them.

Jesus clearly states that the "wage" received from disciplines of right-living can either be received from the Father or received from other people. But one cannot receive a wage from both. The source and the type of wage will depend on before whom one is positioned. This positioning—or "being in the presence of"—Jesus describes as a matter of the person's *intention*.[146]

One is positioned, in one's awareness or heart, *in the presence of* whoever one intends to be seen by. If in performing the deed we intend to be seen by other people, we are in *their* presence. In this case, their recognition is itself the wage that we will earn from men for that deed (Matt 6:2). But there is a different intention and thus a different wage when we are positioned before the Father.

Intrinsic and Extrinsic Benefits

What is the "wage" we receive from the Father? Obviously, payment is some sort of benefit received. But is it an intrinsic or an extrinsic sort of benefit? In other words, is the benefit we receive from secret disciplinary practices something built into the intentional practice itself, or is it an unrelated benefit to arrive later?

Often this passage has been read as promising some extrinsic reward. If I do this act now, I might think, someday God will give me some otherwise unrelated gifts or benefits. Those benefits might even be exactly what I'm renouncing today. So, for instance, I might do good in secret today so that later, in heaven, I can have a big reputation ("have more stars in my crown," people used to say). Or, I might choose to remain sexually chaste in hopes that God will reward me with a lucrative job and successful investments. This kind of bargaining with God—my good deeds in exchange for God's special favors—is familiar to most people. Humans do it rather naturally. But I think Jesus has a different way in mind.

The Father Bestows Intrinsic Benefits

Try to think of the matter this way. Jesus is describing the Father's "wage" as an *intrinsic* benefit. It emerges from the practice. Following the theme of the "wage" throughout Jesus' teaching in Matthew, what emerges is primarily a type of benefit that is *built into the act itself*.[147]

Here is the "wage" of disciplines pursued in the presence of the Father alone: acts of service and devotion engaged in *only* for the sake of interacting with God and helping my neighbor have a built-in capacity to help me grow in partnership with God. By their nature—both intentional and embodied in action—they enable me to learn more about the kingdom of God. These deeds, performed with a tunnel-visioned focus on God, help me to see things from the Father's perspective and to recognize when he's at work. This enables me to engage more consistently in a life of submissive synergy or co-working with God.

The intention directly determines the benefit. This recurs throughout Jesus' teaching. For instance, Jesus says that whoever receives a prophet *in the name of a prophet*—in other words, *because* that person is a prophet—will receive a prophet's wage. Likewise, receiving a righteous person because he's righteous, brings the wage of the righteous. And, even something so small as giving a cup of cold water to a disciple, *only* because he is a disciple, Jesus promises will not be without its wage or benefit. There is an internal, unlosable benefit acquired through acts done only for the sake of interacting with God and helping others.

It's all about *intentionality*. The progress one experiences in any discipline will be directly related to one's "in order to" in the action.

Heart-Attention Chooses the Wage

So, Jesus explains a basic truth of the human heart—a psychological truism we might say. I cannot give money (or do any other discipline) for the sake of making a social impression *and* simultaneously be focused on engaging God alone. The human heart cannot do both at once. Either one or the other motive will be foregrounded. "Therefore, when you practice mercy-giving, do not blow trumpets before you, like the actors do in the synagogues and streets so that they may be esteemed by people. Truly I tell you, they have received their wage" (Matt 6:2).

Our human attention is too limited to split it in both directions and maintain efficacy. I cannot pursue both an intrinsic and an extrinsic reward simultaneously. I must choose between them. If I position myself to make an impression on people, that will be the outcome of my disciplinary deed—no more. If, however, I want to be changed into the Father's own character, that's also possible by focusing my whole attention *in these deeds* on God alone.

Of course, my problem is that it takes me so much effort to do good things, I really think the world ought to know it is happening. "Call the news! I'm doing the dishes and I took out the trash without even being asked!" Jesus warns us that indulging such a thirst for reputation and human recognition will prevent the disciplines from bringing their full, intrinsic benefits. They only work when one gives oneself to God alone in and through them.

But the initially difficult action does become less effortful. Disciplines become easier. Anything we do more than once becomes progressively simpler to repeat. Jesus incorporates this created feature of human life into his theory of how disciplines, rightly focused, produce intrinsic benefits.

The Intrinsic Progress within a Discipline

Jesus describes a progression within the practice of any discipline. While the heart's focused intention determines the type of benefit reaped from a discipline, there are still degrees of benefit. Even in a God-focused series of actions some of those actions will have greater results than others. The greatest growth within this practice comes as I begin to lose my self-awareness in the action and become aware only of interacting with God and benefiting my neighbor.

Here is Jesus' description of that moment: "But when you practice mercy-giving do not let your left hand know what your right hand is doing, in such a manner let your mercy-giving be in secret. And your Father who sees in secret will pay you" (Matt 6:3–4).

Jesus' image of the right and left hands independently working, without awareness of the other, is a concise description of habituation. Or, in terms of Jesus' elements of the human self, that process by which an action or skill is transferred from the heart (focused, conscious choice) to the soul (the less conscious, flowing life-force which can proceed without our choice).

For instance, consider the stages in learning to play a musical instrument. Initially, it requires a great deal of conscious focus—every finger placement and each beat are fully aware. However, at that stage nobody would want to hear you play. Because it would not flow. Full consciousness of the mechanics of playing an instrument, as is the case prior to mastery, produces poor music.

Eventually, the pianist, for example, internalizes the mechanics of body placement, movement, timing, and so forth to such a degree that he is no longer aware of his fingers. All his focus is on the music itself. Musical flow emerges and great performances become possible, but only when the basics are so fully internalized and automatic that the right hand no longer knows what the left hand is doing. In fact, if the mature pianist somehow becomes self-conscious and reverts to noticing his hands—the performance will tank.

Music only flows once we, through practice-formed habituation, forget ourselves. The same is true of growing through disciplines in the kingdom of God. The greater benefit comes to me as I fade away.

The fruitful self-forgetfulness that emerges through well-focused practice becomes obvious later in Jesus' teachings. In Matthew 25:31–46, Jesus telescopes forward to consider the end result of different life-paths among the nations. There will be a separation, like a shepherd makes between sheep and goats, between the blessed and the cursed. It will be based on individual deeds. Their responses to their placement are instructive. The blessed, when invited deeper into a life of co-working, are told it is because "I was hungry and you gave me something to eat; I was thirsty and you gave me drink; I was a stranger, and you invited me in; naked and you clothed me; I was sick, and you visited me; I was in prison, and you came to me" (Matt 25:36–36).

At this point we see the long-term life result of someone who has practiced the disciplines, focusing only on God, until they have become automatic, soul-flowing actions. The blessed cannot recall the occasion! "The right-living will answer, 'Lord, when . . . ?'" Just as Jesus described, these people have given themselves to interacting with God through their mercy-giving to such a degree that they cannot recall the occasions for which they are now rewarded. They've been hearing the music and they can no longer recall having pushed the keys.

This is the greatest benefit—the loss of self-consciousness as we enter ever deeper into the flow of God's work in this world. What do we learn when we develop habits of service in this manner? I believe the intrinsic benefit is nothing less than a deeper understanding of the Father's own way and character, which we accumulate in the depths of our soul. These experiences reshape our underlying idea of God—our default notion to which we revert when not actively thinking about God.

Let me ask you a question. Have you ever wondered what God gets out of serving? Why does he serve? There is no higher being than him from whom he could receive an extrinsic reward. He has no deficiency or lack to be supplied. Yet, he became a servant and consistently seeks the welfare of his creatures. So, what does God get out of his service?

If you enter consistently into service in secret, before the Father alone, *you will know.* Guaranteed. You will know because you will get the same thing out of it that the Father does.[148]

CHAPTER NINE

How the Disciplines Work, Pt. 2

From the Bottom Up (Matthew 25:1–13)

Disciplines: From the Bottom Up

JESUS' EXPLANATION OF THE general or shared features of disciplines in Matthew 6:1–6, 16–18 focused on the importance of *intention* or heart-focus in determining which benefit gets instilled in the less-conscious depths of the soul. It is a top-down account of how disciplines transform us for our work in the kingdom. But Jesus also gives a bottom-up account of the need for this habituated transformation. The key passage is Matthew 25:1–13.

Whereas the top-down account emphasizes our intentional focus during times when we are relatively unpressured and free to choose, the bottom-up account acknowledges that our life will include moments when there is no possibility of unpressured, optimal choice. We will face crisis moments and even seasons. We will have to walk through these in such a weary condition that we are temporarily incapable of choosing well—or perhaps of choosing at all. But those moments are also occasions in which God is doing something right where we are at. The kingdom is still present and, to live well, we still need to enter it. How is it possible to work with God in those moments?

Disciplines and Co-working in Crisis Moments

In these moments of great fatigue and/or surprise—moments when our choices are too weak or too slow to help—our capacity to co-work with God will depend on the habitual residue in our soul. In other words, the intrinsic "wage" that has accumulated during the times of intentional practice before the Father alone.

Jesus communicates this truth through the parable—comparison—of the ten virgins. Here are Jesus' words:

> At that time [i.e., in a crisis moment such as is described in Matthew 24] the kingdom of the heavens [i.e., co-working with God] will be compared to ten virgins, who took their own lamps and went out to meet the bridegroom. Five of them were foolish and five had practical wisdom. The foolish took their lamps but did not bring oil for themselves. However, the practically wise took oil in vessels along with their lamps. While the bridegroom was delaying, they all got drowsy and feel asleep. But in the middle of the night there was a shout. "Look, the bridegroom! Come out to meet him!" Then all those virgins got up and trimmed their lamps. Now the foolish said to those with practical wisdom, "Give us some of your oil, because our lamps are going out." But those with practical wisdom responded, "No, there won't be enough for you and for us. Go instead to the venders and purchase it for yourselves." While they were going to make the purchase, the bridegroom came. Those who were ready entered with him into the marriage feast and the door was closed. Later, the other virgins came and said, "Lord, Lord, open for us." But in response he said, "Truly I tell you; I don't know you." Keep using your waking time, therefore, because you do not know the day nor the hour. (Matt 25:1–13)

A Story about Co-working

This is Jesus' account of co-working with God in the context of a crisis moment. He described the crisis in the chapter leading up to this passage. Unfortunately, there is widespread confusion, in many Christian traditions, about the phrase "the kingdom of the heavens." So we need to be clear about what this phrase does *not* mean. It does not refer to a place of life after death, nor to the entry requirements for getting into heaven after death. Nor does it refer to any religious or sociological institution like the church or some theocratic political system. Instead, this phrase, just like the "kingdom of God," refers first to God in action *in this world.* Second-arily, as in this passage, the phrase may focus on humans interacting or co-working with God in his actions. All that to say, this is a description of co-working with God, in crisis moments, and what is required on the human side to co-work with God under such conditions.

Two Types of Co-workers

Two different types of people are invited to co-work with God—in ordi-nary as well as in crisis moments. Jesus chooses the image of a group of ten virgins—half of them possess a quality that the others lack. Notice that all of them are *virgins*—young and chaste. Jesus does not say that some are good and some bad. Nor is there a distinction here between righteous and unrighteous persons. All ten are depicted as generally good, ethical people. Here's the one difference Jesus highlights: some are foolish and some have practical wisdom—a keen know-how for everyday life.

So, we must ask ourselves: What is the difference between possessing practical wisdom and lacking it? What does someone with real insight into everyday life *do* that those others, who are otherwise moral people, fail to do? In the parable, Jesus encodes the answer in a metaphor.

Disciplines and Their Residue in Character

Jesus introduces a standard rabbinic metaphor here—oil as practice. It is often found in homilies alluding to or interpreting Solomon's comparison of righteousness and wisdom versus wickedness and folly in Ecclesiastes 9. The original text sounded a dark, pessimistic note—it sounded as if wis-dom and right-living didn't profit much. Everyone, good and bad, ends up dead, and that's that. But the rabbis consistently introduced a moral element when interpreting this passage. The Targum's gloss and the Mi-drashim—rabbinic sermons—on the chapter both inserted considerable expansions that encouraged hopeful observance of good deeds. In particu-lar, the rabbis identified the "works" that God has already approved in 9:7 with the "oil," which in 9:8 ought not be lacking from one's head. Oil refers to good deeds or, occasionally, the result of those deeds.[149]

The rabbis lifted this metaphor and routinely encouraged their students to "mix a little oil with your study of Torah." What they meant by "oil" was practicing good deeds.[150] To mix oil with the study of Torah was to engage in daily practices—acts of righteousness—that embody the

Torah.[151] Acts of righteousness (*dikaiosyne*) is the same feature of Jewish life that Jesus used in Matthew 6 to describe how disciplines benefit human beings. Oil is *embodied practice*.

In Jesus' story, a virgin's readiness to co-work with God depends on *the residue* of her embodied practice. This residue is described as *vessels* containing the *oil*. In other words, the everyday practice gets stored somewhere and that stored result is what co-working with God chiefly depends upon in these pressurized moments. When the bridegroom arrives in the middle of the night, *at that moment* one either has a vessel with oil or one does not. If oil is practice, stored practice is character—soul habit.

The Moment of Synergy

Since this parable is about co-working with God, we can lift the topic out of the metaphors of the parable for a moment. When we work with God, we join into a project that the Father has been arranging for a very long time before we entered the scene. In our experience, opportunities present themselves, often which we neither planned nor arranged. Nonetheless, we are in the right place and time to add something needed to complete what the Father has organized.

Perhaps, it would help to briefly recall and relate this to Jesus' description of co-working with God in John 4. He describes it as *completing* or *finishing* the Father's deed. "My food is to do the will of he who sent me and to complete his deed" (John 4:34). So, we find ourselves suddenly aware that several elements of a project are already developed. If we do our little bit, this part of the larger project will be finished. Jesus connects this feature of co-working with how God works through many people over time. He sequentially invites people to step into and to complete what others have prepared but not completed. "I sent you to harvest that for which you have not labored. Others have labored and you have entered into their labor" (John 4:38).

The experience of co-working is, in part, a discovery that you are only one link in a grand chain. God has been moving many others. Through them, over untold spans of time, the Father has set up the conditions for you to do something, with him, at this moment. You can "enter into" their labor. God will use you to complete what he started through others. And, of course, he will use others to complete what he is starting through you. Our individual deeds and opportunities are discreet but connected moments within God's grand project.

So, the moment of opportunity is something that has been prepared beforehand.[152] It cannot be paused or rewound. We either are ready at that

moment, for that particular task with God, or we are not. Time keeps moving. History does not wait for our best condition. Open doors typically don't
stay open for long.

What Synergy Requires in the Crisis Moment

In the parable of the virgins, Jesus emphasizes that in crisis moments our
readiness to join with God in action will depend on something specific.

Notice, first, what it does not depend on. It does not depend on *being*
awake—that is conscious and heart-attentive—at the moment of opportunity. *Both* the practically wise and the foolish fall asleep. Everyone is limited in
their capacity for sustained focus and choice. If our strategy for co-working
depends on active choice at every moment of opportunity, we will only manage to join in God's project on those occasions when we happen to be fresh
and alert and energized. Many other opportunities will pass us by.

Rather, in the crisis moments what will matter is the stored character
or unreflective responses that disciplines have instilled in us. After practicing disciplines, attentive to the Father alone, for a prolonged period, certain
things can now happen without active choice. Those disciplines have transferred virtues from the heart's choice to the soul's unconscious flow and
automatic responses. This residue of the practices is what comes out when
we are too tired or confused to make a genuine choice.

Character: What Cannot Be Shared

The interchange between the practically wise and the foolish virgins highlights the importance, and necessarily individual nature, of this residue of
practice in one's character. Have you ever wondered why the practically
wise would not just give the foolish virgins some oil? Doesn't that seem
selfish? After all, doesn't Jesus teach us to share and to give to those in
need? Are they unwilling to be team players?

Remember that Jesus is using metaphors that *refer* to something. Since
oil refers to personal practices and the vessels refer to the soul-residue of
character accumulated by those practices, these things are by nature *un*share-
able. Some things I must do for myself, and you must do for yourself.

Character virtues in the unconscious depths of an individual soul—
things like patience, gentleness, kindness, self-control, hopeful trust—are
non-transferable. If the moment of opportunity requires me to respond
with patience, for instance, I cannot borrow some of your patience to

complete the task. I'll have to make do with my own. If it's insufficient, I won't be up to the task.

Likewise, some things cannot be acquired instantaneously. If there is no gentleness or kindness or humility in me, at the moment of opportunity, I cannot obtain such virtues on the spot. I can only develop and transfer such qualities into my soul over time, through daily practice.

Moreover, I cannot develop your gentleness by my practice. I must practice for me. You will have to practice for yourself. Some things simply cannot be done for another, no matter how much we may wish to.

The Realistic Necessity of Disciplines for a Life

Here is Jesus' realism. In crisis moments, our ability to join with God in his work *at that moment* will depend upon what comes out of us automatically. In every life, there are times when we must sleep. The heart's focus is insufficient. Fatigue. Surprise. Sadness. Illness. Social chaos. These and other conditions overwhelm our capacity to deliberate and choose. Under such conditions, our capacity to respond to the kingdom opportunities will turn on what comes out of us automatically—not deliberately.

Whether or not I find that I have cooperated with God in that moment will depend completely on the content of my soul's flow and habitual responses. Either it will already have been transformed over time through the oil of practice, or it will have been left unchanged by my failure to practice. My soul's habits will either carry my drowsy self deeper into God's project, or they will leave me on the outside.

If I must go away and gather my thoughts, or wake up enough to choose, the moment will have passed. The door will be closed. That occasion for cooperating in God's work will be lost. Time does not flow backwards.

"While they were going to make the purchase, the bridegroom came. Those who were ready entered with him into the marriage feast and the door was closed. Later, the other virgins came and said, 'Lord, Lord, open for us.' But in response he said, 'Truly I tell you; I don't know you'" (Matt 25:10–12). There are no do-overs in life—not even in the kingdom.

Co-working, Not Heaven or Hell

Again, to be clear, Jesus is describing the loss of an opportunity to co-work with God. Since we were created for co-working—dominion—this is no trivial loss. Nonetheless, he is not speaking about going to heaven or hell after death. This particular chance for contributing to the Father's amazing project is past and unrecoverable. We did not interact with—were not "known" by—God and his project in this instance. That's just the truth. There will be other opportunities, but those also will require our readiness.

Practice: How to Wisely Use One's Waking Time

So, Jesus' counsel of wisdom is this: "Make good use of your waking moments, therefore, because you do not know the day nor the hour." Literally, Jesus says "stay awake" or "keep alert." How do we make sense of this advice?

Some, throughout the ages, have turned this saying into a counsel of regular sleep deprivation. "Systematically reduce your sleep hours. Strive to always stay awake." But the context gives Jesus' word a very different emphasis. Both the practically wise and the foolish must inevitably sleep. There simply *are* human limitations. We share bodies and souls with the beasts. Moreover, sleeping in the middle of the night did not prevent the practically wise from co-working with God—from greeting the bridegroom's arrival. The problem is not sleep in the middle of the night.

Jesus' point is that the real difference was made, before the critical moment of opportunity, by what each gave her attention to when she could stay awake. Some used their waking hours well and some poorly. Five used their waking time to practice and transfer those spiritual skills into their automatic souls. Five failed to practice during their waking time.

They foolishly assumed that they would be sufficiently awake whenever the time came. Then they would make a good choice. They trusted their good intentions. It would have been wiser not to. Instead, practical wisdom uses everyday waking intentions to gradually create a storehouse of character. Through attentive daily practice, a soul is shaped with reserves, which will still work when one cannot form an intention.

"Keep focused" or "keep using your waking time" means to intentionally practice now while we have the energy to do so and the pressure has not yet arrived. After all, we don't know when a crisis will appear, but we can be certain that it will. Within the sweep of his teaching, specifically in Matthew 6, Jesus has already told his students how to "stay awake" in their practice. We stay awake by focusing our attention, in everyday embodied practices, upon God alone.

Disciplines and the Ordinary Life of Discipleship

As we conclude our account of Jesus' theory of the disciplines, perhaps it would be helpful to counter a common misconception. Often people approach the use of spiritual disciplines as if they are a step up from the ordinary life of discipleship. The misunderstanding goes like this: ordinary Christians live the moral life, but a few special people go beyond this to something truly heroic and spiritually impressive—they do spiritual exercise or practice disciplines too.

If we have understood Jesus' teaching about the disciplines, we will immediately see that this is inverted. The act of co-working with God—"the bridegroom's arrival"—is the ordinary Christian life just occurring in a more difficult or fatigue-ridden moment. But it is still the same sort of activity. In these moments we will still be invited to bless those who curse us, to walk extra miles, to forgive, extend compassion, and give cups of cold water in Jesus' name. All this is the ordinary life of a student of Jesus.

In fact, Jesus periodically gave his students such opportunities to assess their readiness for ordinary life tasks under a variety of conditions. Like every other human skill, faith grows by being used.

Consider Jesus' way of teaching. At key moments in his interaction with his students, Jesus calls them to try to do something that they cannot possibly do on their own. Someone brings a demon-possessed person to them, Jesus tells his students "You cast it out." Thousands of people follow them into a wilderness and stay for days to hear Jesus teaching. But they're hungry. They're not going to make it home without fainting. Jesus tells his students "You feed them." The disciples are deeply shaken as storm-tossed waves fill the boat. Jesus is seen walking towards them on the water. "Come to me," he says. These moments require close, thoughtful consideration.

If the truth of human life were that we are disconnected from and unaided by God, such a call would simply be cruel—especially in a moment of stress and fear. But Jesus' invitations are reasonable within the reality of the kingdom of God. The fundamental realities to which we are schooled in Jesus' Way are the Father's character and constant activity right where we are at. You and I never have to be unaided nor alone. Actually, these seemingly unreasonable requests are doorways, which Jesus is opening, into the experience of God working right where his students are.

But Jesus also knows that action under the pressure of risk—action when you feel vulnerable and unstable in your position—is not the only kind of action needed. We need to develop the capacity for it, but that development is a process. Performing well under pressure will usually depend upon what one has been practicing when not under pressure. This type of unpressured daily practice is the source of "roots" or of "vessels with extra oil" in Jesus' Way.

The Disciplines beneath Ordinary Life

The various disciplines are remedial—mere practice for these other moments. As such, the disciplines are not higher but lower than the ordinary Christian life. They are like the thousands of free throws on an empty court, in relation to the free throw required in the championship game. They are preparatory drills, which over time enable us to live the ordinary life in the Way under more extreme and varied circumstances.

So, if you have no difficulty turning the other cheek or blessing those who curse you *under any circumstances even while greatly fatigued*, please don't waste time on these practices. You have no need for them. They are beneath you.

On the other hand, maybe you're more like me. Maybe you find that blessings come out more readily when you're prepared for the confrontation than when you are not expecting it. Or, that you are more cheerful in taking on an extra duty when you're well fed. For lesser people like us, disciplines are wise to engage in.

We need to form soul-habits while we can, so we don't miss opportunities to co-work with God in those crisis moments. We need remedial work. It is a simple matter of humility to acknowledge that fact and arrange our life around it.

Remember. The goal of good practice is not to repeat an action until you can get it right. The goal is to repeat it until you cannot get it wrong. That's why our practice is never complete.

"Make use of your waking time, therefore, because you do not know the day nor the hour of opportunity."

INTERLUDE

The Philosopher
and Society

JESUS ANCHORED HIS MORALITY and social life before the Father alone. He replaced the ancient target of heroism—aiming for social impressiveness—with humility and small acts of trust-filled service. Paradoxically, this produced a life that could only be considered as moral greatness. How do the Greek and Roman philosophers compare? Let's take a glance in their direction.

The ancient philosophers' conversation, when considering their social world, shared a set of common themes and questions. The various schools and the most influential philosophers differed on their answers to those questions, but everyone wrestled with them to one degree or another.

Here are some of the primary concerns that all the philosophers felt compelled to explore:

1. Is there such a thing as a natural community (or society) for human beings, or are we by nature isolated individuals for whom community is an elective? If there is a natural community, who is included in that natural community? And, what constitutes the inner boundaries and outer boundaries of that community? For instance, is the inner boundary drawn around commonality of body type, speech, reason, etc.? Is the outer boundary of one's natural community comprised of proximate physical lineage, one's circle of friends, the city-state, the cosmos, or the gods?

2. What is the relation between the individual and society? Which of the two is deeper, prior, or back of the other? Does humanity start as a bunch of "I's" or an always already connected "We"?

3. What is the relation of morality and society? This must be asked both in terms of the ideals (what constitutes a good act, person, or form of life?) and the means for moral improvement (how does one proceed from worse to better, from blameworthy to praiseworthy character?). Is society good for the person, or bad for the person, or some irreducible mixture of benefits and harms?

Again, Jesus' teachings address these primary questions in distinctive and internally coherent ways. Before we turn to Jesus, however, let's briefly consider the central positions of the Greek philosophers.

The Background Heroic Ethic

The pre-philosophic Greeks—Homer, Hesiod, and a host of tragedians— saw the hero as the epitome of human development. The hero was a nobleman—a person with property, standing, and say over others—who devoted himself to struggling for superiority among his peers. This struggle was always social, whether the specific competition took place in battle, or debate, or athletic event, or song. The hero strove to overcome in *this* moment despite the certainty of eventual loss and death. He faced his dread outcome with mustered courage—in the end broken but unbowed. The determined but measured effort to rise—within a hard to define sense of measure—was itself laudable.

Amidst his life of struggle, the hero held a singular conviction that whatever and whoever is better ought to be acknowledged or honored. This acknowledgment was the goal of a good life and lasted past the individual's demise. Only by attaining acknowledgment from his society did the hero transcend his fated death. Thus, the hero always aimed for the grandest deed possible, within the controlling context of others' estimations.

A paradox emerges from this mix of convictions. The hero seeks grandness, but only the kind of grandness that would be praised by his social peers. This conformity at the heart of the heroic, or honor-based, ethic ultimately stunts the moral development that it initially spurs. Opting out of the heroic goal of impressing "those who matter" led, in the seminal case of Socrates, to a revolution in social and ethical life. But the revolution was short lived.

Why This Matters

Before we dive in—why do we need to know this? The heroic ethic is important *for us* to recognize for two reasons.

First, our age is witnessing a type of neo-heroism in ethics—a resurgent sense of living better or worse based on one's self-presentation to one's peers. Of course, contemporary self-presentations are largely digitized. The manicured images appear on Facebook, Instagram, Snapchat, and other such platforms. But the root impulse is the same—"live to impress!" This has already led in our day to what has been described as "burnout society."[153] The problem is not just ancient. However, we sometimes see things more clearly with the distance afforded by observing them in an ancient setting.

Second, understanding the deep pervasiveness of the heroic ethic among the pagan philosophers helps us see Jesus' philosophy in sharper relief. We will understand Jesus better if we see him against this backdrop. So, please stick with me for this lightening tour of the heroic aspiration in ancient pagan philosophy.

Socrates

Socrates' weirdness—his disregard for social conventions that were geared toward acknowledgment—and his singular focus on questions of truth set him at odds with many in his community. Socrates competed for truth, not for esteem, and this choice made him difficult for Athens to accommodate.

He was just too awkward and disconcerting to have around. It's not simply that Socrates didn't fit, but that his words, when considered, put others out of place too. His questions made them wonder if it was Athens and her customs that were misshaped. Ultimately, Athenians voted for his death. Socrates' competition for truth rather than honor could not be allowed. Hemlock righted the game in the Athenians' favor—at least so they thought.

The death of Socrates was the birth of a new kind of individual and a new kind of community—namely, the philosopher and the philosophic school. But Socrates' aloofness from social convention and public appraisal proved difficult to incorporate except in attenuated forms.

Plato

Plato, moved by Socrates' teaching and exemplary death, founded a small, intentional community, named the Academy, aimed at training and deploying lovers of wisdom for a mission of civic renovation. The Academy existed to produce a new kind of ruler for new kinds of cities.

The chief concern of life, for Plato, is the care of the soul. Soul tending produces a new form of city-craft. City-craft (or "politics" if you can hear that word in a more elemental and not-yet-jaded manner) simply is the art of caring for the soul in its natural communal environment. The two, if considered with enough depth, turn into each other. Moral life is communal.

Aristotle

For Aristotle, too, the human being's natural place is the human society. We are social animals and can only exist in community. If a being lives in solitude, rather than the jostling of city life, "he is either a beast or a god—but he cannot be a man."[154] Like his teacher, Aristotle understands human good as the good of the city. Aristotle, with his penchant for precision and clarity, seeks to provide knowledge (not just true opinion) of that civic, human good.

Knowledge requires understanding first principles and seeing how, in relation to each other, they logically entail particular conclusions. Like the pure sciences, the practical science of ethics or city-craft ("politics") derives its first principles from experience. The requisite experience, however, is the possession of a good set of habits. The habits, which Aristotle uses as first principles, were acquired by being properly brought up within the city. These habits of life, generally praised by the cultured citizen of a great city, are called excellences or virtues.

Thus, for both Aristotle and Plato, the foundation of an ethical life is to be already and always situated in the presence of human evaluation. The constant awareness of what other good people would praise or blame creates a mental substructure for developing good habits and character. These social intuitions acquired by living within a good society with good customs are the axioms for ethical reasoning. We might say they are caught more than taught.

Epicureans

So far, with Plato and Aristotle, the individual arises from and is secondary to his or her society. In the generation following Aristotle, the emphasis flips. To varying degrees, the two major schools that are formed after Aristotle place an emphasis on the individual.

Epicurus is an atomist—an individualist—in both his account of the cosmos and his account of the human good. Societies are collections of human individuals—but the individuals are deeper than and prior to the society. Society emerged because of the particular needs of human individuals.

The primary moral good is to care for oneself. Due to human fragility this entails a limited attention to the good of others. But the natural size of a functional human community, thus contracted, was pretty small. An extended group of friends was the most natural community. The city-state was a bit too large, and the type of city-craft envisioned by Plato and Aristotle did not produce enough benefits for one's personal good. It's best not to get too involved at that level.

Stoics

The Stoics also relativized the importance of the city-state. They emphasized things smaller and larger—the individual and the cosmos—as the proper focus of human moral development. What joins the individual and cosmos is reason itself—the *logos* that pervades both individual minds (to a limited degree) and the cosmos (as the primary unit of perfect rational order).

The Stoics advocated a distinctive cosmopolitanism of reason. In the Stoic imagination, every speck of matter was pervaded by rationality and thus the cosmos was perfectly rational. (Which meant it was also perfectly *necessary* or fated to be exactly what it is.) Of course, only a cosmic mind could perceive the goodness of every minute occurrence. The individual human task, therefore, was to gradually broaden one's perspective, shedding the illusory attachment to oneself as if to a detachable whole, and intensify one's reason until he or she can see all things from this cosmic perspective.

As one approximates this perspective of cosmic reason, what emerges is a singular attachment to reason and a sense of connection or belonging with all things living in accord with reason. The result is a view of the whole cosmos as a single city composed of gods and men—in other words, of all rational beings.[155] A city is simply a group of people living in the same place and administered by law.[156] Shared reason, or *logos*, is the law administering the cosmos as a whole, which makes it a single city.

Jesus and the Moral Paradox

Jesus' Way offers a genuinely new trajectory in social life and ethics. Jesus' approach initiates a distinctly *non-heroic* path. As counter intuitive as it sounds, humanity desperately needed and still needs a non-heroic path to goodness. It's the only path that reliably reaches its destination.

Jesus resituated humanity and the moral goal. Rather than calibrating themselves to the praise and blame of peers, Jesus taught his students how to live before the Father alone. The social boundaries of approval and disapproval are changed. Likewise, humility rather than public impressiveness guides Jesus in his moral trajectory. Jesus teaches his students to give charitable aid in secret and to provide cups of cold water when needed, rather than to turn the tides of a battle and to make ornate public speeches. These two features of Jesus' Way are liberating and empowering for moral renovation. Paradoxically, they are also socially transformative without aiming directly at that end. Ultimately, Jesus' students are the ones whose moral transformation really changed the world.

Here's the paradox: Greek morality was aimed at public, moral heroism—*ostensive greatness*—but, because its implied audience rejected anything that was "excessive" or "too much," it ended in moral mediocrity. By contrast, Jesus' morality aims to live before the Father alone. He replaces heroism with humility. But the result was grand—deeply so. By purposefully living in a social world centered around the Father and embracing the Father's humility and gentleness, Jesus' early followers routinely behaved in ways that their contemporaries could only see as morally heroic. Greatness emerged by not thinking of greatness at all.

Social Identity in Jesus' Way

Human beings require both connection and distinction in relation to other persons. They need both to fit with others and to find their unique, personal significance. A healthy balance is both delicate and difficult to find. In fact, Jesus' life and teaching presuppose that the balance is not only difficult, but impossible, to find within a horizon of merely human interactions. Only a broader horizon will provide the hope of rightly ordered and measured human relations.

So, what are the boundaries—the horizon—of our natural community? How do my ways of connecting and distinguishing myself from others effect my long-term spiritual and moral abilities? Does it really matter if I publish or hide my aims in life? What role do these three social strategies—joining, opposing, and either hiding or manifesting—play in fashioning the person that I will ultimately become? In other words, how does Jesus lead us into new social relations full of morally transformative power?

These questions form the subject matter of the following section.

SECTION IV

Kingdom Social Relations

CHAPTER TEN

Kingdom Social Relations, Pt. 1

The Society of the Open Heavens

Morality and Social Visibility

BOTH ANCIENT GREEK AND ancient Hebrew thought connect morality with seeing and being seen by others. More explicitly, they connect hiding with *im*morality. Two examples will suffice.

Gyges' Ring

In Plato's *Republic*, Glaucon recounts the tale of Gyges and his magic ring. Glaucon is making an argument that morality is only the byproduct of social disapproval with its threat of punishment. If a person were capable of escaping subjection to punishment—either through vast power or through invisibility—then morality would vanish. He presents Gyges as an example. Gyges, a shepherd in the king's service, was in the fields when a great earthquake opened a chasm in the earth. Descending into the chasm, Gyges acquired a magic ring. Once Gyges discovers that the ring will turn him invisible if he twists it, he does all the things he secretly wished but never dared to do while visible. Once securely unobservable, Gyges seduces the queen, murders his master, and takes the throne for himself.[157]

The point? Morality is a social convention. Invisibility exempts a person from social evaluation. With that exemption goes all moral inhibitions. Invisibility cancels morality. Without natural community, anything goes.

Adam's Fig-Leaves

In the Hebrew Bible, Genesis 3 narrates the first act of human rebellion. As soon as Adam and Eve take the forbidden fruit, their eyes are opened. They experience exposure and fragility—nakedness. Moral trespass creates a new kind of vision. In response, they hide, and they sew fig leaves together to cover themselves. Later, in response to God's questions, they say that they were motived by shame and by fear. Humans feel the need to be unobserved in their wrongdoing. Hiding salves immorality. Humanity's shared hiding from God—following sin—redraws the boundaries of their natural community.

The social context matters deeply for our moral resolve. The two stories above illustrate that truth. But what constitutes the boundaries of the natural human community? Whose vision matters for our moral formation?

Jesus' choice to live in a new (yet actually primordial) kind of social sphere provides humanity with the ultimate antidote to fig leaves and magic rings. Aristotle had noticed that morality, in his context, began with the presence of *human* evaluation. Other humans constituted the natural community. Jesus, in contrast, has a distinctive account of the natural community and, indeed, of visibility within it. Judging by its effect, Jesus found a particularly powerful way to leverage this dynamic for personal renovation.

Jesus and the Outer Boundaries of Natural Community

A curious event precedes Jesus' public ministry. After Jesus is baptized by John, he withdraws to the wilderness where he spends forty days in solitude. Mark's account highlights this event in a way that provides a stark contrast with the mainstream of Greek philosophers and their account of natural human community.

Aristotle had said that if one lives in solitude, he must either be a beast or a god, for he cannot be a human being.[158] Why? Not only is human existence social, but, for Aristotle, that society is only ever *human* society. To be a human one must live among humans and internalize their evaluations. Gods and beasts are irrelevant to that process of becoming human in one's habits.

Natural Community among Beasts and Immortals

Mark's words intersect with Aristotle's in a striking manner. First, Mark situates Jesus and his natural community in relation to the heavens—a realm of immortal beings typically invisible to human eyes. Then he tells us that Jesus, while in solitude, lived among angels—those immortal beings that in pagan societies are usually called the gods—and beasts.

Evidently, Jesus' life is rooted outside that sphere which Aristotle would recognize as human. Here are Mark's words:

> And it happened in those days that Jesus came from Nazareth in Galilee and was baptized in the Jordan by John. Immediately, as he was ascending from the water, he saw the heavens torn open and the Spirit, as a dove, descending upon him. And a voice emerged from the heavens. "You are my Son, my beloved, in you I am well pleased." Immediately, the Spirit cast him out into the wilderness. He was in the wilderness forty days being tested by the Satan. He was with the beasts, and the angels ministered to him. (Mark 1:9–13)

To describe Jesus' life Mark must begin by rending and reordering the social world. To remake our lives something analogous must occur.

The Open Heavens: Outer Boundary of Natural Community

As Jesus gives himself to John's baptism—humbly endorsing John's work—the boundaries of his perceived world are ruptured. "The heavens are continuously torn open"—such is the force of the *present* participle in the original. In other words, this is not a freak, one-time experience. Rather, this is something foundational and enduring. The heavens are not sealed. The invisible realm is not closed to human perception.[159] There is no indication that the heavens close again. Jesus lives before the open heavens. Soon he will be teaching his students to do the same.

From the open heavens, Jesus sees and hears things. The Spirit descends upon him in the form of a dove, and Jesus hears the Father speak. The Father affirms an identity—a social relation—for Jesus that is rooted in the heavens. "You are my Son, my beloved, in you I am tickled pink." It is the Father, and the Father alone, who bestows the essential relation, which is Jesus' core social identity. Jesus is the Father's Son—his beloved. Moreover, this Son-relation is identified with Isaiah's servant of the LORD "in whom I am well-pleased."

You will recall that this is the passage in Isaiah from which we discussed the Father's distinctive character in chapter 5 above.

As soon as the Father affirms his relation to Jesus, the Spirit drives Jesus into isolation. Under those conditions, the satan[160] tests or "runs his experiment"[161] on Jesus.[162] Minimally, this means that Jesus' relational web is anchored in the heavens, not among human peers. He receives affirmation from the Father and then is tested, in isolation from any human support or distraction, by a countervailing spiritual voice. The "prosecuting attorney" or the satan attempts to break apart Jesus' confidence in his relation to the Father—his core social identity.

In this forging of his social identity, Jesus transcends what Aristotle could recognize as a human life. He simultaneously is among the wild beasts—thus beneath what Aristotle would consider human—and is served by immortals—thus above Aristotle's human company. Jesus' primary struggle for relational connection and distinction transpires before heavenly society. Later, Jesus will be tried by human beings—but his identity has already been anchored in the open heavens. The human trial is late and derivative in Jesus' experience.

Expanding the Natural Social Horizon

The minimal import of the baptism-temptation passage seems to include this claim. Experiences of relation to other persons includes the experience of relation to non-humans. While these have traditionally been denied, dismissed, or ignored, they play an irreducible role in who a person will become. Our natural social horizon is much broader than we've dared to imagine.[163]

To be clear, this vision of heavenly society, while intelligible within the world of Second Temple Judaism, was far from a general consensus even there. The existence of spirits and angels, and the possible modes of human interaction with them, was one point of the many faceted division between the two most pronounced sects in Jesus' world—the Sadducees and the Pharisees (see Acts 23:8–9).

The Sadducees acknowledged the existence of the Creator God— YHWH—but denied all other heavenly beings. Likewise, they discredited any claims, after Moses, of seeing or hearing God or angelic beings. Prophecy—those things humans heard from God within the heavenly court—was a sham. Nothing but the Torah and its explicit commands was to be credited. Pharisees, on the other hand, acknowledged the possibility of all the above. They received the prophetic texts and shaped many of their hopes accordingly.

The Essenes—or at least the "Yahad," or "Community," of Qumran near the Dead Sea—lived with a host of spirits, good and evil, around and within them. We have found a number of prayers for protection from the evil spirits. Here are some snippets. "Let not any satan rule over me to lead me astray from your way," Levi is depicted as praying.[164] Or, a prayer for deliverance found among psalms in Qumran, "Forgive my sin, YHWH, and cleanse me from my iniquity. Bestow on me a spirit of faith and knowledge. Let me not stumble in transgression. Let not a satan rule over me, nor an evil spirit; let neither pain nor an evil inclination take possession of my bones. . . ."[165] Protection from evil spirits was found primarily through inclusion in the pure community of the sons of light.[166]

We should also note that a broader world—inclusive of heavenly beings—was not unknown to the Greek world.[167] Socrates lived in obedience to his *daemon*—a messenger from the one God—whose voice warned him from taking false paths. The poets and earliest (Pre-Socratic) philosophers all claimed inspiration from heavenly beings.[168]

The primary difference is the degree to which these visions and auditions were to be foundational for social identity. The Greeks knew that other beings—gods, spirits, and *daemons*—were out there, but they were irrelevant to ordinary social identity. Human roles and personas were forged between human players in human society. The gods, like Fate, may intervene and alter courses. But *who* one was emerged from human society. The Hebrew prophets foreshadowed Jesus' approach. They received calls, which rooted their personal identities, within the heavenly court.[169]

For Jesus, there are always more persons in the room than you can see. Human beings and their evaluations are visible in their presence, but there are others invisibly present as well. Healthy social estimation requires also taking these beings into account. He taught his students to approach their social identity this way too.

Dominion: The Inner Boundary of Natural Community

Let's pause to consider Jesus' account of the inner boundary of natural community before we consider how Jesus teaches his students to inhabit this expanded natural community of the open heavens. We now see that Jesus credited a much broader range of participants as social peers than most humans do. But what is the inner point of connection between them all? Why can the heavens be our community? Or, better, should we be included in heaven's community?

The Greek philosophers identified the inner boundaries of human community with something distinctively human, at least as they saw it. For Aristotle, it was the acquired and praised customs of human cities. City customs embodied a type of rationality. For the Stoics, it was rationality itself. Thus, the Stoic intended to live within a cosmic city inhabited by gods and men. This sounds a bit like Jesus' open heavens, except that the gods were simply envisioned as rational principles built into each speck of cosmic matter. By most Stoic accounts, they were not persons.[170]

Jesus also identifies an inner boundary—a shared characteristic—of those included in the natural community of the open heavens. Jesus' focal characteristic is related to the co-dominion with which humans were created. We discussed this above in chapter 6, "Kingdom, or God in Action." Humans were designed with some say over a bit of this world—a range of effective will.

This effective will, and its relation to the Father's will (either in alignment with it or rebellion against it), constitutes the inner boundary of the created community. Consider Jesus' words on this score:

> Jesus' mother came, along with his brothers, and standing outside they sent to him and called him. A crowd was sitting around Jesus, and they told him, "Look, your mother and your brothers [and your sisters] are seeking you outside!" Jesus responded to them. "Who is my mother and my brothers?" Looking around at those seated in a circle around him, he said, "Look, my mother and my brothers! Whoever does the will of God, that one is my brother and sister and mother." (Mark 3:31–35)

The inner relation that constitutes the community of the open heavens is a shared impulse to co-work with God—to practice the Father's will in our own bodies and personal interactions. The inner shape of dominion—of personal agency—is willing. Thus, the inner boundary of humanity's natural community, according to Jesus, is a matter of the will or heart.[171]

An implicit contrast surfaces between those who stand on the outside and those who enter and enact God's will from the inside. If, at this point, Jesus' physical mother and brothers were aiming to co-work with God, they would be inside—seated in the circle asking questions—and not standing outside.

Since Jesus' core social identity was introduced through his vision of the open heavens, we should reflect that the key term "Son" is deeply embedded in the notion of a shared project or dominion. In the ancient world, a "son" is the rightful agent of his father. He should not only possess the same character as his father, but he should be engaged in the same project.

When Jesus teaches his students to align themselves with the Father's will, to address their prayers to "our Father" and other such exhortations, he is also identifying the inner boundaries of the natural community. We are, at least potentially, sons and daughters of the Father. The Creator of heaven and earth, the one who is not dependent on anything else but whose character is full of gentle care—that's the one we were designed to work with and for in this world.

Alignment of our wills with the Father's will produces an inner coherence and communal connection that is broader than just a collection of visible contemporaries. It is larger than just linkages to fellow human persons in proximity. It connects us with immortals as well. Angels are present and interested. Other deathless beings also attend us. (We'll come to that momentarily.) The open heavens, as a social home, is at once larger than human society and less inclusive—for, at the moment, some humans simply will not cede their personal projects to the Father's. They will place themselves outside the open heavens. They will be locked out, at least momentarily, by turning the latch on *their* side, not heaven's.

How the Inner and Outer Social Boundaries Meet

In Mark 8:27–9:1, Jesus addresses his students with a thick cluster of intertwined themes—practical wisdom (that is decision-making about what is possible or impossible, worthwhile or a waste of time), the boundaries and content of social identity, and the presence or absence of deathless beings.

Let's consider this passage in segments. Here is how Jesus connects dominion and social boundaries. It turns on how we use our practical wisdom—a feature of those created for dominion.

> Jesus and his students departed into the villages of Caesarea Philippi. On the way, he asked his students, "Who do people say that I am?" They told him, "Some say John the Baptist, others Elijah, others one of the prophets." And he asked them, "Who do you say that I am?" Peter answered, "You are the Messiah." And Jesus rebuked them so that they would tell no one about him. And Jesus began to teach them that the Son of Man must suffer many things, must be rejected by the elders and chief priests and the scribes, must be killed and on the third day rise again. He was stating the matter frankly. Peter took him aside and began to rebuke him. But Jesus turned around and, looking at his students, rebuked Peter. "Get behind me, Satan, because you are not using practical wisdom based on the things of God but based on the things of human beings." (Mark 8:27–33)

Merely Human Society

Jesus initiates this conversation with his students situated in the merely human social world to which they are accustomed. "Who do people think I am?" A cluster of responses stays within the boundaries of the prophetic category. It makes sense. Jesus has enacted many of the roles of a classical prophet—miracles, oracles, public orations, pronouncements of judgment, ethical exhortation, healings, weather control. All these are prophetic deeds.

Now Jesus individuates—he offers his students an opportunity to step out of the stream of contemporary opinion: "But who do *you* say that I am?"

Peter, as usual, is the first to speak up. He wants to identify Jesus with the Davidic Messiah. (In Matthew, Jesus recognizes that Peter has received a special insight—a revelation—from the Father. But Mark doesn't include that bit.) Peter's category is less obvious. After all, David doesn't multiply food, heal people, or change weather. David excels in battle and at the intrigues and graces of court life, but Jesus hasn't followed his example. At this point in Peter's development, "Messiah" is another—and even less apt—social category for making sense of Jesus' distinct character and calling. Peter is right, but for all the wrong reasons.

Censure or Rebuke

So, the censure—the expression of strong disapproval—begins. This word *epitimao* signifies the act of appraisal or assigning value to something. In other contexts, it may be used for setting a price but in verbal exchanges it means to show how something lacks value—is blameworthy.

Jesus censures his students, not just Peter, and tells them to hold their tongues about such categories. Neither prophet nor Messiah is adequate.

Self-Identification

Instead, Jesus uses a socially amorphous and ambiguous phrase—"The Son of Man"—as his self-referent. One *like* a Son of Man was welcomed in the heavenly court, in the vision of Daniel 7:13–14, and given authority to act on God's behalf and receive worship from the nations.[172] But in Ezekiel and other Second Temple Jewish literature the phrase is used to mean something like "a bloke" or "a guy"—a nondescript reference to a human being—or even "this guy"—a humble, roundabout form of self-reference.[173] At first blush, it is unclear which of these Jesus is evoking. The highest or the lowest? Is he at the right hand of the Ancient of Days or just a humble creature of dust?

Why does Jesus choose such a nearly empty signifier? Probably because the content of the other, ready-made identities is misleading. Jesus' identity is rooted elsewhere, and his personal role will cut at an angle across their categories. To understand what "the Son of Man" is, they'll have to watch Jesus give it content—both in his person and in subsequent statements and allusions. As it turns out, it will be both the highest and the lowest possible meaning in an unforgettable fusion. Human disapproval, and its most painful consequences, will precede the highest honor before God and say over all nations. After total human rejection and punishment, on the third day he will rise again and reign immortal.

Jesus speaks openly and directly about this. But, for the moment, his students lack the perceptual frame to make sense of his words. They'll understand later.

Peter: Dominion from Merely Human Practical Wisdom

At this point, Peter pulls Jesus to the side and censures him. Evidently, Jesus has lost his mind. Jesus' words are not going to help with troop morale, which has to be primary.

Jesus, fixed on guiding his students aright, responds with a word of censure to show both *in what way* and *before whom* Peter's thought process is blameworthy. "Get behind me, Satan, because you are not deliberating (using practical wisdom) based on the things of God but based on the things of human beings" (Mark 8:33).

The cognitive word Jesus uses, *phroneo*, is often translated as "to set one's mind" or "to think about." The noun version is *phronesis*. As we've noted, Greeks had a proliferation of words and distinctions for mental phenomenon. Our vocabulary is relatively poor on this score, so we need periphrases to get the underlying idea across. The word, which I translate as "deliberate" or "use practical wisdom," refers to the sort of thought that issues in bodily action and accounts for what is proper to attempt or do. Questions of what is possible or impossible, right or wrong, wise or foolish, likely to succeed or hopeless—all these are decided by use of *phronesis* or practical wisdom. As such, *phronesis* is the internal process that immediately results in our agency in the world. In biblical terms, there is no dominion without *phronesis*. Humans were created to co-work with God—to exercise co-dominion. So *phronesis* is terribly important.

But our practical wisdom or *phronesis* operates within horizons. We start our deliberations with some sense of what is real and who is watching. Aristotle noticed that feature too, although he didn't really question the horizons his society assumed. The biblical account, from which Jesus works, describes an unnatural shrinking of that horizon following Adam and Eve's rebellion.

That's where Peter is now. The horizon of Peter's deliberation is all human. He is assessing the relative likelihood and possible outcomes *only* by considering human factors.

This shrinking of the horizon—contraction of one's attention—to exclude God as a real factor is, quite simply, the rhetorical strategy of the satan—the prosecuting attorney. Jesus was familiar with it from his time in the solitude of the wilderness when the satan tested him. Now Jesus hears the same deliberative pattern on Peter's lips. So, for the good of Peter and all his students, Jesus censures him.

Practical Wisdom within the Open Heavens

What would it be like to deliberate based on the realities of God? When the horizon for relevant action and social esteem is expanded to include the heavens, what kind of practical reasoning follows? Jesus illustrates.

> Jesus called the crowd with his students and told them, "If any-one wants to follow me, let him say 'no' to himself and take up his cross and follow me. For whoever wants to preserve his soul will destroy it, but whoever would destroy his soul on account of me and the gospel will preserve it. What does it benefit a person to turn a profit on the whole world and to be fined his soul? For what would a person give as a trade-off for his soul? Whoever is embarrassed by me and my words in this adulterous and error-ridden generation, the Son of Man will be embarrassed by him, when he comes in the glory of his Father with the holy angels." And he said to them, "Truly I say to you that there are some who shall not taste death that are standing here until they see the kingdom of God has arrived with power." (Mark 8:34–9:1)

Self, Soul, and Social Order

Notice that oneself, one's soul, and this generation all lump together. The soul—the biological life-force that we experience as a mostly unconscious

flow—is deeply rooted in human social bonds. The soul registers social status and the relative pecking order at a deep level.

In fact, such social layering and hierarchy of influence is a well-stud-
ied and universal feature of bestial life from crustaceans up to the great
apes.[174] Part of what soul does, in order to keep itself alive, is continuously
monitor—in glances and tones and postures and gestures—who is above
and below whom in the social order.

When human alienation from God artificially shrinks our natural
communal boundaries, soul relations take over. This autopilot layer has
been habituated to only consider human acts and their relative potency.
Through long negligence, it has become blind to the open heavens.

Saying "No" to Soul

To exercise proper dominion and to think the things of God, one must directly oppose this feature of the soul. The soul will read the hierarchy of its society
and adjust itself. In Jesus' world that means that temple elites and Romans
are not to be contradicted or ignored. If they shame you, you'd better feel the
shame and shrink away. Because the next stop is a cross.

But to deliberate within the horizon of the open heavens—to think
the things of God—means to tell the soul "no" at this point. The paradox
is that uprooting or destroying the soul's automatic social layering will, by
means of heaven's action, preserve the soul. By contrast, going with the
soul's self-preserving impulses leads to its ultimate destruction. Climb-
ing the social ladder—a soul guided impulse—does not produce what it
promises, instead it brings disaster.

A New Context for Shame and Glory

Finally, Jesus connects the call to deny soul with a contrast in acknowledged
social order and identity. Whoever feels embarrassment or shame, when
owning a connection to Jesus and his teachings, is rooted in the present
generation—his or her social horizon is constricted and ends at the edges
of proximate human opinion. Jesus, however, finds his shame and his glory
in the presence of the Father and his holy angels. Those who do his Father's
will are the natural participants in the community from which he expects
approval. If, at a given moment, not a single human being falls into that category, Jesus is not left alone. He lives before the Father's face.

According to Jesus, the expanded social horizon—enveloping both seen and the unseen persons—is not merely a future but a *present* reality. All around Jesus and his students are a class of persons, which in Jewish thought were called "those who shall not taste death." I've indicated as much in the translation above.

Most translations of this passage will read something like this. "There are those standing here who will not taste death until they see the kingdom of God come with power." This is also a possible translation. It takes the temporal phrase "until they see the kingdom . . ." as modifying "will not taste death" rather than modifying "standing here." It is possible, but it is not the better translation in context. Here's why.

Those Who Will Not Taste Death

The Second Temple Jews had a category of persons whom they knew to have been exempted from physical death.[175] These included both the angels, who are immortal, and a small class of humans who were translated into the heavens without dying. Enoch and Elijah were the primary biblical examples of this category of human. Enoch, in Genesis 5, broke with the pattern of his age. In the seventh generation from Adam, Enoch returns to the sort of interaction with God that Adam enjoyed before sin. "Enoch walked with God and then he was not found for God took him." Later, Elijah is taken into the heavens—caught up by horses and chariots of fire.[176]

A more natural reading of this passage recognizes that Jesus is referring to the presence, in their midst, of these deathless beings. Jesus is not stating that some will die after God's great act of power. Rather, he is assuring his students, presently living within a severely shrunken social horizon, that "those who [like Elijah] will not taste death" are near and watching.

If those watching in the room include people like Enoch and Elijah, does it really make sense to worry what Billy-Bob or Suzy-Q thinks of your decision? Whose opinion should you feel as a pressure to weigh?

Conversely, even when Billy-Bob and Suzy-Q and all other human observers are absent, you are still not alone. There are always more persons in the room than you and I can see.

Moreover, it is their society that we are being prepared to enjoy. We too, assuming we are trusting and enacting Jesus' instruction, "shall not see death" (John 8:51–52). As his early student, John, recalls, Jesus is offering his students an entrance to the ranks of those will never die. It's not just that Enoch and Elijah are great ones whom we could have the privilege of meeting. Rather, they constitute the natural society into which we are pledging through our apprenticeship with Jesus. They are among our eternal companions as distinguished from those with whom we happen to share space right now. They are "our people."

The very next passage brings Jesus' point home. In order to aid them in locating the proper horizon for their deliberations, Jesus takes Peter and the Zebedee brothers up the mountain. Here's what happens:

> After six days Jesus took along Peter and James and John and led them onto a high mountain by themselves alone. He was trans-figured before them. His garments became gleaming—very white—such as no launderer on earth could whiten them. Elijah appeared to them with Moses, and they were chatting with Je-sus. In response, Peter says to Jesus, "Rabbi, it's good that we're here. We'll make three shrines—one for you, one for Moses, and one for Elijah." Peter didn't know how to respond, because they were all freaked out. A cloud overshadowed them, and a voice emerged out of the cloud, "This is my Son, my beloved, keep lis-tening to him." Suddenly, as they looked around, they no longer saw anyone except Jesus alone with themselves. (Mark 9:2–8)

Jesus' students are enabled, briefly, to see some of those who are standing there until they see God complete his project. Those, like Elijah, who shall not taste death are carrying on a conversation with Jesus. This is Jesus' natural community—the ones before whom he lives alongside the match-less Father.

Kingdom Community—We Are Three

The point of Jesus' teaching about the boundaries of our natural community is simply this. There are always more persons—actors and observers—in the room than you and I can see. When you and I meet in private, there are always at least three persons present. We are three. Heaven is present.

Occasionally, when it is needful, we may be granted a glimpse—some vision—of this reality. Most of the time it remains invisible, though never closed. The heavens are all around us. The Father is closer than our next breath. Angels are watching to learn from the Father's work in and through us.[177]

If this is true, then your everyday actions—in word and deed—and social transactions bear consequences that are cosmic in scope. There are no insignificant occasions of trial, no unobserved rebellions, no victories that hearten no one. Your life matters. All of it. And not just for you.

Finally, the Father's attention—ever turned toward you—is your primary relation. All others are secondary, and they are improved by keeping the Father at the center. As you co-work with the Father—enact his will by aligning your own will—you will find human relations reshaping all around you. You will find that you are accompanied and supported also by brothers, sisters, mothers you hadn't known. A family of shared heart, not just of blood, will emerge as you walk with the Father alone.

CHAPTER ELEVEN

Kingdom Social Relations, Pt. 2

Beyond Seduction and Opposition
to a Life of Transparency

Social Relations in This Age

REALITY—EVEN SOCIAL REALITY—IS BIGGER than humans have been comfortable acknowledging. Since Adam and Eve there has been a tendency to shrink the natural community or social world until it includes only humans—and only select, proximate humans at that.

By contrast, Jesus invites his students into the natural community of the open heavens. There we can breathe again—the horizon is expansive enough for healthy deliberation and non-manipulative interactions. But, from within the open heavens, we still must interact with *this age*—in relations with people who don't see past the humans in close proximity. How can we negotiate those relations well?

That's the subject of this chapter.

Social Identity and the Competition for Attention

To hear Jesus' advice concerning interactions with this age or social order, we need to return to the parable of the sower, with which we began this book.

The parable of the sower and the soils is included in three different accounts of Jesus' life: those by Matthew, Mark, and Luke. Evidently, Jesus told it on multiple occasions and in different settings. At least his early followers remember it that way.[178]

In Mark's account, Jesus indicates that this parable is a kind of key to all the parables: "Do you not understand this parable? How will you understand all the parables?" (Mark 4:13). This one has special significance.[179]

In each of these gospels, Jesus' explanation of the parable of the soils, which ends with the problem of social identity, is followed by further teachings concerning social identity. Clearly, whenever Jesus unfolded his big-picture account of lasting personal change, he thought that the social-identity element required a little extra focus. I must say that I've found it the most difficult in my own life. Perhaps Jesus thought this would be the case for many of us. At any rate, I'm grateful for these added clarifications.

The Three Obstacles to Social Identity

Core social ties within the open heavens can be severed by any of three postures toward the present human community—seduction, obsessive opposition, and resignation.

Within the parable of the soils, Jesus' students are cautioned against being overwhelmed by the "worries of the age and the illusion of wealth." Such assimilation to or seduction by the social order constitutes the first obstacle to healthy social identity in the kingdom.

In Matthew, Jesus proceeds from explaining this parable to telling and explaining the parable of the wheat and the tares. The central point of that parable is a warning against becoming too obsessed with and agitated by the effort to correct the wrongs which one witnesses in the world (Matt 13:24–30, 36–43). Here is a second, distinct manner in which our social relations and identity may be distracted from the kingdom.

In Mark and Luke, Jesus invokes a principle of openness—the need to live with public transparency as one learns—and combines it with a warning that failure to enact what one learns will lead to loss of understanding (Mark 4:21–25; Luke 8:16–18).

When these warnings are added together and seen in relation to each other, a composite picture emerges of three primary obstacles to healthy social identity within the kingdom of God. Let's consider each of these in turn.

THE FIRST OBSTACLE

Seduction: Assimilating Oneself
to Human Social Expectations

The primary social problem that Jesus identifies within the parable of the soils is seduction by the world. "Other seeds fell upon the thorns, and when they came up the thorns choked them" (Matt 13:7). In explanation, Jesus elaborates "And the one sown in the thorns, he is the one who hears the word and the worries of the social order [*lit.* age] and the illusory lure of wealth choke the word and it becomes fruitless" (Matt 13:22).

In this scenario, Jesus' student gains an initial understanding of his message and perhaps even adopts some disciplines. Ultimately, however, he fails to bring his relation to the human social world into alignment with Jesus' Way. As a result, this type of student succumbs to the shared priorities, experienced as worries and aspirations, that bind human groups together. The human social order sets the agenda for his or her life.

Choking on Rapport

Jesus' word is instructive. The disparate aims and aversions, which are caught from the social order, "choke" or "smother" the life-giving information that Jesus has given. The person's attention, which is always finite, is divided among too many concerns. It simply does not provide enough focus for Jesus' word to complete its fruit-bearing—in other words, to produce the new type of life to which it would naturally lead.

In so far as we were created to connect with other persons it is natural for us to look at things through their eyes. We are fashioned, after all, to communicate. We can imaginatively put ourselves in others' shoes. Often, thereby, we come to understand why they desire what they desire and fear what they fear. This human capacity—empathy—lies at the heart of much good. We cannot live ethically without it.[180] But it can also be over-activated. Empathy has a dark side.[181] When my impulse to connect is not balanced by concerns for truth—some reality aim—it easily leads me into group-assimilation regardless of the content of the group's aims.

Jesus warns his students. The means by which we connect with people can be twisted. We can easily bend our presentation of self and attunement with others until we are merely mirroring or assimilating to others' aspirations and ideals. Here's the problem: Jesus' message provides distinct aims and trajectories for human life and action, but they cannot be merged without loss into the aspirations of any merely human social order. The "illusion of wealth," which Jesus foregrounds, is a good example of most human societies' misguided aspirations. People routinely and feverishly seek well-being in what cannot deliver it. If we internalize our society's aspirations, perhaps seek to "outperform" them according to their own standards, this will require a great deal of our attention. By sufficiently dividing our attention, the effect of Jesus' own teaching will be stunted in us. Nothing more is needed to distract a person from the fully flourishing life that Jesus offers.

Acknowledgment from Whom?

The social element of life in Jesus' Way is secured through personal relations, which includes those anchored in the heavens. In this regard a distinctive of Jesus' teaching surfaces afresh. Aristotle, you will remember, took the praise and blame of the city's nobles as his first principle for moral reasoning. "Good people praise good things and blame bad things" is Aristotle's founding sense. Ethical reasoning is an attempt to explain the patterned relations between those things which such people praised, on the one hand, and blamed, on the other. All Aristotle's reasoning was conducted within a merely human social order.

In John 5:44, Jesus addressed his generations incapacity to see the significance of his deeds. Jesus points to their rootedness in human social opinion. He asks an important diagnostic question: "How can you believe when you receive glory from one another, and you do not seek the glory that is from the only God?" Internalizing the human competition for honor, rather than looking to the Father for approval and disapproval, prevents people from trusting their own perceptions of the good that Jesus is producing. Jesus repeatedly invites them to consider the deeds themselves rather than filtering them through the estimations of their social order. "If I'm not doing my Father's deeds, stop trusting me; but if I am doing them, even if you wouldn't trust me, trust the deeds so that you may apprehend and keep apprehending that the Father is in me and I am in the Father" (John 10:37–38, see also 14:8–11).

Individuation

In order to make sense of Jesus and his teachings, a person must be willing to look in an unmediated manner at what Jesus does. A degree of individuation is required. Jesus insists on each person evaluating for him- or herself, rather than glancing sideways and mirroring what others think.

Individuation, by its nature, can be painful. Jesus acknowledges as much. Humans feel at peace through envelopment in a larger "we"—participation in some group from which one is relatively undifferentiated.[182] But Jesus' Way requires personal differentiation—individual decision.

> Do you suppose that I've arrived to give peace on the earth? No. I tell you, not peace but division. For from now on five in a household will be divided—three against two and two against three. A father will be divided from his son, and the son from the father, mother against daughter and daughter against the mother, mother-in-law against daughter-in-law and daughter-in-law against mother-in-law. (Luke 12:51-53)

Each must choose. Those choices will divide—or individuate—persons within their close relations. Tight gates and narrow paths cannot be traversed as a crowd (see Matt 7:13–14). There may be a significant gathering on either side of it, but only individuals can pass through. Given the realities of current human social orders and the variable responses of the human heart, Jesus knows that differences will arise as people receive or reject his message.

One must be prepared to stand with Jesus—appropriately blushing and beaming before the Father and his society alone—in order to complete the personal transformation that Jesus' life-giving information provides. A certain oddness—like Jesus' strangeness in his world—must be embraced. People will often not get what you are about or why you care in the way you do.[183] That's okay. You are well understood by the Father and a host of others whose opinion will outlast this generation's. That's good enough.

THE SECOND OBSTACLE

Obsessive Opposition to Wrongs in the World

But assimilation—a failure to individuate—is only one social-psychological posture that prevents stable personal change. Another mistaken social posture, highlighted by the parable of the wheat and the tares, is excessive opposition to the world.

Obsession with correcting all the wrongs one sees in the world is in many ways the psychological contrary of seduction. Nonetheless, this posture too prevents effective co-working with God. Here are Jesus' words on the matter. He presents them in the parable of the wheat and the tares. Notice, especially, the impulse of the slaves and the landowner's counter-advice:

Jesus presented another parable to them. "The kingdom of the heavens [i.e., God's work] is like a man sowing good seeds in his field. While people were sleeping, his enemy came and scattered tares among the wheat, and left. When the stalk sprouted and formed fruit, then the tares also became visible. The slaves of the landowner approached him and said, 'Lord, didn't you sow good seed in your field? Where did the tares come from?' He said to them, 'An enemy did this.' The slaves said to him, 'Do you want us to go out and collect them?' He said, 'No. Otherwise while you are collecting the tares you might uproot the wheat with them. Permit them to grow together until the harvest. At the time of the harvest, I will tell the harvesters to gather first the tares, to bind them in order to burn them, but to gather the wheat together into my storehouse.'" (Matt 13:24–30)

Then Jesus left the crowd and entered the house. His students approached him saying, "Clarify for us the parable of the tares in the field." In response he said, "The one who sows the good seed is the Son of Man. The field is the world. The good seed—these are the sons of the kingdom. The tares are the sons of the evil one. The enemy who sows them is the devil. The harvest is the end-result of the social order [lit. age], and the harvesters are angels. Therefore, just as the tares are gathered and burned with fire, so it will be in the end-result of the social order [lit. age]. The Son of Man will send his angels. They will gather from his kingdom all the offences and those who practice lawlessness, and they will cast them into the furnace of fire. The weeping and the grinding of teeth will be there. Then the right-living will shine forth like the sun in the kingdom of their Father. He who has ears, let him hear." (Matt 13:36–43)

Since ancient times, there has been a tendency to speak of this parable as if the field were the church.[184] The church includes both good and bad, all mixed up at present, but in the next age it will be purified. That may be true of the church, but it is certainly *not* what this parable is about.

Good and Bad Characters in the World

Jesus is clear. The field is the *world*—that might include the church but certainly is bigger. The world is the full horizon of our experiences. The seeds—good and bad—represent different "sons." To be a son of something, in Hebraic thought, was to possess the *character* of that thing. The "sons of the kingdom" possess the character of God's way of doing things—of his distinctive action. The "sons of the evil one" are those who share an evil character.

The difference between the two is not obvious at the beginning. Both good and bad persons share many features of human life and practice. It takes a while for the outcome of different life-approaches and character traits to become obvious. But even when they are obvious, their removal cannot be safely conducted by human hands.

The Enemy's Strategy

A second strategy for preventing human transformation comes to light here. The enemy wants to prevent people from reaching full maturity. In the parable of the soils, the goal was to prevent faith. Now that faith has developed, by introducing "weeds" or "tares" the goal is to prevent growth into love. How? By instigating conspicuous wrongs and glaring hypocrisies right in the middle of the "wheat"—of those acquiring the Father's character. Of course, those who are loyal to the landowner want to fix things—pull up the tares!

Zeal as Spiritual Distraction

The landowner's slaves exhibit an exuberant zeal for purifying the world. They would like to uproot the wrongdoers and right the injustices they see—and they want to do it *now!*

In this parable, Jesus depicts a basic human issue that emerges as we co-work with God. As we begin to develop God's character within ourselves and enact that in the world, we become aware of evil acts and those who routinely perpetrate them. Pain—needless suffering—stands out. This world is not what it ought to be. We can see at least some of the human reasons for its misery. A train of thought easily follows. Shouldn't we devote ourselves to rooting out the wrongs? Surely, we should not rest until the last injustice has been banished! A twitchy, agitated crusader mentality can easily emerge at this point.

The landowner's words are a warning about the process of personal transformation. Beware of fixating on the failures of those around you. It doesn't lead where you think it will. Negotiating one's identity as a student of Jesus does not involve launching an inquisition—relentlessly searching out others wrongs and trying to correct or eradicate them.

Jesus tells his students that the moral crusader posture will prevent lasting personal transformation. Moreover, he explains how and why.

Distracted, perpetual agitation over current wrongs in the world prevent a steady focus on producing good with God. One can easily be set ever against bad things, but without adequately realizing within oneself the goodness of a life as God's son or daughter.[185]

By his choice of words, Jesus connects this parable with the parable of the soils and thereby specifies how the moral crusader is prevented from spiritual maturation. An echo resonates between these parables—with the thorns in the soil and the tares in the field. Jesus intends his students to consider their relation.

Thorns in the soil of my heart will stifle personal maturation and growth. Tares in the world will not. I need to settle my priorities and develop focus within my attention. Without that I cannot grow. But I don't need to hunt down and stop every evil in the world. In fact, fixating on evils around me actually becomes a thorn—a cluttering of my attention—in the imagery of the adjacent parable.

Our Roots and "Uprooting" Wrongs

Some key words to notice are roots and scandals or offences. The overeager crusader wants to gather all the tares immediately, but the wise landowner says, "You may uproot the wheat too." You will remember that the "roots" needed for growth, in the parable of the soils, represent spiritual disciplines or daily practices. The attitude of perpetual threat-detection and error-correction directed toward others tends to uproot—to encroach upon the focus needed in basic spiritual practices—the good as well as the bad.

In the parable of the soils, failure to strengthen one's attention through daily practice produces a flimsy weakness. Such a person cannot sustain attention for more than very brief spells. He is "temporary" (13:21). When difficulties come, either through ordinary sufferings or through external hostilities, he is "scandalized" or "offended." In the parable of the tares, Jesus says that the angels will later gather all "scandals" or "offenses" to be bundled and burned.

Weaponizing Authenticity

Jesus is addressing a paradox in the virtue of sincerity or, as we say today, "authenticity." Of course, we live in a world fairly obsessed with demanding authenticity and exposing failures in authenticity. But here is the paradox: while sincerity is irreplaceable as a gauge for directing one's own moral development, it becomes toxic and death-dealing when I focus on assessing others' sincerity. Directing sincerity as a measure for others, not only for oneself, weaponizes it. Suspicion is unleashed, which has no intrinsic boundaries. The persistent aim to unmask and expose produces serious collateral damage—not least to oneself and to others who are developing the Father's character. (After all, it directly counteracts the redemptive self-forgetfulness acquired in the deeper stages of disciplinary practices *before the Father alone*. Insisting on "authenticity" means that the left hand must always know what the right hand is doing.) When I target wrongdoers and set myself to expose every hypocrisy, the collateral roots destroyed just might be mine!

What Do We Do about Evil?

So, what is to be done about evil? What's my task in regard to it? Primarily my task is to make sure my roots—regular practices—are sound and my attention well-focused so it cannot gain entry into my heart. My primary task is to keep myself from committing evil.

I am sure some would respond, "But I cannot just do *nothing*!" But tending one's own heart and directing one's own actions is *not* doing nothing. This is concentrating on the one part of the world I really can change—that's *me*. Through my own change, other things will change too.[186]

In general, it is misguided to imagine that one is placed here primarily to counter all the wrongs and injustices in the world. A purely negative, reactionary stance in one's social relations follows. It tends to narrow one's awareness by zooming in on the points of wrongdoing. This prevents one not only from noticing the substantial good already in the world but also the purely creative goods one could introduce.

In fact, God has created beings who are charged with uprooting evil in the world at the proper time. But that time is not now, and you are not one of those creatures. The holy angels will play that role. You don't have to. Focus on growing roots to withstand the current scandals. In the long run, you'll produce more good in the world. And, in time, God will take care of removing the offences himself.

Perhaps you are thinking, "But there is evil out there!" Indeed, there is. But if you are attending to Jesus' teaching and acting accordingly, then you are focused on producing good with God. That sustained focus—aligning yourself with God and co-working in the place where you are—*is doing something*!

You have no idea how God will use that change in you to effect other changes in the world out there. Historically, God has orchestrated startling improvements in societies that began with small, personal obediences in individual people. It's more likely that God will do it again than that you, single-handedly, will turn the tide of injustice through a direct onslaught. That's a hero's fantasy. We're students of Jesus and called to smaller, but paradoxically more effective, ways in this world.

Overwhelming Evil with Good

There is a story told about Karol Wojtyła during his early pastoral work in rural Niegowić.[187] In Poland of 1948, following the "decapitation of Poland" by the Soviets, young Karol focused on embodying love and cultivating faithfulness among the young people with whom he was charged. His ministry, by necessity, was discreet and mostly underground—inconspicuously conducted to avoid the prying eyes of ever-present communist informants.

The conditions were harsh, but Karol continued undeterred. He organized a drama club, recruited young people, and directed a play in which Christ shows up in the disguise of a beggar. He gathered a focused prayer group and mentored its leaders. He led the young people in hikes, outdoor singing, sports, and discussion groups. A light set on a hill, however, cannot be hid.

Inevitably, some communist informers caught wind of these activities. One day they cornered one of his teenagers and roughed him up. They wanted to scare him and make him inform. Karol's words to his young friend bespeak the Christ-like confidence in the victory of goodness. "Don't worry about them, Stanisław. In time, they'll finish themselves off."

And so it happened. There were some decades and much suffering to intervene. But the Soviets finished themselves of. The work of Karol Wojtyła and his faithful youth, however, continues and flourishes to this day. It is the nature of evil that it cannot last; the nature of good that it's effects can ripple outward forever.

Some Basic Truths

This approach to overwhelming evil with good, rather than directly counteracting it, rests upon a few truths.

I. OUR FATHER'S WORLD

First, this world is our Father's field. The main thing going on in the world is our Father's project—his kingdom. His project is centered on transforming persons. Moreover, he is watching over his world and is not unaware of his enemy's activities. The Father has a different strategy for dealing with evil—an approach we would not have chosen. The Father deals with evil through redemption more than prevention. We want to prevent evil. The Father specializes in redeeming those touched by it.

Jesus' basic point is that God is capable of achieving a redemptive purpose even through the ongoing presence of bad people and countervailing forces within the world. They can stay for the moment. The process of trying to remove them all now would prevent a person from the personal disciplines that enable a good life even in hostile and difficult circumstances.

II. JESUS IS STILL SOWING

Second, the Son of Man is still sowing good seed—producing people with the Father's character to work in his world. Jesus makes a significant distinction that can easily be lost in translation. When he speaks of the one who sows the good seed, Jesus uses a present participle. This implies continuous, ongoing sorts of action. But when Jesus speaks of the one who sows the bad seed, he uses an aorist participle—which leaves the duration of action undefined. In other words, Jesus emphasizes that, while it is unclear how long the wrongdoers will be around, the production of morally transformed persons is the Son's unceasing activity in this world. This is a reason for great hope.

Whatever wrongs we see around us, and they are real, we have the assurance that the Son continues in our day to reshape people and reform the Father's world. Whatever our momentary perception of the situation, God is not inactive in this world.

III. CO-WORKING AS CHILDREN

Third, if we will risk focusing on our own apprenticeship and allow the Father to unmask others, the end result will be that "the right-living will shine forth like the sun in the kingdom of their Father" (Matt 13:43). This phrase begs for our reflection. Why does Jesus speak of the "kingdom *of their Father*," rather than simply the kingdom of God or of the heavens? And, what is the shining supposed to mean?

We will shine in the kingdom of our Father because, at this point, we are not going to feel like servants or subjects as we co-work with God. We will be children—bearing the Father's likeness—who have finally found ourselves at home in God's project. His project is also ours. We work as sons and daughters, not as slaves or hired hands.

And we will *shine* as we co-work with the Father because death will be no more. In the ancient world, shining is a way of indicating immortality. This tells us of the ultimate horizon within which our work is rightly measured. It's good to have six-month, one-, two-, and five-year work schemes. But that's really too short to measure the Father's project. "When we've been there ten thousand years bright shining as the sun" as the old hymn has it—we really will just be starting the project.

Especially for those susceptible to the crusader's zeal—a twitchy, agitated opposition to the world—this deathless timeframe is essential. We can indeed wait for the Father's action, because the sky really is not the limit and death is not the end.

THE THIRD OBSTACLE

Resignation, or the Failure to Appear

There is a third defective social posture that prevents adequate maturation and personal change: *resignation*. Those who resign themselves hide or meld into the social context. Hiding, as Jesus describes it, is not so much seduction toward other goals as resignation to a supposed unchangeability in the current order.

The one who hides fails to enact. She does not show up to clearly be and do what she knows to be right and true. This person is stilted. Inside, at least initially, she knows that Jesus' Way is best. But she holds back from going public. She camouflages. Maybe she thinks there would be unsettling consequences and she lacks confidence in the power of Jesus' Way to negotiate them.

So, she silently goes along with the world. She holds Jesus' message within herself. But she does not dare to believe that her little light—small truths spoken and enacted—could affect the human social world, which seems so fixed. Ultimately, she resigns herself to anonymity and cedes responsibility for what really is within her power and within her right to do. The result is a tendency to lose even her original insights.

Advice on Transparency

Let's look at Jesus' words on this social defect. Following the parable of the soils, Mark and Luke both narrate additional instructions. On both occasions, Jesus focused on his student's need to live *openly* in the Way in order to continuously grow. Let's consider these passages together. First, Mark:

> Jesus was saying to them, "The lamp isn't brought in in order to place it under a grain basket or under the bed is it? Isn't it brought in in order to be placed on a lampstand? For there is nothing hidden except in order to be revealed, nor has anything been covered up except in order that it should become obvious. If anyone has ears to hear, let him hear." And he was telling them, "Watch out what you listen to. By the measure you are using it will be measured to you, and it will be intensified for you. For whoever has, to him it will be given. And whoever does not have, even what he has will be taken from him." (Mark 3:21–25)

Now Luke:

> No one having lit a lamp hides it in a vessel or places it underneath a bed. Rather, he places it upon a lampstand so that those who enter may see the light. For nothing is hidden that will not become visible, nor covered over that will not be known and become visible. Therefore, watch out how you listen. For whoever has, to him it will be given. And whoever does not have, even what he presumes to have, will be taken from him. (Luke 8:16–18)

The general goal seems to be an easy openness about oneself as Jesus' student. There is no need to be significantly different depending on whom one is around. Jesus' student can naturally speak about what he's learning—about his insights as well as his confusions and failures—without making it unduly weird. This doesn't mean that one must embark upon a branding campaign and squeeze every interaction into an occasion for saying something about Jesus. It just means that a person who is learning from Jesus can do that anywhere, everywhere, always. No masks are needed. In fact, what is most needed is an absence of masks.

Jesus' exhortation about openness—or not hiding—includes three observations about the dynamic involved.

I. Truth Will Out

First, a key belief underlies our open transparency as Jesus' students: *truth will out*. Light, when it enters darkness, is not extinguished by the darkness. Hiddenness is necessarily a temporary affair. Eventually, whatever is covered gets uncovered. In fact, very often the deep secret of one generation is not only known but *obvious* to the next. Just because Jesus' teaching is out of step with the current social order does not mean that it cannot work. Count on the truth becoming public—it will happen eventually and its always best if you have been living there all along.

II. Consider How You Listen

Second, given that Jesus' message and the dominant social order are out of sync with each other, pay close attention to *how* and *to what* you are listening. There is a need for personal discernment in processing both Jesus' message and the social input around us.

Others' claims, evaluations, predictions, and preferences, if uncritically focused upon, may influence the self in detrimental ways. A thousand claims to the contrary cannot change the fact that light dispels darkness. But, if absorbed uncritically, those claims can significantly alter a person's expectations and social habits. They could lead a person to hide or camouflage the thing she most needs to openly own.

It is interesting, in this regard, to note that the opening chapters of Genesis depict two contrasting accounts of guided discovery—one led by the LORD God and the other by the serpent.[188] In both cases, humans come to see something they had not yet noticed through the influence of another's guidance.

In Genesis 2, the LORD God brings all the beasts before Adam. Adam gives names to them and also realizes his loneliness. None of them were a sufficient counterpart to Adam. Only after this realization does the LORD God fashion the woman and present her to Adam. Adam's exclamation, "At last, bone of my bone and flesh of my flesh, she shall be call woman" (Gen 2:23), dramatizes Adam's own discovery of his appropriate counterpart. This was a process of guided discovery—assisted knowing—led by the LORD God.

In contrast, Genesis 3 depicts another form of guided discovery. This time the serpent leads Eve by words. At their creation, *all* the fruits of the garden had been depicted as "pleasing to the eye and good for food" (Gen 2:9). Under the sway of the serpent's speech, however, Eve now seems to only notice that the one forbidden fruit looks "good for food and a delight to the eyes" (Gen 3:6). Through the guidance of another's speech, she sees differently. In this case, the guidance does not help and the angle of vision includes a significant blind spot. Moreover, the LORD God's moral evaluation of the situation for Adam points out that the problem arose by his choice of whom to listen to. Adam was listening to Eve, who was listening to the serpent, rather than listening to God (Gen 3:17).

As Jesus says, "Be careful *how* you listen" (Luke 8:18) and "Be careful *what* you listen to" (Mark 3:24). It will not change what is true, but it will certainly change what you notice and how much confidence you have in your current opinions.

It's worth reflecting on how you listen and to whom you listen most regularly. The consequences are not trivial, as Jesus indicates in his next point.

III. Notice Feedback Loops

Third, be aware of positive feedback loops in your cognitive and social habits. Our mental and social lives are full of positive feedback loops—moments in which one thing is altered that creates the conditions for something else to intensify its effects, which in turn creates conditions for further intensification, and so on. The body has a few such positive feedback loops (for instance, contractions in childbirth stimulate oxytocin, which stimulates more contractions, etc.). Most of the body's feedback loops, however, are negative or inhibitory—designed to prevent rapid changes. No doubt there is wisdom in our biological inheritance here. But human thought and social interaction are less resistant to rapid, cumulative change.

With regard to internalizing Jesus' teachings this means that habitual openness in practicing Jesus' life-instructions leads to a multiplying effect in one's personal growth. The life-experience of socially embodying Jesus' Way leads to receiving new insights, which set up the possibility for fuller social embodiment, and so on. But the contrary is true as well.

Hiding one's insight and failing to socially embody Jesus' Way, will lead to a loss of the little understanding that one had. The understanding becomes fuzzy and gradually fades as one refrains from openly living in it. "For whoever has, to him it will be given. And whoever does not have, even what he presumes to have, will be taken from him" (Luke 8:18). *Use it or lose it.* That's how moral insight works in Jesus' Way.

Back to the Father

All three of these approaches to social identity share a common downfall. They transfer the center—the reality principle—in our social relations from the Father to the particular human group among whom we find ourselves. The kingdom—God and God's project in this world—ceases to supply the basic relations that make me the person that I am. "We" ceases to be primarily "My God and I—and those who do my Father's will." Instead, the primary relations, around which my persona is fashioned, are the attractions, repulsions, and intimidations of human groups.

CHAPTER TWELVE

Around the Table

The Gift of a Communal
Spiritual Exercise

At the Teacher's Table

"REMEMBER THAT TIME WHEN Jesus touched the leper?"

About fourteen or fifteen of us, from several different nations, were seated around a table in Thessaloniki, Greece. It was Sunday; the last evening of a long weekend gathering filled with teaching. We'd been hard at it since Friday afternoon. On the table, apart from our Bibles, pencils, and a flickering candle, there was just a loaf of bread and some wine. Throughout the weekend we had plumbed the depths of Jesus' teachings. But this moment—this communal exercise—was different. It was for remembering. Not for remembering this teaching or that saying, but for remembering Jesus.

"The leper cried out in faith for healing. Jesus could have just *spoken* him clean, but instead Jesus touched him. It's like Jesus wanted to heal his isolated soul and not just his rotting skin."

"Yeah," offered another. "And remember that time when the disciples were in a heated debate about which of them was the greatest—who would get to be prime minister once Jesus took power. They came to Jesus to make his choice between them. And what does Jesus do? He invites a small child into the circle. 'If you want to work with God,' Jesus says, 'you'll have to become like a small child.'"

On and on the stories went. Different moments and interactions popped into each of our minds, and we shared them with each other. We were remembering Jesus and we were awaiting—welcoming—Jesus in our midst.

The Table: Integrating Understandings, Practices, and Social Relations

Throughout this book we've been examining how Jesus, intentionally and intelligently, remakes human life. He explains at least part of how it happens in the parable of sower. By supplying new understandings, initiating new practices, and fostering new social relations, Jesus' teaching enables humans to undergo startling moral and spiritual transformation. And so, we have taken a closer look at key aspects of Jesus' teachings focused on these three elements.

Now it is time to consider a practice, which Jesus passes on to his students, that intertwines all three elements. It is a shared meal, in Jesus' memory and through which he is present. Over time, his early followers started calling this meal the Eucharist—"gratitude" or "thanksgiving"—because of the specific words spoken and the experience evoked through the shared practice. Gratitude emerges because this practice encapsulates a vision of salvation—of the restoration of well-being to human life.

Jesus' Theory of Salvation 1: Teaching

Jesus has a bi-focal theory, really a functional model, of salvation. The aspect foregrounded in the Gospels, and in this book, is that *Jesus' teaching ministry is itself salvific*. Jesus leads with teaching and example when he begins the process of remaking people in his own generation. No one who attentively examines the witness of the canonical Gospels can miss this.

Salvific teaching, however, does not make human salvation a matter of self-improvement—just following some needed tips. Rather, Jesus' teaching and example constitute invitations into something *God* is doing. Receiving a place within God's overarching action saves, it restores well-being. Jesus' message provides the entry point for a restored life of submissive synergy with God.

That Jesus sees his teaching as salvific is built into the metaphor he uses to describe it. The message is a seed or sperm resulting in new life. The new birth—or, more accurately, generation from above—is affected by Jesus' word. When Jesus opens his mouth, he is implanting the seed of a new kind of human life in any heart that would receive it.

As we pointed out in the prologue, Jesus is offering the life-giving information that Socrates cannot provide. Thus, we have focused, throughout this book, primarily on the first element of Jesus' account of human transformation—salvific teaching.

Jesus' Theory of Salvation 2: Cross and Resurrection

But teaching was not Jesus' only means by which to remake humanity. While his teaching was necessary, it alone would not be fully sufficient, to woo twisted humans into a life within God's overarching project. A second aspect of Jesus' work would complete his teaching and make it effective in human transformation—namely, *his self-sacrifice*. This element is not an addition conjured by later followers, but Jesus' own understanding as depicted in the Gospels.

Jesus saw his cross and resurrection as playing a specific role within his overall work. Moreover, he had a theory, or big-picture understanding, of how his cross and resurrection would be effective. Jesus' predictions of his crucifixion include a basic outline of what he thought the cross would do.

Jesus' predictive statements all imply a continuity of his project. Jesus saw a throughline, not a series of disjunctions, from his teaching along the seaside to surrendering himself to a mock trial, hanging on a Roman cross, and bursting forth from the tomb three days later. In his teachings, Jesus clearly connected his overall life-example and teaching to his crucifixion. He almost always predicts his death while teaching about discipleship and life in God's kingdom. We already looked at one of these occasions—his clarification of kingdom power as service despite suffering (Mark 10:35–45).

However, Jesus most fully explains the significance of his death at his Last Supper—an enhanced Passover meal. Let's take a closer look at his explanation and at that meal.

The Passover

The Passover, or *Pesach*, was the liberation festival of Israel. In Jesus' day, Jews flocked to Jerusalem for the feast. And, often enough, there was trouble for the Romans surrounding this feast. The meanings attached to this symbolic meal evoked ancient memories of defeated Egyptians and thus inflamed current hopes for a new Jewish state—one born from defeating the Romans.

The upper room was already stocked with meaning-thick symbols, therefore, when Jesus reclined at the table with his students. But the meal was about to get yet more meaningful. Jesus would add significances, centered on his impending crucifixion, to those already resident in the bread and wine of Passover.

> When the hour had come, Jesus reclined and the apostles with him. He said to them, "I have intensely desired to eat this Passover with you before I suffer. For I am telling you that I will not eat this until it is fulfilled in the kingdom of God." And when he had received a cup and given thanks, he said, "Take this and divide it among yourselves. For I am telling you that I will not drink from the fruit of the vine from now until the kingdom of God comes." And when he had taken a loaf and given thanks, he broke it and gave it to them saying, "This is my body that is always given for you. Do this in my memory." And in the same way, the cup after dinner, saying, "This cup is the new covenant in my blood which is always poured out for you." (Luke 22:14–20)

The Lord's Supper

Through the symbols of the loaf and cup, Jesus establishes two meaningful connections between his life and teaching, on the one hand, and his approaching crucifixion, on the other. Notice the continuity. Jesus does *not* say, "The teaching approach didn't work so I'll go die for you instead." Rather, Jesus says, "Here is how my death encapsulates and completes what I've been teaching you all along." Jesus gives us the practice of the Lord's Supper as a point of integration between his teachings and his cross.

Divide It among Yourselves

As his students gather around the table, Jesus expresses a deep longing for this time together. He has been waiting for the opportunity. He will use the symbols at hand to more intimately reveal how God will act through his suffering.

Jesus begins by twice emphasizing that God's project—his kingdom—will be fulfilled or arrive within the events that would ensue. In fact, God would accomplish his greatest act before Jesus would eat or drink again. He makes the point first with reference to eating and again with reference to drinking. Jesus doesn't want anyone to miss the point. Something big is coming. God's project, Jesus intimates, is about to turn a corner—to enter a new phase.

In light of that change, Jesus delegates authority to his students. Here they are identified more specifically as apostles because they are sent to represent Jesus. The word apostle refers to someone who is sent on another's behalf. So, Jesus gives thanks for a cup and invites his apostles, "Take this and divide it among yourselves. . . ." To share the cup of a king is, implicitly, to be entrusted with some measure of his authority.

Their immediately ensuing argument about who is the greatest shows their inability, even at this hour, to grasp Jesus' Way and the nature of his power (Luke 22:24–27). Jesus' kingly authority is to be shared among them all, not passed to a single apostle or student. There would be no greatest among them—unless by "greatest" people understand the one who most fully serves.

Nonetheless, Jesus begins by dividing authority among his apostles. Momentarily, Jesus will make this division and investiture more explicit.

> You are those who have stuck with me in my trials. And I am investing you, just as my Father invested me, with a kingdom, so that you may eat and drink at my table in my kingdom and sit on thrones judging the twelve tribes of Israel. (Luke 22:28–30)

Jesus' presence in the world will soon change. He wants his apostles to share in extending his work after his death. They will have personally assigned projects—a kingdom—granted to them and will play key roles in the remaking of the twelve tribes of Israel.

The nature of genuine effectiveness has already been explained—service is potentially unlimited in the scope of its effects because it can synergize with other forms of goodness. True power works under and alongside others for their benefit. Evidently, Jesus' students still don't get that. But soon they will see. Now is the time to give them a practice, which will be part of how they will come to see.

The Loaf: What Is a Body For?

Having voiced his desire for this meal and for his students' sharing in his project, Jesus takes the loaf. He gives thanks and breaks it. "This is my body that is always given for you. Do this in my memory."

By means of the loaf, Jesus interprets the cross as encapsulating an operational principle by which he has conducted his entire life and ministry. "My body is always given for you." In the original language the present participle has durative aspect. In other words, the action is described as *ongoing*. That's important. The gift of Jesus' body is not a one-time event, something that occurred only at a specific time on the cross. Rather, Jesus' bodily self-giving is an ongoing posture of his life—it is something that he has done and is doing and will continue as he goes to the cross. This is the first layer of a very dense symbol. Before we consider the second layer, which is implicit in the Passover context, we need to reflect on Jesus' understanding of his body.

Have you ever wondered: What are bodies and what are they for?

I saw a T-shirt several years ago. The words on it stuck with me. "My body is not a temple, it's an amusement park." That T-shirt really sums up a shift in how bodies are considered today—not as a place to serve and behold the sacred but as a site for sensory manipulation and entertainment.

One may think of bodies as focal points for personal presence in the world, which also supply a certain degree of independent power—a capacity to act. Both dimensions are significant.

I. The Body: A Focal Point for Personal Presence

As a focal point for my presence, my body is where you access me. If you want to get my attention, interacting with my body will eventually draw it to you. My daughters long ago realized that, mentally, Daddy was not always in the room. That was especially the case if I was reading or working on something. If they wanted to talk to me, words weren't initially enough to break through whatever my mind was focused on. They learned to tug on my arm or my clothes and say, "Daddy." Then I was there—and cheerfully so! By accessing my body, they got in touch with me. They enabled me to hear them. Personal life intensifies around and shows up through our bodies.

II. The Body: An Independent Power Source

Moreover, bodies supply a measure of independent energy for life. They're vivified by soul. Such energy is limited and must be constantly replenished by means of food and rest. But it is real. God supplied us with soul-fueled bodies as an expression of his delight in delegating effectiveness. By God's design, the human body is a limited vehicle for making things happen without any necessary reliance on God. This gives humans a measure of freedom—both positive and negative—and with it the dignity of causality in this world.

Characteristically, humans approach their bodies either as occasions for self-gratification or for dominating and exploiting themselves and other people. The self-gratification approach gets plenty of negative attention by moralists. "Tsk. Tsk. An amusement park, indeed!" On the other hand, self-domination tends to be celebrated. Maybe the T-shirt for this approach would be "My body is not a temple, it's a 24/7 factory" or, perhaps, "it's a heavy-duty machine." But both approaches degrade the human person. Jesus offers a different relation to our bodies.

What Jesus' Body Is For

In taking the loaf, Jesus articulates what his body is for. "My body is always given for you." Jesus sees his body—this part of the world where his person is concentrated and from which he has a measure of independent power—as *for* God, *for* others. And that's not something new to arrive in his life on the eve of the cross. The understanding has been there all along.

Run through the storyline of the Gospels and you will see this principle throughout. For instance, Jesus is worn out and emotionally spent. He has just found out that his cousin, who baptized him, has been beheaded. He knows this portends something of his own destiny. He wants to be alone, so he gets in the boat and heads across the lake for some recovery time in solitude. The people, however, guess where he is going and run around the lake. When Jesus comes ashore, they're waiting for him. What does he do? In compassion, Jesus teaches and feeds the multitudes. "My body is always given for you."

Jesus is teaching. Small children approach him wanting his attention—his touch. The disciples are indignant. "Control your brats! How about some decorum around here!" But Jesus says, "Let the little children come to me. God's action belongs to them." What does this mean? "My body is *always* given for you."

They crucified Jesus between two brigands. The Roman governor's hands were still damp from his washing them of the matter. Passersby jeered. The Sadducean leaders taunted him. How did Jesus respond? "Father, forgive them. They don't understand what they're doing."

From the beginning to the climax of his ministry, Jesus' operational principle for life in the body is the same. "My body is always given for you." The cross culminates, it does not originate, that approach.

The Loaf: Liberation from Slavery

But Jesus' body-understanding intersects with another layer of this rich symbol. In the context of the Passover meal, the loaf already had a very specific meaning. According to Gamaliel, the unleavened bread symbolizes liberation—redemption from Egyptian slavery (m. Pes. 10.5). Year by year, Passover after Passover, the children of Israel drew attention to the unleavened bread. In so doing, they remembered that they once were enslaved but the LORD had "brought [them] out from bondage to freedom, from sorrow to gladness, and from mourning to a Festival-day, and from darkness to great light, and from servitude to redemption."[189] The bread is freedom from slavery.

Now put the two meanings together. Jesus invites you to think them at the same time.

What are bodies for? They give us something to expend on behalf of God and others. Our bodies are a primary way in which our lives are unfinished acts of God's love for God's world. "My body is always given for you."

But the loaf is also redemption—liberation from slavery! Jesus, through embodying this principle, buys people back from slavery.

Connected, these two meanings produce something like this: When you receive and inhabit this truth—this complex of understandings, habitual practice, and style of social relation—you are genuinely set free. Once my body—my little capacity to show up in the world and independently make things happen—is received as for God and for others, there is nothing that can enslave me. If the Son sets you free, you are free indeed.

Do This in My Memory: A Communal
Spiritual Exercise

As Jesus interprets his life and cross for his students, he simultaneously provides a communal spiritual exercise. By means of this communal practice, their shared attention would be drawn to his cross and its layered depths of meaning. "Do this in my memory." One could translate this phrase more robustly as "Keep doing this in my memory." Grammatically, the aspect of the present imperative is durative. In ordinary language, that means that Jesus is calling his students to a continuous practice, not a single deed. Jesus establishes this meal as a regular communal exercise for his students.

Memory, especially in the context of a Passover meal, anticipates more than cognitive rehearsal. Each year the families of Israel would gather and remember their liberation from slavery. But the memory was not just of a distant event that their ancestors experienced, rather it was a way of making the exodus, in which they had each participated, present again.[190] "Why is this night different from all other nights?" the youngest in the room would ask. The oldest, who hopefully had accumulated sufficient experience to really inhabit the truth of his words, would respond, "*We* were slaves to Pharaoh in Egypt and the LORD our God took *us* out from there with a strong hand and with an outstretched arm . . ." (*Passover Haggadah*; see also Deut 16:3, 12). Each successive generation in Israel participated in the LORD's liberation from Egypt. The Passover meal was part of how they learned that they too were there.

Likewise, with the Lord's Supper, the practice itself is essential. Jesus was wise enough to not say, "*Explain this* in my memory." He said, "*Do this* in my memory." There is something in the *practice* that can never be exhausted or fully conveyed in its interpretation. Try it. You will see. Words about it may prime and focus the heart. However, doing it—intentionally breaking bread and drinking wine as Jesus' remembering community—works upon us at levels deeper than the heart's focal awareness. The communal practice is part of how God's love, demonstrated in Jesus' cross, sinks down to those subterranean levels of our souls. Nothing can adequately substitute for the doing in community. An entire ecology of practices grows from this meal and plays an indispensable role in transforming human life.

The Cup: New Covenant in Jesus' Blood

Finally, Jesus takes the cup. "This cup is the new covenant in my blood which is always poured out for you" (Luke 22:20). Thus Jesus completes the interpretation of his cross in continuity with his soul-pouring life for others. As with the loaf, the symbolism of the cup is dense and multilayered. In essence, Jesus is inviting us to see that his life and death instigates a renewal of social relations and an internalization of God's character within the human person. That's a lot. Let's look at it piece by piece.

1. COVENANT: A CONNECTION DEEPER THAN SOCIAL CONTRACT

The covenant regulates social relations by establishing a loyalty prior to and overarching any and all subsequent connections.[191] God approaches humans and establishes relations that will order the rest of that person's or people-group's life.

In biblical thought, the covenant is the primary basis for social relations. The covenant is not a social contract—a direct agreement between primordial individuals with natural rights that founds society by ceding some
individual rights to the collective.[192] It's an entirely different basis for social
belonging and personal connection. Since the social contract has largely replaced covenant in contemporary thought, it is worth noting the difference.

The covenant is not rooted in any direct agreement between individuals. Rather, the covenant regulates human relationships *indirectly*.
Those human persons within the covenant are connected to each other by
means of a prior, shared relation to God. The human-to-human relation
is mediated by God. Moreover, the covenant is not initiated from the human side. God establishes his covenant with humanity in Adam and Noah.
Subsequently God covenants, in differing manners, with particular people
groups within humanity, beginning with Abraham.[193]

When Jesus establishes this meal practice, he is claiming to be renewing that covenant bond—the triangular relation between God and
those persons who constitute his people. A renewed loyalty to God will
link human beings to each other in a deeper manner. Henceforth, those
who come to Jesus will inhabit a new web of social relations that span both
visible humanity and the open heavens.[194] They will be connected to each
other via a deeper connection to God and God's ways in Jesus. Hope for a
deeper connection was already resident in Israel's prophetic tradition and
is implicit in Jesus' words.

II. THE *NEW* COVENANT: INTERNALIZING GOD'S LIFE-INSTRUCTIONS

The symbolism is thick. Jesus' words create a three-way connection between
his life-culmination on the cross, the blood of the covenant imagery in Exodus 24:8, and the promise of a new covenant found in Jeremiah 31:31–34.
To inhabit Jesus' angle of vision, one must consider all three together.

A) BLOOD OF THE COVENANT

The covenant God made with Israel at Sinai, following the exodus, was
sealed with sacrificial blood. "Behold the blood of the covenant, which the
LORD has cut with you, over all these words" (Exod 24:8).

In biblical thought, blood represents soul—the life-force flowing
through a body—and thus is given in sacrifice to restore or create harmoni-
ous relations (Gen 9:4; Lev 17:11, 14; Deut 12:23). The covenant is ratified

or publicly enacted by symbolically surrendering a measure of independent life-force. Blood was symbolically necessary.

Israel was receiving the covenant, encapsulated in "all these words" spoken from Sinai. In other words, they were accepting the fusion of their life, symbolized by the blood, with the God-relation thereby created. The symbolism is appropriate. In Hebraic thought, the soul is in the blood. Shared life is found in covenant bonds. But there is always a concomitant relinquishment of independent life. Thus, soul—individual life-force—must be surrendered to some degree in order to have a shared life. Hence the surrender of blood to seal entrance into a covenant.

As he lifts the cup, Jesus evokes this imagery. Jesus' lifeblood is continuously being poured out for others to create this possibility of God-initiated and God-mediated relations. His life has been spent to this end. But the covenant is not simply the one sealed at Sinai.

b) New Heart: Transformed Consciousness and the Ingathering

Jesus sees his self-sacrifice, already initiated and soon to be completed on the cross, as the effective reception of the *new* covenant promised by Jeremiah. The promise had gained widespread circulation in exilic times. To understand Jesus' intention, we should consider this promise.

Judah's Babylonian exile constituted the social context of the promise. But the spiritual and moral context went deeper. Because the exile was not simply a tragedy—an inevitable result of human limitations stymieing someone's well-intended best efforts. Rather, it was the product of sin. The Judeans were aware that the exile—both of North Israel by the Assyrians and of Judah by the Babylonians—was the direct consequence of their own moral and spiritual failures.

Yes, there were vertical betrayals of the covenant. They had wandered from YHWH's way, making idols, and attempting to become an empire rather than the nation YHWH made them. But there were also horizontal betrayals of the covenant, for Israel and Judah had betrayed each other.

Judah was acutely aware that North Israel's exile was the result of strife among the covenant people.[195] North Israel had aligned itself with the Syrians against Judah. Judah called to Assyria for help. As a consequence, Assyria destroyed and exiled North Israel. Judah knew that it was, in part, her own fault. But that wasn't the end of her guilt. Subsequent prophets highlighted the ways in which Judah continued to corrupt herself morally and spiritually even after the exile of the northern ten tribes. Despite prophetic warnings, she refused to listen, persisted in her rebellions, and suffered an analogous exile at the hands of the Babylonians.

No, the exile was not just a sociological, political, or geographic problem. Geographic dispersion exposed moral and spiritual decay—betrayals both of their God and of their brothers.

Thus, promises of God gathering the exiles always included a moral and spiritual transformation of the people gathered. It would do no long term good to return the twelve tribes, simply as they were, to the promised land. Without any moral or spiritual alteration, idolatry and communal fratricide would lead to another exile. For all Israel to really be gathered and renewed, they would need to be changed *from the inside out*. In both Ezekiel and Jeremiah, a transformation of Israel's consciousness—her heart—plays a key role in God renewing his covenant and gathering the exiles (Ezek 36:16–36; Jer 31:31–34; 32:36–42).

Jeremiah took the issue deeper still. In Jeremiah, the transformation of Israel's heart meant receiving a new relation to the Torah—to God's instructions for human life among his people. Jeremiah lends this promise its iconic words. However, the deep roots of this hope are Moses' words in Deuteronomy 29–30.

THE NEW HEART IN DEUTERONOMY

Moses scolds Israel for its failure to attend to God's action and words among them. "You have seen all that the LORD did before your eyes in the land of Egypt. . . . Yet to this day the LORD has not given you a heart to know, nor eyes to see, nor ears to hear" (Deut 29:2, 4). Moses seems to imply that true words and external signs are not enough. For genuine understanding to occur, God will have to supplement human attention—our hearing, seeing, and heart-focus. Human agency, we've seen, requires incorporation into God's larger project to be truly effective. Perhaps in an analogous manner, human attention cannot quite grasp God's way without some added help. Without divine aid, the deficits of human attention will lead to compounding moral and spiritual failures, political and military defeat, and exile.

In the next chapter, however, Moses promises a restoration on the other side of exile. Restoration will begin with the exiles giving attention—"cause these things to return to your heart"—and listening anew to God's voice (Deut 30:1–2). When the captives attend and listen, God will not only gather them into the land, but he will also augment their attention. "The LORD your God will circumcise your heart and the heart of your seed, to love the LORD your God with all your heart and with all your soul, so that you may live" (Deut. 30:6). Moses anticipates a synergy of attention—as the exiles turn to God, God amplifies their capacity to focus, he "circumcises their heart."

THE NEW HEART IN JEREMIAH

With Moses' promise in the background, Jeremiah tells of a day when God will gather and renew his people. On that day, God's instructions for life—the Torah—will no longer be experienced as external requirements at odds with one's internal thoughts and desires and judgments.

> Behold the days are coming, declares the LORD, when I will make a new covenant with the house of Israel and with the house of Judah. It won't be like the covenant which I made with their fathers in the day that I took them out of the land of Egypt—my covenant which they broke, though I was a husband to them. . . . But this is the covenant which I will make with the house of Israel after those days: . . . I will put my instruction within them. I will write it on their heart. I will be their God and they will be my people. They will not teach each man his neighbor and each man his brother saying, "Know the LORD," because they will all know me—from the least of them to the greatest of them. . . . (Jer 31:31–34)

God will, in a manner akin to writing, effect a transfer of his instructions from the outside to the inside of each person's consciousness or heart. Every Israelite, great and small, will interact with God—possess real knowledge of God. This is the only viable resolution to the human problem at the heart of Israel's exile.

c) JESUS' LIFEBLOOD AND THE NEW HEART

With his words, Jesus evokes this whole cluster of hopes and promises. "This cup is the new covenant in my blood which is always poured out for you" (Luke 22:20). In accepting the cross, Jesus expects that God will use it to produce within his students a new understanding of God's character and ways. Through the cross, God will remake human hearts—augment our attention and perception—so that his instructions for life are now inside us. Such a people's deeds would naturally manifest God's word on the outside since it had been inscribed on the inside.

By his life conduct and choice of the cross, Jesus poured out his life-blood—his soul—for others. Thereby he effects the internalization of God's character within any bound to him.

Full Circle

It is worth pausing to notice something. Conceptually, we've come full circle. The parable of the sower, encapsulating Jesus' theory of moral transformation, centers on the problem of how Jesus' message can be received in the heart and allowed to be fruitful. The accent in that account falls on the human side—our multifaceted reception of the word. What shall we do to cooperate with God's work when we hear? In other words, Jesus conducts his teaching ministry with a concern to enable an internalization of God's ways within the human heart and soul. "He who has ears, let him hear." That's our side.

But then there's God's side. God has a way to make our reception possible. By his own interpretation, Jesus goes to the cross to affect an internalization of God's ways within the human heart. He is ushering in the new covenant—activating the content of Jeremiah's promise. By pouring out his life, Jesus is enacting God's way of augmenting human attention and perception. The new heart, capable of the multifaceted reception envisioned in the parable of the sower, will be given just as Moses and Jeremiah had promised.

In other words, Jesus' words and Jesus' blood aim at the exact same result. His words spoken and his body given are two moments in a single life-aim—our transformation within a new relation to God. Jesus interprets the cross as the direct consequence and cumulative act of his teaching and life example. His teaching and his cross are not two projects. They're one.

Why Did Jesus Have to Die?

So, why did Jesus have to die? Because, without the cross and resurrection, Jesus' teachings would not have sunk deep enough into us to change our hearts. There undoubtably are other reasons too, but this one must not be missed. It is the one that Jesus himself emphasizes.

God could have forgiven us with just a word. But he could not have saved us—restored our well-being—with just a word. To save us took an entire life. Jesus' personal presence in his body, his moral and spiritual example, the profundity and insight of his teaching, his palpable love shining through his everyday life and culminating in the cross and the resurrection—*none of it* was dispensable for our restoration. God could have forgiven us with a word, but to *save* us—that required Jesus in his fullness.

It would be folly, therefore, to think that we could excise Jesus' teachings from his cross and resurrection and still get their full effect. His life was too integrated for any of it to be regarded as mere accident. The cross is not a mishap. The cross, coupled with the resurrection, completes what Jesus began saying. For his words to bear fruit, we'll have to listen, see, and focus our hearts upon his cross.

However, it would be equally foolish to expect Jesus' cross and resurrection to effect this great change in us apart from his teachings. The cross, after all, was intended to enable us to truly internalize the things about which Jesus taught. In the cross and resurrection God captures and augments our attention. These acts reveal his character and encode Jesus' teaching so that we can, with God's help, understand and practice and relate anew based upon them. Only by attending to Jesus' teachings, therefore, can we receive all that the cross was meant to give.

His teaching and his cross are not two projects. They're one and, thus, must be received together.

The Gift of a Recurrent Meal

And, so, as Jesus steels himself to face the cross, he leaves one last gift for his students. It's a meal but it is also a spiritual exercise that reshapes hearts within new social relations.

Meaning-saturated bread and wine. Attention focused on Jesus and his ongoing manner of life for others. Tastes and smells. Faces and bodies with Jesus' memory between them—connecting them anew to God and each other. "*Do this* in my memory," Jesus said. He didn't say, "*Explain it* in my memory." There is wisdom and grace in his charge—in the practice.

Back to the Teacher's Table

So, as we gathered around that table in Thessaloniki, we remembered Jesus. Some in the group had seen more dying with Christ. They had lost family and homes and earthly citizenship by walking this path. Some had seen more rising. They had experienced prodigious responses to prayer, or unexpected gifts that made everyday life possible, or effectiveness that could not be explained by their own talents and resources. But ultimately, both dying and rising marked each of our lives. That's the shape of life in the kingdom.

Among us were those with unbearably difficult marriages. There were a few who had suffered repeated miscarriages—some were eventually enabled to bear children, some were not. One person had experienced a healing, after we prayed for him, that the doctors couldn't explain. "Something must have been wrong with the original bloodwork," the doctor said, "because there's no trace of that disease now." It was a mixed bag. Moral failures. Spiritual breakthroughs. Betrayals. Costly acts of care for each other. Miraculous interventions. Lingering suffering. Unanswered questions. It was all there around that table.

And, suddenly, Jesus was there too. His memory could not stay put in the past.

"Remember when Jesus stood outside Lazarus' tomb and shouted, 'Lazarus come out!'? Jesus did that for me too." And Jesus had.

Many years ago, before he converted, this Iranian brother had overdosed on drugs. In the West one might say that he went through a near-death experience. But *his experience* was not of a near death. It was of death and then life restored. While he was dead, Jesus spoke to him and called him back into this world. Jesus said that he wasn't done here. After coming back to life in this world, he encountered Jesus for the second time, in the scriptures, and understood who had called him.

Of course, he also knew that sometimes Jesus called people from the other side of the veil instead. God makes choices that we are not yet in a position to understand. His own little brother, with whom he had shared the gospel, was subsequently executed in an Iranian prison because he openly embraced Jesus. When Jesus stood to embrace his little brother, Jesus was not calling him back into this earthly realm but into the heavens beyond.

All of this belongs around the table. "Do this in my memory," Jesus said. For thousands of years now, Jesus has shown up at tables like this one. He makes his presence felt and speaks through faces not immediately recognizable as his own. But the voice—the character and weight of the words spoken—those are clearly Jesus'. When people who are committed to learning life from Jesus engage in the practice, he will be there.

That's true for you and for the people among whom you live too. I don't know what Jesus would say and do when he visits you there. He'd be addressing your life and your community, not mine. But he's the Soul Whisperer. He'll know what needs to be said. Try it and see. You'll be glad—actually, grateful—that you did.

EPILOGUE

From Spectator to Apprentice

How to Read the Gospels in the Way

Too often we read the Gospels assuming our relation to Jesus is that of a spectator. Jesus acts. We look on. Jesus heals a blind man on the road to Jericho. We applaud him. Jesus stumps the Sadducees. We chuckle. Jesus dies as a martyr for God's cause and our salvation. We thank him. Jesus rises again. We worship him. But it's all something we do passively and from a distance. Bleacher seats wouldn't get in the way.

Jesus' early followers wrote the Gospels to be read differently. They assumed personal practice and imitation of Jesus by the readers. In Jesus' world, rabbis welcomed their apprentices into their lives. Within a mentoring relation, the apprentice learned his master's teachings by heart and followed his example in the minutest detail. Jesus' disciples did the same as they followed Jesus. Later they invited others to imitate them as they imitated Christ.

As these earliest followers neared the end of their time in the flesh, the Gospels were composed as surrogates for the living voices who passed on Jesus' way of life in person. Thus, in the second century, Justin the Martyr referred to our Gospels as "memoirs of the apostles"—life notes sketched about their time with Jesus by those committed to becoming like Jesus. They were composed for and read as guides to life as Jesus lived.

So, the Gospels should be read much more the way a novice chess player scrutinizes the games of a chess grandmaster. The novice doesn't initially know why the master makes a particular move. But he knows there *must be* a reason—probably several reasons. This is, after all, the *grandmaster's* move! By attentively imitating, the novice eventually comes to understand the brilliance of each move. Something irreplaceable happens through reenactment—taking the moves from the recorded page and again playing through them on the board. Practice reveals the rationale in time. Insight follows personal imitation. The needed angle of vision is bestowed through placing oneself in the master's shoes. Embodied experience, through creative reenactment, begets insight.

The same is true of Jesus' life and teachings. The apprentice's singular goal is to become like her or his master. The Gospels were written because the first few generations of apprentices found these stories effectively made people like Jesus when they not only read them, but also *attentively enacted them.* Placing oneself in Jesus' shoes, and in the shoes of his earliest followers, enabled ordinary people to see differently and respond freshly to life's challenges.

The Gospels can still do this work in our lives. We too can open the Gospels and read stories about Jesus in order to enact them in our lives. No doubt we will be puzzled at first, but we will search and await insight into the logic of Jesus' deed or word. We'll try to *do* the things Jesus taught and modeled in our everyday lives. Occasionally we'll fail, but we'll do so attentively. Thus, our next reading will be primed with a new set of questions rising from the experience of apprenticeship. And our next attempt will be a little different that the last. This is reading as an apprentice, not just as a spectator. Obedience—embodied engagement—still produces insight.

May I invite you to read and live them out with me? I've related some of my discoveries through following this process. But there's *sooo* much more to be learned there. You just might meet Jesus anew and, with him, discover a form of life that you've longed for but didn't know was possible.

I'll look forward to seeing you there—another step or two down this path.

Endnotes

1. Napier, *En Route to the Confessions.*

2. Robb, "Kingdom among Us."

3. A BRIEF WORD TO SCHOLARLY READERS—whether philosophers, historians, theologians, or biblical exegetes: In this book, I engage Jesus' teachings and write in a mode that Paul Ricoeur calls "second naïveté." Anyone concerned to grasp the "secondness" involved will want to consult the notes. My engaged exposition foregrounds the fact, often obscured in modern scholarship, that both Jesus and the other philosophers to whom I refer explicitly intended to make claims on our existence—our forms of life—rooted in correlative claims about how things really are. No honest account can ignore that fact. If I've done my job, the reader will feel the weight of those claims and be in a better position to authentically assess, for her- or himself, how to respond.

4. Jesus and Socrates share another feature. Since neither wrote, contemporary scholars may doubt the possibility of recovering the philosophy of either or both. Nonetheless, Pierre Hadot, among the most illustrious historians of ancient philosophy, takes as his focus the "figure of Socrates" rather than a hypothetical reconstruction of an "historical Socrates." The figure—as presented focally in Plato, but peripherally in such authors as Xenophon, Aristophanes, Aristotle, Diogenes Laertius, Libanius, and Maximus of Tyre—echoes through the ages. See Hadot, *What Is Ancient Philosophy?*, 22–38, and Hadot, *Philosophy as a Way of Life*, 147–78. It is, after all, the figure who has been historically decisive. One may bracket any skepticism about the correspondence of the figure to the "historical person" and reflect philosophically on the figure. For a helpful overview of the origins of the "Socratic problem" and its dissolution, from which Hadot proceeds, see Dorion, "Rise and Fall of the Socratic Problem," 1–23.

    I am claiming that an analogous attention to the "figure of Jesus" is also philosophically interesting and fruitful. The "figure of Jesus" is presented focally in the earliest accounts of his life (found in the canonical Gospels) and peripherally through the writings of his early followers and his early critics (such as Celsus' *On the True Doctrine* among the pagans and the Ben Pantera passages in early rabbinic literature among Jewish critics). There is no shortage of textual material for the figure of Jesus. In modern scholarship, there has been little philosophical attention to the figure of Jesus. A notable exception is Gooch, *Reflections on Jesus and Socrates*. Two more recent titles seem to promise such a focus but offer a more diffuse approach—drawing from Paul and the whole of the New Testament rather than focusing on the Gospels' figure and his teachings. Kreeft, *Philosophy of Jesus*; and Pennington, *Jesus the Great Philosopher*. In my estimation, by shifting focus outside the Gospels' figure of Jesus, these texts lose in depth what they gain in breadth.

5. See, e.g., Matt 7:13–14; Acts 9:2, 18:25–26, 19:9, 23, 22:4, 24:14–16, 22. Of course, this metaphor is not the exclusive property of Jesus' movement. In other places and times, some have endeavored to discover and teach "the Way"—a form of living best suited to the nature of human life. The most famous of these is Lao Tsu, author of the *Tao Te Ching*.

6. To calibrate one's understanding of ancient philosophy as ways of living, see Hadot, *What Is Ancient Philosophy?*; Nussbaum, "Therapy of Desire in Hellenistic Ethics"; Nussbaum, *Therapy of Desire*. More recently, Cooper, *Pursuits of Wisdom*, provides a needed corrective to a homogenizing tendency in Hadot.

7. As an indication of the expansive scholarly discussion behind this point, I will simply gesture toward such seminal works as Malherbe, *Paul and the Popular Philosophers*; Engberg-Pedersen, *Paul and the Stoics*; Engberg-Pedersen, *John and Philosophy*. For a principled critique of the terms of this comparative project, see Rowe, *One True Life*. Rowe offers an account, post-Wittgenstein and MacIntyre, of the inherent incommensurability of traditional discourses and argues to juxtapose Christian and Stoic stories as in conflict.

8. Consider, e.g., Justin Martyr, *Dialogue with Trypho* as well as his *1 Apology* and *2 Apology*; Tatian, *Address to the Greeks*, and Athenagoras, *Embassy*.

9. Among Hellenistic Jews this trend goes back at least as far as Aristobulus in the second century BC. However, there is also an important argument to be made for a philosophical form of thought embedded in the Hebrew Bible itself. See Hazony, *Philosophy of the Hebrew Scripture*; Johnson, *Biblical Philosophy*. For a deep background to the modern comparison between Near Eastern thought and philosophy, see the various essays in Frankfurt et al., *Intellectual Adventure of Ancient Man*. For a more recent whistle-stop tour of ancient Mediterranean thought, which includes the Jews among the philosophers, see Clark, *Ancient Mediterranean Philosophy*.

10. See ch. 1 and 4 of Hadot and Davidson, *Philosophy as a Way of Life*.

11. Of course, teachings about God and the nature of divinity held a central place in Jesus' movement, as it did in most ancient philosophies. "Theology," however, was a word Jesus' earliest followers avoided, likely due to prior connotations in their context.

    "Theology," as a label for a form of teaching, had pagan connotations in the early centuries. Three forms of "theology" were commonly recognized by the ancients: mythic, physical, and political. Mythic or poetic theology was storytelling about the gods. Homer and Hesiod were theologians in this sense. Physical or natural theology referred to the gods as personifications of the forces of nature. Civic or public theology, as the Stoics described it from Panaetius of Rhodes onward, was the attribution of divine qualities either to rulers, such as the Caesar, or civic aims, such as "Justice" and "Peace," in order to solidify a social group. Tertullian and Augustine of Hippo, both of whom cite Varro, are primary sources of testimonia for these views. See Tertullian, *ad Nationes* 2.1ff., and Augustine, *City of God* 4.24–27; 6.12, etc.

In addition to these three, we might note that Aristotle used the word to designate one of the three branches of speculative philosophy: mathematics, physics, and theology (*Metaphysics* 6.1). In this sense, theology designated his theory of being *qua* being as developed in *Metaphysics* book 12. The Stoics included Aristotle's usage in their category of "physical theology," but it probably should be counted as a fourth usage.

12. The depiction of Jesus' teachings in second- to fourth-century Christian literature as a philosophy has long been known, though has rarely entered popular discussions of Jesus. The implicit self-identification of first-century followers is becoming better known. Nonetheless, these facts have not been widely used in the scholarly literature to revisit Jesus' own teachings.

13. See, for instance, Didache 2–3, 5 and Justin Martyr, *1 Apol.* 14–16.

14. Plato, *Theaetetus. Sophist* (translation modified).

15. Socrates is not isolated among the Greek philosophers in his dependence upon revelation. See Jaeger, *The Theology of the Early Greek Philosophers*.

16. *Apology* 31d, 40a–b.

17. This message is also called "the word of God" or simply "the word." Below we will examine the meaning of "kingdom." For now, one may consider the "word of the kingdom" as informative descriptions of how God is acting in this world now and how humans can cooperatively interact with God's actions.

18. That is, in Matthew, Mark, and Luke's accounts of Jesus' life and teachings.

19. Mark 4:1–20, 26–32; Matt 13:3–35; Luke 8:4–15.

20. In Second Temple Jewish thought, a similar metaphor was employed to speak of how YHWH, in calling Israel, planted the Torah to develop a new kind of people. See Flusser, *Judaism of the Second Temple Period*, 199–206, for discussion and references.

21. John 3:1–8; 1 Pet 1:23; 1 John 3:9.

22. 1 Cor 4:15; Phil 10.

23. John 3:1–8; 1 Pet 1:3, 23.

24. According to Liddell and Scott, *Greek-English Lexicon*, 344, this verb is used "mostly of the father."

25. Nicodemus misunderstands Jesus in John 3 as meaning "born again." Commentators often note the ambiguity of the *anōthen* particle. It could mean either "again" or "from above." However, a similar ambiguity resides in the word *gennaō*. Nicodemus is doubly confused.

26. Of course, neither generation nor birth are the endpoint of the metaphor complex. Once a newly begotten life comes to term, he or she enters the world as an infant and gradually grows to full maturity. The spiritual pregnancy issues in a life that initially requires specially adapted spiritual and moral nutrition to grow (1 Cor 3:1–3; Heb 5:11–14; 1 Pet 2:1–3; see also Odes of Solomon 19). Different forms of nutrition are required for each stage—first milk then meat. For an exposition of this metaphor complex, which is connected to the metaphor of the word as seed, see Napier, "Finding Words to Nourish."

27. *Strom.* 1.5 et passim.

28. Examples of this line of argument and personal testimony may be found in Justin Martyr, *Dialogue with Trypho the Jew*; Tatian, *Oration to the Greeks*; Theophilus, *To Autolycus*; Athenagoras, *Embassy for the Christians*; Clement of Alexandria, *Stromateis*; Lactantius, *Divine Institutes*; Eusebius, *Preparation for the Gospel*; and perhaps most thoroughly, Augustine, *On True Religion*.

29. This pithy saying is preserved in Diogenes Laertius, *Lives of Eminent Philosophers* 5.19. For the sort of reasoning behind it, see the beginning chapters of Aristotle, *Nichomachean Ethics*, book 9.

30. Socrates and the old Stoics rest their whole theory on the rational mind and find moral goodness there alone. Plato places goodness there too, but acknowledges inevitable and irresolvable competition between reason and the appetites. His account of the emotions places them as potentially good and potentially vicious. Aristotle conceives of a polity that trains the irrational parts for goodness through what we would call social conditioning.

31. While Aristotle thought of the rational mind, to the limited degree present in a human being, as physically located in the heart (as opposed to the brain), the heart was not, for Aristotle, the faculty itself but only a physical site for that faculty. For Jesus, the heart *is* the faculty. For an account of how Jesus' theory of the heart finds, through Augustine of Hippo, its characteristically Western formulation, see chapter 3 of Napier, *En Route to the Confessions*.

32. See, e.g., Dan 4:13; 5:20–22.

33. See Carasik, *Theologies of the Mind in Biblical Israel*, esp. 104–24.

34. We should note, however, that a *primary* site or focus does not, in Jesus' case, mean *exclusive* site or focus. While Jesus' theory has a primary focal point in the heart, he sees the heart's attention as interacting with several irreducible features of human life. Each of these aspects of personal activity must be transformed for personal change to endure and produce genuine human flourishing. In this particular respect, Jesus is closer to Aristotle, and to a lesser degree Plato, than to the pure cognitivism of Socrates and the old Stoics.

35. For the range of modern interpretations of this parable, the reader may consult the summaries offered in the works to follow. I will not reproduce such a narrative

of alternate interpretations here. See Boucher, *Mysterious Parable*; Davies and Allison, *Critical and Exegetical Commentary*, 373–406. Also Snodgrass, *Stories with Intention*, 145–77.

36. In the broad sweep of New Testament writings, moreover, "fruitfulness" continues to be primarily moral (Rom 7:4–5; Col 1:10) and sometimes cognitive (1 Cor 14:14; Col 1:10). "Unfruitful" consistently depicts immoral dispositions or immoral deeds (Eph 5:11; Titus 3:14; 2 Pet 1:8; Jude 12).

37. This is true in both the East and the West. See Irenaeus, *Against Heresies* 5.36.2; Augustine, *Questions on the Gospels* 1.9; and Chrysostom, *Homilies on the Gospel of St. Matthew* 44.4–6.

38. For the historical exegesis behind this, especially the meaning of "kingdom of God" in the Targumim, see chapter 6 below.

39. There is probably a background allusion to Isaiah 6:13 and, perhaps also, 55:10–11 here. The "holy seed," in Isaiah's vision, represents the remnant or "stump" from which a restored Israel would again grow. The restoration of Israel, from exilic remnants, was always understood as a moral and spiritual, not purely geographical, transformation. Both North Israel and Judah went into their respective exiles because of spiritual and moral failure—toward the LORD and toward each other. Thus, the exile could not be ended without a change of heart—moral transformation. The key prophecies promise moral transformation (see Jer 17:1; 31:33–34; 32:37–41; Ezek 11:17–20; 36:24–28). Jesus' seminal insight seems to be that individuals' reception of the "word of the kingdom" initiates the moral transformation whereby God's promises of restoration will be fulfilled. The parable of the sower explains that process for his students.

40. For early examples, see John 1:12–13; 3:1–8; 1 Peter 1:3, 23; 1 John 3:9; 1 Cor 4;15; Phil 10. For the corollary metaphor complex of subsequent levels of teaching as milk and solid food, one may consult Napier, "Finding Words to Nourish," 17–32.

41. Whether or not one agrees with Jesus on this point, I think anyone who cares to consider the matter could imagine how one's daily behavior might be altered by an enduring belief that God is paying close attention and personally acting in the very details of one's life. Conversely, we have ample historical examples from the last hundred years of how many people, though certainly not all, behave when they believe that there is no God with any interest in their behavior.

Jesus' later followers would also remark on the moral stimulus that genuine belief in a coming judgment supplies to the convert. See for instance Origen, *Contra Celsum* 1.38; 3.57, 67–69; 4.26, 53; 7.35. While we find substantial overlap of content between ethical exhortation in the philosophic schools and in early Christian sources, the results of Christian moral exhortation were generally more transformative. Why? According to early Christian thinkers, the difference could largely be explained by the distinctive role of eschatology. Although other philosophers preached moral truths, they didn't have the power to consistently change their behavior because they lacked a broader belief in the judgment to come and the resurrection of the body. Solid hope fuels moral transformation. See Origen, *Contra Celsum* 3.67–69; 4.53; and Augustine, *On True Religion* 1.1–4.7.

42. In Jesus' age, some Jewish teachers said that the fruits of the garden in Eden, which Adam and Eve were told to cultivate or "work," symbolized the virtues. Different

virtues were signified by the diversity of trees. Different symbolic meanings attached to the leaves, wood, etc., but the roots were said to be something produced by "working" or "tilling"—in other words through bodily disciplines. See Philo of Alexandria, *Allegorical Interpretation* 1.89. The generalizability of this notion of virtuous "roots" being produced through labor or discipline may be seen in his other writings, for instance, *Every Good Man Is Free* 68–69, and *On the Sacrifices of Abel and Cain* 39–42, esp. 40. See also *Avot* 3.22 in the Mishnah. For the presence in Philo of such rabbinic interpretations, see Toblin, *Creation of Man*.

43. Jesus' words indicate as much. In the original, there is a noticeably mixed use of plural pronouns as subjects for singular verbs in the parable. For instance, in Matt 13:5–6, "others (plural) fell (singular) upon the rocky places, . . . it was scorched and because it did not possess a root, it was dried up (all singular)." Grammatically, this is fairly common in Greek. However, in this case it could hold a deeper significance. When Jesus offers his interpretation of the parable, in Matthew 13:18–23, the plural classes of seeds are all interpreted as individual *persons*. Everything becomes singular. Because bodies individuate us, Jesus signals the personal disciplinary work needed by using the singular.

44. This is the core insight behind Augustine of Hippo's philosophy of history—his notion of the city of God and the city of men. Shared loves create social orders. Shared aversions are the flipside of shared loves. See his *City of God*.

45. Dalman, *Arbeit und Sitte in Palästina*, 153–65. Also, Jeremias, *Parables of Jesus*, 150, citing Dalman.

46. Occasionally an exegete will refer to Isaac reaping one hundred-fold (Gen 26:12) as proof that this was a common occurrence. However, in context, this hundred-fold crop is depicted as an instant wealth production uncanny enough to scare Isaac's neighbors. It provokes a request that he move away (26:13–16).

47. For the sake of lay readability, I use the language of "parts." The technical term, in Husserlian phenomenology, would be "moments"—distinguishable but dependent and thus non-detachable elements of a whole. For instance, the branches, leaves, and bark are detachable parts of a tree. Their color, texture, and aroma, however, would be moments of them. In this context, I understand heart, soul, discursive thought, body, and social relations to be moments of the human person. Of course, other moments of the self could be identified, but these moments have particular utility in focusing Jesus' practical philosophy.

48. The close association of soul (*nephesh*) with a body is highlighted by its use to speak of corpses. In Leviticus and again in Numbers, when purity codes are given, a corpse is called a "dead soul" (see Lev 21:11), which the Septuagint translates as a "finished soul" (ψυχῇ τετελευτηκυίᾳ). This seems to be the fuller phrase implied when in other passages the command is simply not to touch "a soul" (Lev. 19:28; 21:1; 22:4; Num. 5:2; 6:6, 11; 9:6, 7, 10; 19:11, 13, etc.).

49. In the first creation account of Genesis, "living soul" is created first in fish (Gen 1:20) and then in land animals (1:24) before humans, in the second account, are also made to be living soul (Gen 2:7). The rest of the scriptures continue to affirm the shared soul-nature of humans and the lower animals.

50. In the Greek philosophical tradition, soul connects us with plants too. (See Aristotle's *On the Soul*.) At a very basic level, soul is a power to engage an environment, at different levels of complexity, and for a creature to incorporate elements of that environment into itself. The most basic level of this process is nutrition, which plants also do by incorporating minerals and amino acids from the soil and converting those into aspects of themselves.

51. The language of "flow" is more than metaphor. With regard to the Hebrew Bible's mindset, soul (*nephesh*) is always described with liquid characteristics. It is poured out, leaks away, dries up, is split on the ground, etc. See Isa 53:12; Ps 119:28; Num 11:6; 1 Sam 1:15; 2 Sam 14:14; Job 14:10–11, etc. Moreover, when located in relation to the physical body (our "flesh and bone"), the soul of the flesh is in the blood—the liquid element. See Lev 17:11, Deut 12:23–24. Blood (containing *nephesh*), when spilt, flows down to its natural abode in Sheol—the watery netherworld. See Ps 31:18, etc. See Dor-Shav, "Soul of Fire," esp. 88–90.

52. I've benefited in this section from aspects of the phenomenological description found in Frank, *Man's Soul*. A similar emphasis on flow in soul phenomena marks Dallas Willard's discussion of soul in Willard, *Renovation of the Heart*, ch. 11, especially pp. 203–5.

53. Dallas Willard, whenever he taught on the disciplines of solitude and silence, routinely pointed out that "when you enter solitude, what you will learn is that you have a soul."

54. For a similar finding, from the eminent psychologist who developed the experience sampling method of research, see Csikszentmihalyi, *Flow and the Foundations of Positive Psychology*, and his numerous papers on "time alone" for various demographics. In sum, with rare exceptions, Csikszentmihalyi found that when people are alone and not engaged in work or otherwise distracted, they drift toward lower moods and thoughts of hopelessness, dissatisfaction, and worthlessness. However, these lowered mood periods in solitude seem to prepare a person for higher than usual moods when they again enter into community.

55. An early follower of Jesus, Paul, analyses this experience in Romans 7:7ff. The person may be confused and saddened by unintentional sinning and frustrated failures to do the good he or she has chosen. It doesn't last forever, but it is an unavoidable stage in the transformation process.

56. This is fully intelligible in a Second Temple Jewish setting. The question of priority and posteriority among the various commandments was a standard problem for the Second Temple Jews. Mostly, it was raised to resolve local, occasional conflicts between particular commands. If several priests are working on multiple sacrifices, each to fulfill a commandment, which goes first at the altar? Here's their principle. "Whatever is more holy than the other precedes that other" (*Mishnah Horayoth* 6.1; see also *Zebahim* 10.2). The rabbis extrapolated this principle as standing behind the instructions given in Leviticus 16:17 that when the High Priest offers his sacrifice nobody else should be in the tent of meeting—in other words, sacrifices for others must wait for his more important sacrifice to be completed. Then others' sacrifices may be offered.

57. See below chapter 4 on "The Father's Name" for the meaning of these strange and wonderful four letters.

58. For the distinctively Jewish, and then Christian, conception of spirit see, Napier, "Alexandrian Jewish Roots."

59. Again, the connection of soul with water is not mine, but permeates the Hebrew Bible. It's already an established understanding in Jesus' world. See the subsection "What Is Soul?" including the notes in the chapter above for references.

60. For a discussion of the meaning of this strange and unpronounceable name, see chapter 4 below.

61. Of course, the inability of miracles to compel belief has always been the case and was intended by God to be so. See Deut 13:1–5 for warnings about wonder-workers that entice toward false-gods.

62. Consider, as an example, brainwashing practices.

63. Among the ancients, Augustine described this role of authority in enabling a first apprehension of the subject matter at hand. "Faith seeking understanding," as his view gets summarized, simply means that learning begins with trusting someone's introductory description and then going to see for oneself. See Augustine, *De utilitate credendi* (On the Advantage of Believing).

    The work of Dru Johnson highlights a similar theme, positively and negatively construed, in Genesis 2 and 3, and then echoed through the Hebrew Bible and New Testament. He argues persuasively for a reading of Genesis 2 in which God guides Adam through a process of discovering, or coming to know, the woman as his proper mate. This guided knowing provides the implicit point of contrast for knowledge acquisition in the next chapter. In Genesis 3, a new guide usurps the role of God as the guide who verbally highlights what to notice so as to see well. Perverse, though not inaccurate, verbal guidance results in a perverse knowing or "seeing as" in which the primordial couple see their bodies in a new way as shameful. See Johnson, *Biblical Knowing*, 22–64. Also, summarizing and repeating his case, in Johnson, *Biblical Philosophy*, ch. 8.

64. In the Bible there are two types of knowledge of God. I will call one of them "mere knowledge." This is what Paul describes in Romans 1:18ff. There are some things we cannot help knowing about God simply because we are the kind of creatures that we are and living in this world. "Mere knowledge" is universal. Everybody has some basic concept of divinity. But there's a second, deeper form of knowing God, which is the subject of this chapter. This type of knowledge is not just knowing *about* God. It involves first-hand interaction and personal familiarity with God. There's a great difference between knowing facts about a person and really knowing that person. We will find that this second form of knowledge—firsthand, interactive knowledge—comes through personal obedience. But let's take this one step at a time.

65. For this temporal feature, implicit in accounts of truth within the Hebrew scriptures, see Hazony, *Philosophy of the Hebrew Scripture*, 193–218.

66. Again, I'm grateful to Dallas Willard for this clear formulation. See *Knowing Christ Today* for his popular exposition. For a slightly more thorough but still accessible account see two articles: Willard, "Truth in the Fire," and Willard, "How Concepts Relate the Mind to Its Objects." The two indispensable accounts for those wanting to plumb deeper are Willard, "Knowledge," 138–67, and Willard, *Logic and the Objectivity of Knowledge*.

67. For beautiful and insightful reflections on the degrees and prerequisites for knowledge of God in the Torah, see Hazony, "Torah from Heaven," 3–76. Also, see Hazony, *Philosophy of Hebrew Scripture*, esp. ch. 6.

68. By "frictional cross-referencing" I mean the practice of juxtaposing contrary sayings from Scripture, as well as contrary opinions of the rabbis, as part of the interpretive process by which a halachic judgment finally emerges.

69. To be clear, this acknowledgment of limitation does not contradict the claims of Hebrew scripture at all. The Torah itself depicts the highest knowledge of God yet achieved, in the case of Moses, as still only a glimpse at God's "back." To see God's face is impossible for a mere human to survive (Exod 33:17–23). See Hazony, "Torah from Heaven" for discussion. What is more shocking is Jesus' claim to offer what Torah alone cannot. However, even here, one will notice the harmony between what one learns in Jesus' yoke (see below) and what Moses heard of God's character when viewing God's back on Mount Sinai.

70. To refer back to the prologue, infants are those who have already learned the Socratic lesson of their own ignorance. They know that they don't know, and thus are ready to receive the life-giving information from Jesus.

71. See *Mishnah Aboth* 3.5; cf. also "yoke of the commandments" in *Mishnah Berakoth* 2.2.

72. We'll consider the nature of the kingdom and "entering the kingdom" in chapter 6 below.

73. What follows may be considered an attempt to perform, with contemporary cosmology, something analogous to the perspective offered in such passages as Isa 40:6–8, 12–26; Job 38–41; Jer 10:6–16.

74. We will return to the Father's gentleness in chapter 5 below. For a beautiful mediation on the concept of gentleness, specifically as what is excluded from but haunts standard ontologies of affect, see Dufourmantelle, *Power of Gentleness*.

75. I.e., along with the Father and the Spirit, the Son is on the Creator side of the Creator-Creature distinction.

76. Of the three categories of discourse, ethics was the only one that was absolutely necessary in order to be acknowledged as a philosophy. The test case for this claim is Cynicism. The Cynics' physics and logic were left completely implicit. Their speech focused solely on ethics—preaching at the crowds on the street. Nonetheless, they were accepted as philosophers because they taught and lived a distinct ethic.

77. Before we continue toward an account of God's being, allow me to offer a brief word about the strange letters (YHWH) in that last sentence. How does one pronounce a word without vowels? Well, one *doesn't*—and purposely so. These four letters constitute the unpronounceable name by which Israel's God revealed himself.

  In so far as this name was never to be used in an empty or pointless manner, over the course of the first few centuries of the Second Temple era the Jews collectively decided its sanctity was best guarded by not pronouncing it at all. At least two centuries before Jesus' birth, this name had been reverently retired from vocal pronunciation and, in its place, they would insert *Adonai*—"My Lord."

  The Septuagint translation, which was produced beginning about two hundred years before Jesus, is an important case in point. There is no attempt to transliterate the four letters, despite doing so for all other names. Rather, the translators render it by a translation of the phrase that was substituted in liturgical and everyday life, "LORD."

In Hebrew conversations today, Jews often substitute "HaShem," meaning "the Name," when they are referring to "YHWH." I would encourage you to do the same, or to simply say: "LORD." As I read and write this, those are the sounds I reproduce in my mind to remember the God beyond all names. The silent sanctity of the four-consonant name has been part of the universally shared understanding of Jesus and his people—both Jew and gentile—until very recently. And this unspeakable sanctity is an important indicator of the very being of YHWH as he reveals himself.

Although it has become vogue, especially in seminaries, to insert vowels and to voice the name with a speculative pronunciation (e.g., "Yahweh"), I see no basis for this in Jesus' Way. In fact, in the Gospels we see evidence of the circumlocutions used by Jesus' community to avoid pronouncing the Name (such as Jesus' abundant use of divine passives in all four Gospels and Matthew's use of "the kingdom of the heavens"). For further examples and discussion, see Soulen, *Irrevocable*, esp. chapters 2 and 5. I see no record of its pronunciation by subsequent Jesus followers in the New Testament or among the church fathers. As best I can tell, the silent sanctity of this four-consonant name was part of the shared understanding of Jesus and his people—both Jew and gentile—in the early church.

For anyone whose curiosity drives them to nonetheless attempt pronunciation, notice that pronouncing the name *as it is written*—without any conjectured vowels—simply sounds like a breeze blowing through a place. Perhaps that's not an accident. After all, we are told that the voice of YHWH God came to Adam and Eve with the breeze of the day (Gen 3:8).

78. See the nearly exhaustive collection of references to Jews, their practices, their and beliefs by Greco-Roman authors in the volumes of Stern, *Greek and Latin Authors*.

79. See Staples, *Idea of Israel in Second Temple Judaism*, for a thorough and compelling review of the differentiated self-understandings of those claiming descent from Israel in the Second Temple period. Staples clarifies the pervasiveness of "restoration eschatology," which anticipates a restoration of all twelve tribes as the promised end of Israel's various exiles, within both the Hebrew Bible and the various strands of Second Temple Jewish thought.

80. God divides the nations according to the number of the angels of God (LXX) or of the "gods" (Qumran). (For an attempt to appreciate the Greek experience of living under a distributed and mutually conflicting plurality of powers or "gods," see Vernant, *Myth and Society in Ancient Greece*, 92–109. Israel, however, is supposed to be the LORD's special property or "inheritance." In Deuteronomy 4, idols are assigned by God to the other nations—something like the "handing over" of Romans 1—but Israel is to know the truth and thus is not to use any such image. Likewise, Deuteronomy 4:37 emphasizes YHWH's personal, unmediated action in Israel.

The LORD's unmediated action is also at issue in Moses' argument with the LORD in Exodus 32–34 following Israel's sin with the golden calf. In Exodus 32, Moses convinces the LORD to not destroy the people. In 33:1–3, however, the gist of what the LORD tells Moses is "Go on to the land with an angel overseeing you, but I'm done. I'll destroy this people if I go." In other words, on such an arrangement, Israel would become just another nation under a spiritual inter-mediary. That's the point at which Moses has a sit-down protest in 33:12–16. He refuses to continue on to the land with only an angelic intermediary.

81. As a point of interest, the Syriac-speaking church of the East has maintained this optic of the Creator's educational project in important ways that are often ob-scured or even lost in the West. See, for instance, Kitchen, *Syriac Book of Steps*. For an example of the same, as yet unobscured, understanding in the Western church, see Augustine, *On True Religion*.

82. Since most groups in Jesus' day did not consider the canon complete or closed, the terms "Hebrew Bible" and "Old Testament" are somewhat anachronistic. None-theless, the appeal to specific sacred ancestral texts is widespread in Jesus' day. See, for instance, the prologue to Sirach; 2 Macc 15:9; 4 Macc 18:1–24; Josephus *Contra Apion* 1:31–44; Luke 24:27, 44–45. Since these sacred ancestral writings, for the most part, are found in the canons of the Hebrew Bible and Old Testament we will use the more familiar terms in our discussion.

83   There's a primordial conceptual density to the idea of YHWH. Besides being underivative, YHWH also speaks and listens, creates and intervenes, in history; he loves, chooses, angers, grieves, has compassion, shows mercy, etc. Later, when philosophical paganisms move in the direction of describing and emphasizing a meta-divine realm as the object of contemplative devotion, they must remove all the personal character of their divinities to think it. But in Israel it is YHWH alone, in all his personal complexity, who stands behind all things.

84. For the most developed and profound articulation of this understanding, see Kaufmann, *Religion of Israel*, esp. 1–121. For an accessible and easily read intro-duction see Untermann, *Justice for All*, 1–14. A helpful evaluation of Kaufmann's work may be found in Greenberg, *Studies in the Bible and Jewish Thought*, 175–88, "Kaufmann on the Bible: An Appreciation."

85. See Paul, *Studies in the Book of the Covenant*. Similarly, every student of Plato will encounter "the Euthyphro question"—are certain deeds pious and good be-cause all the gods like them, or do all the gods like them because they are pious and good? The tendency in paganism of all forms is to resolve the tension in the direction of the second, meta-divine explanation. In Israel, the question is unintel-ligible because there is no meta-divine realm.

86. A very accessible, and darkly humorous, window into this element of the pagan worldview may be found in Lucian, *Zeus Catechized*. For an accessible medita-tion on the long attempt, through Christianity, to move beyond this worldview by reframing human failure in terms of guilt and forgiveness rather than honor and shame, see Visser, *Beyond Fate*.

87. A good survey of the range of Greek assessments of Fate, which is still worth read-ing, may be found in Greene, *Moira*.

88. Aristotle noted the inconsistency in Hesiod and the mythic poets' account of the gods, specifically at the point in which the gods sought nourishment from the me-ta-divine realm. If they're eternal, Aristotle reasoned, then they don't need nectar. If they need nectar, they cannot be eternal. See *Metaphysics* Book 3.1000a5–19.

89. O'Flaherty, *Rig Veda*, 211–12.

90. Lest I confuse, I'll offer a word here about the Trinity. Retrospectively, of course, Jesus' students came to understand that there are three *whos* but still only one *what* in God—three persons, sharing a single being. I would like you to consider the *what* of God with me. In ancient Greek thought, the *ousia* (in Latin *essentia*) of something is the answer to the question "*What is it?*" When you look at the being of the one God who exists as these three persons, you find a revelation of his unique way of existing. Or, if you prefer, if you consider the three persons who exist as a singular divine being from all eternity, you will find the following revelation of their singular way of existing.

91. For instance, see "the Great Hymn to the Aten" in Hays, *Hidden Riches*, 357. Or, the invocations to prayers to Ea and Nebu in Lenzi, "Invoking the God," 303–15. See also the invocations in Lenzi, *Reading Akkadian Prayers and Hymns*.

92. See Budge, *Egyptian Magic*, ch. 5, "Magical Names."

93. Within the sweep of Israel's library, the Hebrew Bible, it is worth noting that this is the second of three occasions when God is asked to reveal his name or true character. The first person to ask is Jacob as he wrestles with God in Genesis 32:29. He receives no answer. Here, in Exodus 3, Moses receives an answer focused on God's distinctive type of existence. The third request for God's self-revelation, also spoken by Moses, occurs in Exodus 33:12—34:9 and is answered with a deeper revelation of God's character as fundamentally gracious and compassionate. This is continuous with the covenantal emphasis found here in Exodus 3:15–16.

94. Many translations use the latinized old English word, "profane," for the Hebrew word *hol*, but it just means "outside the temple" or common.

95. The Hebrew root *q-d-sh*, from which the word for holiness and sanctify comes, means something that is cut from, set off, separated, apart.

96. In passing, let's also note that we're called to be holy too. When we come to be holy to God, we are no longer just one more example of the human species. To be holy means we too have become uniquely, irreplaceably special as we are dedicated to God. This relation as son or daughter to the Father makes us unlike any other person *to the Father*.

97. As we noted in chapter 3 above, there is a generic notion of divinity, which Paul comments upon in Romans 1:18ff. and that constitutes a base layer of "mere knowledge" of God. Before Paul, Stoic philosophers had made a similar case based upon the universality of *some conception* of divinity among human persons and societies throughout history. See Cicero, *On the Nature of the Gods* 2.12–15.

98. The word *perushim*, "separatists," is the word translated by Pharisee. For an accessible introduction to the Pharisees in Jesus' day, see Skarsaune, *In the Shadow of the Temple*, 117–22.

99. Of course, it is the servant who enacts this gentleness, but in so doing he reveals the Father's character and way—he displays that in which the Father's soul is well pleased.

100. For a detailed portrait of this patient, gentle character at work among Jesus'

followers in the first few centuries, see Kreider, *Patient Ferment of the Early Church.*

101. A good place to start for this perspective is Mangalwadi, *Book That Made Your World.* For an accessible socio-historical account of Rome's conversion see, Stark, *Cities of God.* Also, for Christianity's impact on later Western history, see Stark, *Victory of Reason.* For the role of Christian conversion in stabilizing and enabling the survival of sub-Saharan African cultures, see Sanneh, *Translating the Message.* A similar story concerning the origin of Indian vernaculars, specifically Hindi, in Christian mission, see Mangalwadi, *Book That Made Your World,* ch. 10. For an thoroughly researched introduction to the global picture, see Sanneh, *Disciples of All Nations.* Also, for an emphasis on how the North-South axis in our day is replacing the old East-West tension, see Jenkins, *Next Christendom.*

102. Of course, in the ancient world the Stoics viewed hope as a vice—not a virtue. Hope, for the Stoics, was something like a blind optimism, which denied the harsh goodness of what *is* and tried to substitute for it an imaginary future that is more to one's taste. Closer to our day, Hannah Arendt revives the Stoic position and speaks of the dark side of hope. It is often a means of manipulating oneself and others—a tool of immorality. Hopefulness, swallowed as part of an Enlightenment "progress" narrative, prevented European Jews from responding with realism to the threats they should have noticed leading into the Holocaust. At least, that is Arendt's claim. There are important warnings in the Stoics and Arendt. Hope is not always intelligent nor always good. For that matter, there is a comparable warning already found in Jeremiah's writings in the Hebrew Bible. Hope is not always founded and when unfounded is not good. Only profound insight into the Father's character and the Father's project alongside a clear-eyed apprehension of what's happening around us allows hope and realism to coincide.

103. Regarding Jesus' appeal to birds and grass, Manson's words from nearly a century ago are still on target. "We must not take this as an anticipation of the Argument from Design. It is something much simpler and much deeper. . . . The whole emphasis is on the personal relation of the Creator to his creatures. God clothes the lilies of the field and God feeds the birds, one might almost say, because God is fond of beautiful flowers and fond of birds. As Jesus sees it, the material universe reveals chiefly the love of God. The picture of God making clothes for flowers and preparing meals for the sparrows is the picture of a God who is Lord of Creation by being the servant in love of all his creatures. The statement: 'He that would be chief among you must be the servant of all,' has its application even in the heavenly places." Manson, *Teaching of Jesus,* 163.

104. Two rich yet accessible discussions of this broader doctrine of God's reign may be found in Bright, *Kingdom of God.* Also, see Gray, *Biblical Doctrine of the Reign of God.*

105. A lector would read the Hebrew text, then an Aramaic translation would be delivered from memory by a "*meturgeman*" or interpreter. The interpreter was not permitted to look at a text while translating "so that they [the listeners] will not say the translation is written in the Torah" (Bav. 32a). The two were performed in alteration. One verse from the Torah would be followed by one verse of Targum. Up to three verses of the Prophets could be followed by a Targum of those verses. For a basic introduction to the Targums and their character, see Alexander, "Jewish Aramaic Translations of Scriptures," 217–53.

106. Chronology of content is a specialized issue in Targum research. Recognizing tradition necessarily plays an important role in dating these texts. In particular, the way these glosses were memorized and passed on as tradition, requires a methodological distinction between various dates of (oral) composition and the eventual date of writing. There are often several layers of composition and scholars differ on the dates given. For an overview of the issues involved see Chilton, *Galilean Rabbi and His Bible*, 35–147. Also, see McNamara, *Targum and Testament Revisited*, and Alexander, "Jewish Aramaic Translations of Scriptures."

107. Chilton, *Isaiah Targum*.

108. In many instances including this one, Memra may simply be equivalent to "the Word of God," however, in other cases it seems to be a circumlocution for the ineffable name of God or identified as the light which shone at the beginning. Thus, it is transliterated, rather than translated, in this series. For a thorough discussion of the literature on the subject, see McNamara, *Targum and Testament*, 154–66.

109. Chilton, *Isaiah Targum*.

110. Cathcart and Gordon, *Targum of the Minor Prophets*.

111. Cathcart and Gordon, *Targum of the Minor Prophets*.

112. Cathcart and Gordon, *Targum of the Minor Prophets*.

113. The closest arguments for this emphasis are found in the two works by Bruce Chilton: *God in Strength* and *Glory of Israel*.

114. For the Second Temple idea of "revelation," see, e.g., 4Q427 fr. 7i.18ff.; 1QpHab7.1–14; 11.1ff.; 1QS 1.9; 5.4–12. Flusser, "'The Secret Things Belong to the LORD' (Deut 29:29): Ben Sira and the Essenes," notes divergent views in Second Temple Judaism concerning inquiry into "mysteries." For a solid overview of Second Temple and early Rabbinic notions of revelation, see Bockmeuhl, *Revelation and Mystery*, 7–126.

115. Isaiah 40 is the exception that proves the rule. This text is rendered in view of the initial return from Babylonian exile, thus the kingdom had been temporarily revealed in that mighty deed.

116. For an overview of twentieth-century scholarly positions on the kingdom as present, future, or "inaugurated," see Willis, *Kingdom of God*.

117. Thanks to Nathan Mosher for bringing this contrast into focus for me.

118. I'm grateful to Dallas Willard who first helped me see this biblical linkage and to grasp the important concept behind it in existential terms. See Willard, *Divine Conspiracy*, 21–30, for a very helpful exposition.

119. For instance, see 1QS 3.13–4.26. A helpful discussion is found in Newsom, *The Spirit within Me*, 102–11; also see Schwartz, "The Exegetical Character of 1QS 3:13–4:26."

120. For an introduction to the priestly worldview behind Genesis 1, see Blenkinsopp, *Sage, Priest, Prophet*, 101–14.

121. Notice the primal role of agency for the "life-world" in the phenomenological descriptions of Husserl, *Crisis of the European*. This description of the "life-world" is also fruitfully developed in Merleau-Ponty, *Phenomenology of Perception*. For an adjacent approach, also emphasizing agency, see MacMurray, *Self as Agent*.

122. Here, as Dallas Willard did, I utilize an age-old philosophical strategy. Observation of infants and young children provides a clue to human nature as yet largely unshaped by social convention. For the ancient debate over what sort of human nature is seen in infancy, and the most influential Christian response, see Napier, *En Route to the Confessions*, ch. 5, "Mirror of Fallen Nature." This strategy continues to be utilized in various permutations and to very different ends through the modern period as found, for instance, in Rousseau, Freud, and Merleau-Ponty.

123. Newsom, *Spirit Within Me*, 28–47, includes an investigation of "divine co-agency" as a narrative trope in the Hebrew Bible. While prescinding from any claims concerning its existential reality, Newsom's descriptions of the *narrative* features bear a strange resemblance to what is found in this and the following parable.

124. Stern, *Greek and Latin Authors on Jews and Judaism* (2 vols.) enables one to easily trace the relevant literary remains of this animosity in Greco-Roman literature beginning with Manetho in the third century BC and reaching to Tacitus in the early second century AD.

125. See, for example, LXX Zech 2:11 and Joseph and Asenath 15.6. For secondary discussions see, Jeremias, *Parables of Jesus*, 146ff., more dubiously Dodd, *Parables of the Kingdom*, 142–43, a concise discussion in Meyer, *Aims of Jesus*, 163–64, Gnilka, *Jesus of Nazareth*, 141–42, briefly Wright, *Jesus and the Victory of God*, 241, Bird, *Jesus and the Origins of the Gentile Mission*, 73–77. To put this concern for gentile conversion within the larger context of Second Temple Jewish views, see Dickson, *Mission-Commitment in Ancient Judaism*, 1–89.

126. Ladd, *Gospel of the Kingdom*, 52–65, provides an overview of the surprises regarding power, as expected in Israel, in contrast to Jesus' teaching on the kingdom's presence.

127. The acknowledgment, within the Bible, of human problems related to finitude as well as to sin is argued in Via, *Hardened Heart and Tragic Finitude*. See also the more scattered discussion in Tillich, *Systematic Theology*, 2:19–96.

128. Plato, *Protagoras* 320d–23c.

129. Hesiod, *Works and Days*, 42–105.

130. Hesiod, *Theogony*, 507–616.

131. For helpful commentaries on the Prometheus myth see the work of Jean-Pierre Vernant. A good start may be found in Vernant, *Myth and Thought among the Greeks*, 263–74. Also, Vernant, *Myth and Society in Ancient Greece*, 183–201.

132. Plato, *Protagoras* 321c–d.

133. The most profound recent attempt to inhabit this Greek picture of "prosthetic nature" is Stiegler, *Technics and Time*. In many ways, Steigler seems indebted to the seminal revification of this myth in Illich, *Deschooling Society*, ch. 7, "Rebirth of Epimethean Man."

134. Power and its pervasiveness are, of course, a dominant theme in postmodern streams of thought. While theorists see a proliferation in forms of power, the tendency is to see all power as coercion—whether overt or covert. Most power is covertly coercive. Even the one wielding it may not admit the coerciveness to him- or herself.

This covert exercise of power became a dominant theme in Nietzsche. The "will to power" pervades Christianity, for instance, through a subterfuge— overtly speaking of love while harboring a covert intent to induce guilt. Guilt then becomes a form of coercion. In the founding myth of philosophy, likewise, Socrates is embodying a will to truth in opposition to the sophists will to power. But, for Nietzsche, this turns out to be a subterfuge too. Socrates wields the idea of truth as a covert exercise of the will to power. See Nietzsche, *Birth of Tragedy and the Genealogy of Morals*.

The thinker who has most developed and popularized this idea of coercive power hiding everywhere, and everything being reducible to such underlying power, is Michel Foucault. For an accessible entry point to the theme in his thought, see Foucault, *Power/Knowledge*.

135. The terms became popular through the political philosophy of Joseph S. Nye Jr. See Nye, *Soft Power*.

136. Here I echo elements of James Allen Francis' famous sermon delivered on July 11, 1926, to the Baptist Young People's Union at a Los Angeles Convention. A memorable portion of that sermon is now known as "One Solitary Life" and regularly appears anonymously on posters. The full sermon was published in Francis, *The Real Jesus and Other Sermons*, Sermon XII.

137. Paul refers to the kingdom in 1 Thess 2:10–12; Gal 5:21; 1 Cor 4:20; 6:9–10; 15:24, 50; Rom 14:7. For a overview of these passages, highlighting Paul's mixture of present and future aspects of the kingdom, see Donfried, "Kingdom of God in Paul," 175–90.

138. The term spiritual exercise, and its near synonym spiritual discipline, emerges because of how *askesis* was translated into Latin (*exercitatio animi*) and subsequently developed in the West. For an overview, see Hadot, *Philosophy as a Way of Life*, and Hadot, *What Is Ancient Philosophy?*

139. In the same period, we find Josephus representing differing Jewish religious groups to outsiders as so many philosophic schools. Unsurprisingly, Josephus has a project of depicting Judaism as a philosophy and thus downplaying revolutionary associations after the Jewish War of AD 66–70.

140. A few verses later, we are told that the conceptual content of Paul's ongoing conversation with Felix was "about faith in Jesus . . . discussing justice, self-mastery and the judgment to come" (Acts 24:24–25). The primary aim of the philosophic exercises was to produce human beings that were just (the same word can be translated as "righteous") and capable of prodigious feats of self-control. Paul sandwiches these between two distinctives of the early Jesus movement—faith in Jesus and the coming judgment. Clearly Paul is self-consciously presenting the Way in terms indigenous to the philosophic enterprise among the Greeks and Romans. The early Jesus movement, almost unanimously, followed suit for the next three centuries.

141. After all, one might use and prescribe such disciplines, but without any precise understanding of how and why they work. This unreflective use might even be quite effective. People, for instance, submit to medicines and therapies all the time without any personal understanding of how or why they work. But Jesus takes care not only to introduce his students to specific exercises for practice, but to offer a clear account of how they work within us.

142. This is Dallas Willard's definition of a discipline, upon which I cannot improve.

143. Here we may simply notice that Jesus' account of moral weakness and personal transformation is multifaceted—more so than was common among ancient theories. Cognitive exercises play an important role for Jesus. But they cannot carry the sole responsibility for moral success nor the sole blame for moral failure. Likewise, bodily habits and the malleability of our physical and social life each play critical roles in both moral weakness and transformation. While necessary factors, however, they are not sufficient conditions in themselves.

  According to Jesus' theory, it is the interactions between these factors and their overall coherence or incoherence that will determine the ultimate success or failure of the moral transformation that is initiated in the heart. Moral weakness, or failure to successfully live out the ideals one consciously espouses, results from the incoherence or disintegration of these factors.

  As such, Jesus offers a nuanced account of moral weakness and of moral transformation. He resists the common philosophical temptation to reduce the plurality of human moral experience into one or two conceptual themes within a prepackaged system. Jesus intends his theory to posit as many elements as are needed for adequate description of human moral experience. Because of the intrinsic complexity of human persons, simplicity in such matters is not always a virtue.

144. This must be distinguished from the old Enlightenment fantasy notion of "progress." Its adherents imagined that world conditions inevitably must get better and better with time.

145. Unvaried repetition of these features, while addressing diverse practices, raises the repeated features to the status of universals—qualities capable of instantiation in multiple individuals while being reducible to none of them alone. In more rhetorical terms, this may be an instance of what Dru Johnson describes as "pixilation" in his account of the "Hebraic philosophical style." See Johnson, *Biblical Philosophy*, 84–88.

146. πρὸς τὸ θεαθῆναι αὐτοῖς—the preposition πρὸς followed by the articular infinitive is the standard grammatical form for describing the intention or mental goal of an action.

147. Conversely, one might consider another intrinsic consequence described in scripture: "the wages of sin is death" (Rom 6:23). There's a different word translated "wage" here, but the concept of intrinsic consequence is the same.

148. Notice also that Paul, one of Jesus' early followers, uses the "wage" in a similar manner. In 1 Corinthians 9:17–18 Paul speaks of the "wage" that he gets from not exercising his right to accept money from those to whom he preaches. What is the "wage" Paul gets? Nothing other than the goodness that is produced through his self-renunciation.

149. In *Targum Qoheleth* the oil is reputation—the social result of good deeds. But in the Midrashim the oil refers to the good deeds themselves as they change the person. See *Numbers Rabba* 13.15–16 and *Qoheleth Rabba* 9.8.

150. See the rabbinic sermons in Numbers Rabba 13.15–16 and Qoheleth Rabba 9.8.

151. m. Avot 2:1–2, commending the combination of study of Torah with everyday work, is often connected with this metaphor in later rabbinic sources.

152. In the next generation, one of Jesus' early followers reflects on this feature of life with God. "For we are God's handiwork, created in Christ Jesus for good deeds, which God prepared beforehand so that we could walk in them" (Eph 2:10).

153. Han, *Burnout Society.*

154. Aristotle, *Politics.* 1, 1253a 27–29.

155. Arius Didymus, the testimony to his view is preserved in Eusebius, *Preparation for the Gospel* 15.15.

156. Dio Chrysostom 36.20 (SVF 3.329).

157. *Republic* 2.359d–360b.

158. *Politics* 1, 1253a 27–29.

159. We might notice that there are only a handful of events that are narrated across *all four* Gospels. John's preaching, Jesus' feeding of the multitudes, the cross, etc. The witness that the heavens were open at Jesus' baptism belongs in this very short list of events narrated in all four. Evidently, the open heavens were too important for any early follower of Jesus to leave to the side.

160. That is, the "prosecuting attorney" or "accuser" in the heavenly court.

161. The root sense of "temptation" or "testing" is to attempt or make an experiment of something. The same root produces the Greek word for "experience."

162. Matthew and Luke, in their accounts of Jesus' life, relate the content of that trial in terms of three primary twists or distortions of proper relation to the Father, which Jesus must overcome.

163. As it happens, there is now some neurophysiological corroboration of this fact in brain scans. Interaction with God is experienced as a social relationship. Researchers found that "improvised praying" activates the same regions of the brain that light up when people talk about a friend. See Schjoedt et al., "Highly Religious Participants," 199–207.

164. Aramaic Levi Document, 4Q213a.17–18.

165. 11Q5 XIX.13–16.

166. For a broader horizon, within which to place this belief, see Flusser, *Judaism of the Second Temple Period*, 1:1–31.

167. For a depiction of pagan experiences of seeing a god or hearing from a god or spirit, see Fox, *Pagans and Christians*, 102–261.

168. See Jaeger, *Theology of the Early Greek Philosophers.*

169. See, for instance, 1 Kgs 22:19–23; Isa 6:1–13; Jer 23:16–22; Ezek 1–2, etc. In the Second Temple Jewish texts from Qumran, consider also 1QH hymn 10 for a similar claim. See also, 1QH 3.20; 11.10ff.; 1QS 11.6ff.; 1QM 10.8ff.

170. However, there are minority reports. In Epictetus we find an outlier among the Stoics who seems to think of Zeus in more personalistic terms. See Long, *Epictetus*, especially ch. 6.

171. Augustine's essentially eternal and invisible, yet occasionally manifest, "city of God" (in contrast to the "city of man") may be seen as a development of Jesus' notion of the natural social boundary of those created for co-working with God. See Augustine, *City of God*, book 14, and *Literal Commentary on Genesis* 11:15.

172. A similar, exalted picture may be found in 1 Enoch 48.

173. Geza Vermes brought forth several examples indicating that in the Galilean dialect of Aramean *bar nasha* was used as a circumlocutionary first-person reference in contexts wherein self-reference requires a foregrounding of humility. So, the sense might be more like "this bloke" (a.k.a. "me"). See Vermes' article and Matthew Black's response in Black, *Aramaic Approach*, 310–30.

174. Peterson, *12 Rules for Life*, 1–28, has popularized this fact. See, for a taste of the background literature, de Waal, *Good Natured*, and de Waal, *Chimpanzee Politics.*

175. See Gen 5:24; 2 Kgs 2:11ff.; and, in Second Temple literature, 4 Ezra 6:26.

176. By a bit of fancy, highly improbable exegesis, some Second Temple Jews even got Moses, whose body was never found, enrolled in this class. See Josephus, *Jewish Antiquities* 4.325.

177. For the persistence of this understanding among Jesus' earliest followers see, for instance, Eph 3:4–10; Heb 12:22–24; 1 Pet 1:1–12.

178. A non-canonical memory of the parable, without any interpretation, is also extant in the Gospel of Thomas 9.

179. Matthew thinks so too. Notice Matthew's placement of this parable in chapter 13. It is the structural center of his whole book. In ancient composition, the center is often symbolic. Moreover, these parables frame a quotation from Isaiah, which Matthew says is fulfilled in Jesus' parables, that God will use parables to reveal mysteries hidden since the foundation of the world (Matt 13:34–35).

180. See Gibbs, *Moral Development and Reality.*

181. Among other traits found in highly empathetic people is a tendency to prescribe more severe, vindictive judgments against those perceived as outside one's circle of empathy. See Bloom, *Against Empathy.*

182. This principle was self-consciously exploited in the public strategies of German National Socialism and the various fascisms of the mid-twentieth century. It continues in several regimes of our own day.

183. One of Jesus' early students, Paul of Tarsus, considers this element of life as a student of Jesus in 1 Corinthians 2:15.

184. See Augustine's anti-Donatist writings. For a start, consider *Letters* 76 and 105.

185. This teaching is part of a larger reevaluation of the zeal worldview in Jesus' life and teachings.

Even in the Hebrew Bible, Levitical zeal received a mixed review. Zeal or violent, ruthless imposition of righteousness on a community is the primary characteristic of Levi. Everything is right or wrong. There are no extenuating circumstances worth considering. The Levi type is personal judge, jury, and executioner on behalf of truth and righteousness. Moses shows this trait when he kills the Egyptian whom he finds beating a Hebrew (Exod 2:11–12). Later, when the people of Israel have gone after the golden calf, it is Levi who comes to Moses' side and goes through the camp killing those caught in idolatrous revelry (Exod 32:25–28). Finally, the Levite Phineas displays the archetypical "zeal"—devout extremism—when he strikes down the offending Simeonite man and Midianite woman without any trial or communal process.

As noted, zeal receives mixed reviews. There's a role in Israel for this single-minded devotion, even in forcing righteousness, but it will not be as the leader of the people. Phineas will have a perpetual priesthood. But he'll receive no portion of the land nor be given political power. The king needs to come from a different type of character. Zeal is needed in some places and for specific crisis moments, but it cannot be the only rule of the land. When Levitical zeal in Phineas assumes political leadership, Israel comes to the brink of self-annihilation (Judg 20–21). Those with zeal are best contained within the tabernacle and their righteous killing limited to animal sacrifices.

A thorough study would also include zeal in Elijah, Ezra, and the Maccabees. But for this note, I'll simply point out that Jesus seeks to transform zeal in important ways. When James and John want to call fire down from heaven, evoking Elijah's zeal, Jesus rebukes them (Luke 9:55). Nonetheless, Jesus does not utterly dispense with zeal but remakes it in, for instance, John 2:13–17.

The zeal worldview—left untransformed—paradoxically distracts from God. The threat-detection-and-response system in the human soul can be over-activated to ill-effect.

186. Jesus' early followers articulated an important corollary of the Israelite mono-theistic account of creation. If there is no meta-divine realm and God created all things good, then evil itself must be a privation or lack somehow acquired by things that are good in themselves. This means that evil cannot exist independently of good things. In essence, evil is parasitic. Should something progressively worsen until it was nothing but evil, that thing would simply disappear—cease to exist. Because goodness is a feature of existence within God's creation. Pure evil would be nothingness. Although Jesus does not spell out this corollary explicitly, it seems to be presupposed in his teachings concerning non-resistance to evil in Matthew 5. Why not resist the evil person? Because it would be redundant. Evil self-destructs. We can persistently insert goodness, and, in time, this will overwhelm evil. The evil person either repents and returns to goodness, or self-destructs. There's no third destination.

187. See Berstein and Politi, *His Holiness*, 77; Weigel, *Witness to Hope*, 93.

188. See Johnson, *Biblical Knowing*, 22–64, for the main argument of the next few paragraphs.

189. m. Pes. 10.5 (Danby's translation).

190. One may find some minimal similarity to Plato's notion of learning as a memory of things experienced prior to birth in the Israelite sense of memorial presence. See for instance *Phaedo* 72e, 92d. But the meaning is quite different. Plato's memory participates in something outside of history. The Israelite memory makes history present for successive generations.

191. For a profound meditation on the covenant, in contradistinction to social contract, see the work of Shmuel Trigano. Especially, Trigano, *Philosophy of the Law*. For the downstream consequences of the social contract as originary myth, see Trigano, *Democratic Ideal and the Shoah*.

192. From the late sixteenth through the seventeenth century, the notion of a social contract as the basis of political rule took hold in Western thought. Beginning with Hugo Grotius, jurists, followed by political and social philosophers, began to consider individual persons as primordial. Individuals had rights as possessions. Prior to this many assumed the social or political collective to be primary. So, by imagining individuals as primary, the problem requiring an answer shifted. Since individuals are primordial, how did society ever come to exist? Why is humanity—by nature only so many individuals—found always in communal clumps and usually living together under states? In many ways this was a reboot of the old Epicurean individualism.

   Of course, the various social contract theories, as articulated by the likes of Hobbes and Rousseau, were new myths of origins. They knew as much. After all, if one were to ask for the *names* of the original signatories, they would have replied that you had missed their point. We all implicitly and tacitly executed the contract by our very place in the world of civilization. To their minds, the only conceivable alternatives to the social contract theory would be a straightforward tyranny of might or the divine right of kings. Those wouldn't do. They couldn't imagine a God-rooted society that was not a divine-right monarchy. So, God couldn't be let in. For good and for ill, the social contract became the new founding myth in Western society.

193. God's covenant is not coercive. That's not God's way of making things happen. God initiates but humans still must receive the covenant for it to be effective. Human response is an essential part of the covenantal relation. So, while the covenant is not rooted in consensual choice, it is still voluntary in an important sense. God would not keep anyone against their will. But the nature of human life is such that our willing always comes too late to initiate the primary relations of life.

   If that sounds distasteful, one might make a serious attempt to think through the social contract approach in detail. Try *realistically imagining the process* by which some number of primal individuals, originally without any substantive or binding social connections, nonetheless developed adequate intelligence and language to voluntarily enter into a social contract. (For instance, from whom would they have learned a shared language?) It would be an understatement to call the process miraculous.

   In the alternative biblical conception, creatures, by nature, are receivers and responders. Thus, God initiates the connection and then through his instructions regulates human interactions with each other and with God.

194. Later Paul marvels at how Jesus reconciles all things, whether in the heavens or upon the earth, to himself through the blood of his cross (Col 1:20).

195. See Staples, *Idea of Israel*.

Bibliography

Alexander, Philip S. "Jewish Aramaic Translations of Scriptures." In *Mikra: Text, Translation, Reading, and Interpretation of the Hebrew Bible in Ancient Judaism and Early Christianity*, edited by M. J. Mulder and Harry Sysling, 217–53. Assen: Van Gorcum, 1990.

Berstein, Carl, and Marco Politi. *His Holiness: John Paul II and the Hidden History of Our Time*. New York: Doubleday, 1996.

Bird, Michael F. *Jesus and the Origins of the Gentile Mission*. London: T. & T. Clark, 2006.

Black, Matthew. *An Aramaic Approach to the Gospels and Acts*. 3rd ed. Oxford: Oxford University Press, 1967.

Bloom, Paul. *Against Empathy: The Case for Rational Compassion*. London: HarperCollins, 2016.

Blenkinsopp, Joseph. *Sage, Priest, Prophet: Religious and Intellectual Leadership in Ancient Israel*. Louisville: Westminster John Knox, 1995.

Bockmuehl, Markus N. A. *Revelation and Mystery in Ancient Judaism and Pauline Christianity*. Grand Rapids: Eerdmans, 1990.

Boucher, Madeleine. *The Mysterious Parable: A Literary Study*. Catholic Biblical Quarterly Monograph Series 6. Washington, DC: The Catholic Biblical Association of America, 1977.

Bright, John. *The Kingdom of God: The Biblical Concept and Its Meaning for the Church*. Nashville: Abingdon, 1953.

Budge, E. A. Wallis. *Egyptian Magic*. London: Global Grey, 2018.

Carasik, Michael. *Theologies of the Mind in Biblical Israel*. Studies in Biblical Literature 85. New York: Peter Lang, 2006.

Cathcart, Kevin J., and R. P. Gordon. *The Targum of the Minor Prophets*. Collegeville, MN: Liturgical, 1989.

Chilton, Bruce D. *Galilean Rabbi and His Bible: Jesus' Use of the Interpreted Scripture of His Time*. Wilmington, DE: Glazier, 1984.

207

————. *The Glory of Israel: The Theology and Provenience of the Isaiah Targum.* Journal for the Study of the Old Testament, Supplement Series. Sheffield, UK: JSOT, 1982.

————. *God in Strength: Jesus' Announcement of the Kingdom.* Freistadt: Plöchl, 1979.

————. *The Isaiah Targum.* Collegeville, MN: Liturgical, 1990.

Clark, Stephen L. *Ancient Mediterranean Philosophy: An Introduction.* London: Bloomsbury, 2013.

Cooper, John M. *Pursuits of Wisdom: Six Ways of Life in Ancient Philosophy from Socrates to Plotinus.* Princeton, NJ: Princeton University Press, 2013.

Csikszentmihalyi, Mihaly. *Flow and the Foundations of Positive Psychology.* Dordrecht: Springer, 2014.

Dalman, Gustaf. *Arbeit und Sitte in Palästina.* Band III. *Von der Ernte zum Mehl. Ernten, Dreschen, Worfeln, Sieben, Verwahren, Mahlen.* 1933. Reprint, Jerusalem: SLM, 2013.

Davies, W. D., and Dale Allison, Jr. *Critical and Exegetical Commentary on the Gospel according to Saint Matthew.* Vol. 2. International Critical Commentary Series. Edinburgh: T. & T. Clark, 1991.

De Waal, F. B. M. *Chimpanzee Politics: Power and Sex among Apes.* Baltimore: Johns Hopkins University Press, 2007.

————. *Good Natured: The Origins of Right and Wrong in Humans and Other Animals.* Cambridge: Harvard University Press, 1996.

Dickson, John P. *Mission-Commitment in Ancient Judaism and in the Pauline Communities: The Shape, Extent and Background of Early Christian Mission.* Tübingen: Mohr Siebeck, 2003.

Dodd, C. H. *The Parables of the Kingdom.* New York: Scribner, 1961.

Donfried, Karl Paul. "The Kingdom of God in Paul." In *The Kingdom of God in 20th-Century Interpretation,* edited by Wendall Willis, 175–90. Reprint, Eugene, OR: Wipf & Stock, 2020.

Dorion, Louis-André. "The Rise and Fall of the Socratic Problem." In *Cambridge Companion to Socrates,* edited by Donald R. Morrison, 1–23. Cambridge: Cambridge University Press, 2011.

Dor-Shav, Ethan. "Soul of Fire: A Theory of Biblical Man." *Azure* 5766 (Autumn 2005) 78–113.

Dufourmantelle, Anne. *Power of Gentleness: Meditations on the Risk of Living.* Translated by Katherine Payne and Vincent Salle. New York: Fordham University Press, 2018.

Engberg-Pedersen, Troels. *John and Philosophy: A New Reading of the Fourth Gospel.* Oxford: Oxford University Press, 2017.

————. *Paul and the Stoics.* Edinburgh: T. & T. Clark, 2000.

Flusser, David. *Judaism of the Second Temple Period.* Vol. 1, *Qumran and Apocalypticism.* Grand Rapids: Eerdmans, 2007.

————. *Judaism of the Second Temple Period.* Vol. 2, *The Jewish Sages and Their Literature.* Translated by Azzan Yadin. Grand Rapids: Eerdmans, 2009.

Foucault, Michel. *Power/Knowledge: Selected Interviews & Other Writings 1972–1977.* Edited by Colin Gordon. New York: Pantheon, 1980.

Fox, Robin Lane. *Pagans and Christians.* New York: Knopf, 1989.

Francis, James Allan. *The Real Jesus and Other Sermons.* King of Prussia, PA: Judson, 1926.

Frank, S. L. *Man's Soul: An Introductory Essay in Philosophical Psychology.* Athens, OH: Ohio University Press, 1993.

Frankfurt, H., and H. A. Frankfurt, et al. *The Intellectual Adventure of Ancient Man: An Essay on Speculative Thought in the Ancient Near East*. Chicago: University of Chicago Press, 1946.

Gibbs, John C. *Moral Development and Reality: Beyond the Theories of Kohlberg and Hoffman*. New York: Sage, 2003.

Gnilka, Joachim. *Jesus of Nazareth: Message and History*. Peabody, MA: Hendrickson, 1997.

Gooch, Paul W. *Reflections on Jesus and Socrates: Word and Silence*. New Haven, CT: Yale University Press, 1996.

Gray, John. *The Biblical Doctrine of the Reign of God*. Edinburgh: T. & T. Clark, 1979.

Greenberg, Moshe. *Studies in the Bible and Jewish Thought*. Philadelphia: Jewish Publication Society, 1995.

Greene, William Chase. *Moira: Fate, Good, and Evil in Greek Thought*. New York: Harper & Row, 1944.

Hadot, Pierre. *Philosophy as a Way of Life*. Edited by Arnold I. Davidson. Oxford: Blackwell, 1995.

———. *What Is Ancient Philosophy?* Translated by Michael Chase. Cambridge: Belknap Press of Harvard University Press, 2002.

Han, Byung-Chul. *The Burnout Society*. Translated by Erik Butler. Redwood City, CA: Stanford University Press, 2015.

Hays, Christopher B. *Hidden Riches: A Sourcebook for the Comparative Study of the Hebrew Bible and Ancient Near East*. Louisville: Westminster John Knox, 2014.

Hazony, Yoram. *The Philosophy of the Hebrew Scripture*. Cambridge: Cambridge University Press, 2012.

———. "Torah from Heaven: Moses and Sinai in Exodus." In *The Revelation at Sinai: What Does "Torah from Heaven" Mean?*, edited by Yoram Hazony et al., 3–76. New York: Ktav, 2021.

Husserl, Edmund. *The Crisis of the European Sciences and Transcendental Phenomenology: An Introduction to Phenomenological Philosophy*. Evanston, IL: Northwestern University Press, 1970.

Illich, Ivan. *Deschooling Society*. New York: Harper & Row, 1972.

Jaeger, Werner. *The Theology of the Early Greek Philosophers: The Gifford Lectures 1936*. Eugene, OR: Wipf & Stock, 2003.

Jenkins, Philip. *The Next Christendom: The Coming of Global Christianity*. Oxford: Oxford University Press, 2011.

Jeremias, Joachim. *The Parables of Jesus*. 2nd ed. Hoboken, NJ: Prentice Hall, 1972.

Johnson, Dru. *Biblical Knowing: A Scriptural Epistemology of Error*. Eugene, OR: Cascade, 2013.

———. *Biblical Philosophy: A Hebraic Approach to the Old and New Testaments*. Cambridge: Cambridge University Press, 2021.

Kaufmann, Yehezkel. *The Religion of Israel: From Its Beginnings to the Babylonian Exile*. Chicago: University of Chicago, 1960.

Kitchen, Robert A. *The Syriac Book of Steps: Syriac Texts and English Translation*. Texts from Christian Late Antiquity. 3 vols. Piscataway, NJ: Gorgias, 2009–14.

Kreeft, Peter. *The Philosophy of Jesus*. South Bend, IN: St. Augustine's, 2007.

Kreider, Alan. *The Patient Ferment of the Early Church: The Improbable Rise of Christianity in the Roman Empire*. Grand Rapids: Baker Academic, 2016.

Ladd, George Eldon. *The Gospel of the Kingdom: Scriptural Studies in the Kingdom of God*. Grand Rapids: Eerdmans, 1977.

Lenzi, Alan. "Invoking the God: Interpreting Invocations in Mesopotamian Prayers and Biblical Laments of the Individual." *SBL* 129.2 (2010) 303–15.

———. *Reading Akkadian Prayers and Hymns: An Introduction*. Atlanta: SBL, 2011.

Liddell, Henry George, and Robert Scott. *A Greek-English Lexicon. With a Revised Supplement (1996)*. Edited by Henry Stuart Jones. Oxford: Clarendon, 1996.

Long, A. A. *Epictetus: A Stoic and Socratic Guide to Life*. Oxford: Oxford University Press, 2002.

MacMurray, John. *The Self as Agent*. New York: Harper and Brothers, 1957.

Malherbe, Abraham J. *Paul and the Popular Philosophers*. Minneapolis: Augsburg Fortress, 1989.

Mangalwadi, Vishal. *The Book That Made Your World: How the Bible Created the Soul of Western Civilization*. Nashville: Thomas Nelson, 2011.

Manson, T. W. *The Teaching of Jesus: Studies in its Form and Content*. Cambridge: Cambridge University Press, 1931.

McNamara, Martin. *Targum and Testament Revisited: Aramaic Paraphrases of the Hebrew Bible: A Light on the New Testament*. Grand Rapids: Eerdmans, 2010.

Merleau-Ponty, Maurice. *Phenomenology of Perception*. London: Routledge, 2002.

Meyer, Ben F. *The Aims of Jesus*. London: SCM, 1979.

Napier, Daniel Austin. "The Alexandrian Jewish Roots of the Concept of Immaterial Spirit." In *Gestures of Grace: Essays in Honor of Robert Sweetman*, edited by Joshua Harris. Eugene, OR: Wipf & Stock, forthcoming.

———. *En Route to the Confessions: The Roots and Development of Augustine's Philosophical Anthropology*. Late Antique History and Religion 6. Leuven: Peeters, 2013.

———. "Finding Words to Nourish: 'Milk' and 'Solid Food' in Earliest Christianity and Today." *Christian Studies* 29 (2017) 17–32.

Newsom, Carol A. *The Spirit within Me: Self and Agency in Ancient Israel and Second Temple Judaism*. New Haven, CT: Yale University Press, 2021.

Nietzsche, Friedrich. *The Birth of Tragedy and the Genealogy of Morals*. Translated by Francis Golffing. New York: Anchor, 1956.

Nussbaum, Martha Craven. *The Therapy of Desire: Theory and Practice in Hellenistic Ethics*. Martin Classical Lectures. Princeton, NJ: Princeton University Press, 1994.

———. "The Therapy of Desire in Hellenistic Ethics." In *Antike Philosophie Verstehen = Understanding Ancient Philosophy*, edited by Marcel van Ackeren and Jörn Müller, 218–42. Darmstadt: Wissenschaftliche Buchgesellschaft, 2006.

Nye, Joseph S., Jr. *Soft Power: The Means to Success in World Politics*. New York: Public Affairs, 2005.

O'Flaherty, Wendy Doniger. *The Rig Veda: An Anthology*. New York: Penguin, 1981.

Paul, Shalom M. *Studies in the Book of the Covenant in Light of Cuneiform and Biblical Law*. Dove Studies in Bible, Language, and History. Eugene, OR: Wipf & Stock, 2006.

Pennington, Jonathan T. *Jesus the Great Philosopher: Recovering the Wisdom Needed for the Good Life*. Grand Rapids, MI: Brazos, 2020.

Peterson, Jordan B. *12 Rules for Life: An Antidote to Chaos*. New York: Random House, 2018.

Plato. *Theaetetus. Sophist.* Translated by Harold North Fowler. Loeb Classical Library 123. Cambridge: Harvard University Press, 1921.

Robb, Michael Stewart. "The Kingdom among Us: Jesus, the Kingdom of God and the Gospel according to Dallas Willard." PhD diss., University of Aberdeen, 2016.

Rowe, C. Kavin. *One True Life: The Stoics and Early Christians as Rival Traditions.* New Haven, CT: Yale University Press, 2016.

Sanneh, Lamin. *Disciples of All Nations: Pillars of World Christianity.* Oxford: Oxford University Press, 2008.

———. *Translating the Message: The Missionary Impact on Culture.* New York: Orbis, 2009.

Schjoedt, U., et al. "Highly Religious Participants Recruit Areas of Social Cognition in Personal Prayer." *Social Cognitive and Affective Neuroscience* 4.2 (2009) 199–207.

Schwartz, Ethan. "The Exegetical Character of 1QS 3:13–4:26." *Dead Sea Discoveries* 27.1 (2020) 31–65.

Skarsaune, Oskar. *In the Shadow of the Temple: Jewish Influence on Early Christianity.* Downers Grove, IL: IVP Academic, 2002.

Snodgrass, Klyne. *Stories with Intention: A Comprehensive Guide to the Parables of Jesus.* Grand Rapids: Eerdmans, 2008.

Soulen, R. Kendall. *Irrevocable: The Name of God and the Unity of the Christian Bible.* Minneapolis: Fortress, 2022.

Staples, Jason A. *The Idea of Israel in Second Temple Judaism: A New Theory of People, Exile, and Israelite Identity.* Cambridge: Cambridge University Press, 2022.

Stark, Rodney. *Cities of God: The Real Story of How Christianity Became an Urban Movement and Conquered Rome.* New York: HarperOne, 2007.

———. *The Victory of Reason: How Christianity Led to Freedom, Capitalism, and Western Success.* New York: Random House, 2005.

Stern, Menahem. *Greek and Latin Authors on Jews and Judaism.* 3 vols. Jerusalem: Israel Academy of Sciences and Humanities, 1976–84.

Stiegler, Bernard. *Technics and Time.* Vol. 1, *The Fault of Epimetheus.* Translated by Richard Beardsworth and George Collins. Palo Alto, CA: Stanford University Press, 1998.

Tillich, Paul. *Systematic Theology.* Vol. 2, *Existence and the Christ.* Chicago: University of Chicago Press, 1957.

Toblin, Thomas H., SJ. *The Creation of Man: Philo and the History of Interpretation.* Catholic Biblical Quarterly Monograph Series 14. Washington, DC: Catholic Biblical Association, 1983.

Trigano, Shmuel. *The Democratic Ideal and the Shoah: The Unthought in Political Modernity.* Translated by Gila Walker. Albany, NY: SUNY Press, 2009.

———. *Philosophy of the Law: The Political in the Torah.* Translated by Gila Walker. Jerusalem: Shalem, 2011.

Untermann, Jeremiah. *Justice for All: How the Jewish Bible Revolutionized Ethics.* Philadelphia: Jewish Publication Society, 2017.

Vernant, Jearn-Pierre. *Myth and Society in Ancient Greece.* Hassocks, UK: Harvester, 1980.

———. *Myth and Society in Ancient Greece.* Translated by Janet Lloyd. Brooklyn, NY: Zone, 1990.

———. *Myth and Thought among the Greeks.* Translated by Janet Lloyd with Jeff Fort. Brooklyn, NY: Zone, 2006.

Via, Dan O. *The Hardened Heart and Tragic Finitude.* Eugene, OR: Cascade, 2012.

Visser, Margaret. *Beyond Fate.* Toronto: House of Anansi, 2002.

Weigel, George. *Witness to Hope.* New York: Cliff Street, 1999.

Willard, Dallas. *The Divine Conspiracy: Rediscovering our Hidden Life in God.* New York: HarperCollins, 1997.

———. "How Concepts Relate the Mind to Its Objects: The 'God's Eye View' Vindicated." *Philosophia Christi* 1.2 (1999) 5–20.

———. "Knowledge." In *Cambridge Companion to Husserl,* edited by Barry Smith and David Woodruff Smith, 138–67. Cambridge: Cambridge University Press, 1995.

———. *Logic and the Objectivity of Knowledge.* Athens, OH: Ohio University Press, 1984.

———. *Renovation of the Heart: Putting on the Character of Christ.* Colorado Springs: NavPress, 2002.

———. "Truth in the Fire: C. S. Lewis and the Pursuit of Truth Today." Paper given at the C. S. Lewis Centennial conference, Oxford University, July 21, 1998. https://www.pintswithjack.com/wp-content/uploads/2021/11/Lewis-and-Truth-Dallas-Willard.pdf.

Willis, Wendell Lee. *The Kingdom of God in 20th-Century Interpretation.* Peabody, MA: Hendrickson, 1987.

Wright, N. T. *Jesus and the Victory of God.* London: SPCK, 1996.